Course	Strategic Management
Course Number	**MGT 490**
	University of Massachusetts Dartmouth
	MANAGEMENT

http://create.mheducation.com

ISBN-10: 1308110995   ISBN-13: 9781308110998

Contents

i. Preface 2
1. Strategy, Business Models, and Competitive Advantage 17
2. Charting a Company's Direction: Vision and Mission, Objectives, and Strategy 29
3. Evaluating a Company's External Environment 53
4. Evaluating a Company's Resources, Capabilities, and Competitiveness 84
5. The Five Generic Competitive Strategies 108
6. Strategies for Competing in International Markets 131
7. Corporate Strategy: Diversification and the Multibusiness Company 153
8. Ethics, Corporate Social Responsibility, Environmental Sustainability, and Strategy 183

Credits

i. Preface: *Chapter from Essentials of Strategic Management: The Quest for Competitive Advantage, Fourth Edition by Gamble, Peteraf, Thompson, 2015* 2

1. Strategy, Business Models, and Competitive Advantage: *Chapter 1 from Essentials of Strategic Management: The Quest for Competitive Advantage, Fourth Edition by Gamble, Peteraf, Thompson, 2015* 17

2. Charting a Company's Direction: Vision and Mission, Objectives, and Strategy: *Chapter 2 from Essentials of Strategic Management: The Quest for Competitive Advantage, Fourth Edition by Gamble, Peteraf, Thompson, 2015* 29

3. Evaluating a Company's External Environment: *Chapter 3 from Essentials of Strategic Management: The Quest for Competitive Advantage, Fourth Edition by Gamble, Peteraf, Thompson, 2015* 53

4. Evaluating a Company's Resources, Capabilities, and Competitiveness: *Chapter 4 from Essentials of Strategic Management: The Quest for Competitive Advantage, Fourth Edition by Gamble, Peteraf, Thompson, 2015* 84

5. The Five Generic Competitive Strategies: *Chapter 5 from Essentials of Strategic Management: The Quest for Competitive Advantage, Fourth Edition by Gamble, Peteraf, Thompson, 2015* 108

6. Strategies for Competing in International Markets: *Chapter 7 from Essentials of Strategic Management: The Quest for Competitive Advantage, Fourth Edition by Gamble, Peteraf, Thompson, 2015* 131

7. Corporate Strategy: Diversification and the Multibusiness Company: *Chapter 8 from Essentials of Strategic Management: The Quest for Competitive Advantage, Fourth Edition by Gamble, Peteraf, Thompson, 2015* 153

8. Ethics, Corporate Social Responsibility, Environmental Sustainability, and Strategy: *Chapter 9 from Essentials of Strategic Management: The Quest for Competitive Advantage, Fourth Edition by Gamble, Peteraf, Thompson, 2015* 183

PREFACE

The standout features of this fourth edition of *Essentials of Strategic Management* are its concisely written and robust coverage of strategic management concepts and its compelling collection of cases. The text presents a conceptually strong treatment of strategic management principles and analytic approaches that features straight-to-the-point discussions, timely examples, and a writing style that captures the interest of students. While this edition retains the 10-chapter structure of the prior edition, every chapter has been reexamined, refined, and refreshed. New content has been added to keep the material in line with the latest developments in the theory and practice of strategic management. Also, scores of new examples have been added, along with fresh Concepts & Connections illustrations, to make the content come alive and to provide students with a ringside view of strategy in action. The fundamental character of the fourth edition of *Essentials of Strategic Management* is very much in step with the best academic thinking and contemporary management practice. The chapter content continues to be solidly mainstream and balanced, mirroring *both* the penetrating insight of academic thought and the pragmatism of real-world strategic management.

Complementing the text presentation is a truly appealing lineup of 12 diverse, timely, and thoughtfully crafted cases. All of the cases are tightly linked to the content of the 10 chapters, thus pushing students to apply the concepts and analytical tools they have read about. Eight of the 12 cases were written by the coauthors to illustrate specific tools of analysis or distinct strategic management theories. The four cases not written by the coauthors were chosen because of their exceptional linkage to strategic management concepts presented in the text. We are confident you will be impressed with how well each of the 12 cases in the collection will work in the classroom and the amount of student interest they will spark.

For some years now, growing numbers of strategy instructors at business schools worldwide have been transitioning from a purely text-cases course structure to a more robust and energizing text-cases-simulation course structure. Incorporating a competition-based strategy simulation has the strong appeal of providing class members with *an immediate and engaging opportunity to apply the concepts and analytical tools covered in the chapters in a head-to-head competition with companies run by other class members.* Two widely used and pedagogically effective online strategy simulations, *The Business Strategy Game* and *GLO-BUS,* are optional companions for this text. Both simulations, like the cases, are closely linked to the content of each chapter in the text. The Exercises for Simulation Participants, found at the end of each chapter, provide clear guidance to class members in applying the concepts and analytical tools covered in the chapters to the issues and decisions that they have to wrestle with in managing their simulation company.

Through our experiences as business school faculty members, we also fully understand the assessment demands on faculty teaching strategic management and business policy courses. In many institutions, capstone courses have emerged as the logical home for assessing student achievement of program learning objectives. The fourth edition includes Assurance of Learning Exercises at the end of each chapter that link to the specific Learning Objectives appearing at the beginning of each chapter and highlighted throughout the text. *An important instructional feature of this edition is the linkage of selected chapter-end Assurance of Learning Exercises and cases to the publisher's Connect Management web-based assignment and assessment platform.* Your students will be able to use the online *Connect* supplement to (1) complete two of the Assurance of Learning Exercises appearing at the end of each of the 10 chapters, (2) complete chapter-end quizzes, and (3) complete case tutorials based upon the suggested assignment questions for all 12 cases in this edition. With the exception of some of the chapter-end Assurance of Learning exercises, all of the *Connect* exercises are automatically graded, thereby enabling you to easily assess the learning that has occurred.

In addition, both of the companion strategy simulations have a built-in Learning Assurance Report that quantifies how well each member of your class performed on nine skills/learning measures *versus tens of thousands of other students worldwide* who completed the simulation in the past 12 months. We believe the chapter-end Assurance of Learning Exercises, the all-new online and automatically graded Connect exercises, and the Learning Assurance Report generated at the conclusion of *The Business Strategy Game* and *GLO-BUS* simulations provide you with easy-to-use, empirical measures of student learning in your course. All can be used in conjunction with other instructor-developed or school-developed scoring rubrics and assessment tools to comprehensively evaluate course or program learning outcomes and measure compliance with AACSB accreditation standards.

Taken together, the various components of the fourth edition package and the supporting set of Instructor Resources provide you with enormous course design flexibility and a powerful kit of teaching/learning tools. We've done our very best to ensure that the elements comprising this edition will work well for you in the classroom, help you economize on the time needed to be well prepared for each class, and cause students to conclude that your course is one of the very best they have ever taken—from the standpoint of both enjoyment and learning.

Differentiation from Other Texts

Five noteworthy traits strongly differentiate this text and the accompanying instructional package from others in the field:

1. *Our integrated coverage of the two most popular perspectives on strategic management positioning theory and resource-based theory is unsurpassed by any other leading strategy text.* Principles and concepts from both the positioning perspective and the resource-based perspective are prominently and comprehensively integrated into our coverage of crafting both single-business and multibusiness strategies. By highlighting the relationship between a firm's

resources and capabilities to the activities it conducts along its value chain, we show explicitly how these two perspectives relate to one another. Moreover, in Chapters 3 through 8 it is emphasized repeatedly that a company's strategy must be matched not only to its external market circumstances but also to its internal resources and competitive capabilities.

2. *Our coverage of business ethics, core values, social responsibility, and environmental sustainability is unsurpassed by any other leading strategy text.* Chapter 9, "Ethics, Corporate Social Responsibility, Environmental Sustainability, and Strategy," is embellished with fresh content so that it can better fulfill the important functions of (1) alerting students to the role and importance of ethical and socially responsible decision making and (2) addressing the accreditation requirements that business ethics be visibly and thoroughly embedded in the core curriculum. Moreover, discussions of the roles of values and ethics are integrated into portions of other chapters to further reinforce why and how considerations relating to ethics, values, social responsibility, and sustainability should figure prominently into the managerial task of crafting and executing company strategies.

3. *The caliber of the case collection in the fourth edition is truly unrivaled* from the standpoints of student appeal, teachability, and suitability for drilling students in the use of the concepts and analytical treatments in Chapters 1 through 10. The 12 cases included in this edition are the very latest, the best, and the most on-target that we could find. The ample information about the cases in the Instructor's Manual makes it effortless to select a set of cases each term that will capture the interest of students from start to finish.

4. *The publisher's Connect Management assignment and assessment platform is tightly linked to the text chapters and case lineup.* The *Connect* package for the fourth edition allows professors to assign autograded quizzes and select chapter-end Assurance of Learning Exercises to assess class members' understanding of chapter concepts. In addition, our texts have pioneered the extension of the *Connect Management* platform to case analysis. The autograded case exercises for each of the 12 cases in this edition are robust and extensive and will better enable students to make meaningful contributions to class discussions. The autograded *Connect* case exercises may also be used as graded assignments in the course.

5. The two cutting-edge and widely used strategy simulations—*The Business Strategy Game* and *GLO-BUS*—that are optional companions to the fourth edition give you unmatched capability to employ a text-case-simulation model of course delivery.

Organization, Content, and Features of the Fourth Edition Text Chapters

The following rundown summarizes the noteworthy features and topical emphasis in this new edition:

- Chapter 1 focuses on the importance of developing a clear understanding of why a company exists and why it matters in the marketplace. In developing such an understanding, management must define its approach to creating superior value for customers and how capabilities and resources will be employed to deliver the desired value to customers. We introduce students to the primary approaches to building competitive advantage and the key elements of business-level strategy. Following Henry Mintzberg's pioneering research, we also stress why a company's strategy is partly planned and partly reactive and why this strategy tends to evolve. The chapter also discusses why it is important for a company to have a *viable business model* that outlines the company's customer value proposition and its profit formula. This brief chapter is the perfect accompaniment to your opening-day lecture on what the course is all about and why it matters.

- Chapter 2 delves more deeply into the managerial process of actually crafting and executing a strategy—it makes a great assignment for the second day of class and provides a smooth transition into the heart of the course. The focal point of the chapter is the five-stage managerial process of crafting and executing strategy: (1) forming a strategic vision of where the company is headed and why, (2) developing strategic as well as financial objectives with which to measure the company's progress, (3) crafting a strategy to achieve these targets and move the company toward its market destination, (4) implementing and executing the strategy, and (5) evaluating a company's situation and performance to identify corrective adjustments that are needed. Students are introduced to such core concepts as strategic visions, mission statements and core values, the balanced scorecard, and business-level versus corporate-level strategies. There's a robust discussion of why *all managers are on a company's strategy-making, strategy-executing team* and why a company's strategic plan is a collection of strategies devised by different managers at different levels in the organizational hierarchy. The chapter winds up with a section on how to exercise good corporate governance and examines the conditions that led to recent high-profile corporate governance failures.

- Chapter 3 sets forth the now-familiar analytical tools and concepts of industry and competitive analysis and demonstrates the importance of tailoring strategy to fit the circumstances of a company's industry and competitive environment. The standout feature of this chapter is a presentation of Michael Porter's "five forces model of competition" *that has long been the clearest, most straightforward discussion of any text in the field.* New to this edition is the recasting of the discussion of the macro-environment to include the use of the PESTEL analysis framework for assessing the *p*olitical, *e*conomic, *s*ocial, *t*echnological, *e*nvironmental, and *l*egal factors in a company's macro-environment.

- Chapter 4 presents the resource-based view of the firm, showing why resource and capability analysis is such a powerful tool for sizing up a company's competitive assets. It offers a simple framework for identifying a company's resources and capabilities and another for determining whether they can provide the company with a sustainable competitive advantage over its competitors. New to this edition is a more explicit reference to the widely used VRIN framework. Other topics covered in this chapter include dynamic capabilities, SWOT analysis, value chain analysis, benchmarking, and competitive strength assessments, thus enabling a solid appraisal of a company's relative cost position and customer value proposition vis-à-vis its rivals.

- Chapter 5 deals with the basic approaches used to compete successfully and gain a competitive advantage over market rivals. This discussion is framed around the five generic competitive strategies—low-cost leadership, differentiation, best-cost provider, focused differentiation, and focused low-cost. It describes when each of these approaches works best and what pitfalls to avoid. It explains the role of *cost drivers* and *uniqueness drivers* in reducing a company's costs and enhancing its differentiation, respectively.

- Chapter 6 deals with the *strategy options* available to complement a company's competitive approach and maximize the power of its overall strategy. These include a variety of offensive or defensive competitive moves, and their timing, such as blue ocean strategy and first-mover advantages and disadvantages. It also includes choices concerning the breadth of a company's activities (or its scope of operations along an industry's entire value chain), ranging from horizontal mergers and acquisitions, to vertical integration, outsourcing, and strategic alliances. This material serves to segue into that covered in the next two chapters on international and diversification strategies.

- Chapter 7 explores the full range of strategy options for competing in international markets: export strategies; licensing; franchising; establishing a subsidiary in a foreign market; and using strategic alliances and joint ventures to build competitive strength in foreign markets. There's also a discussion of how to best tailor a company's international strategy to cross-country differences in market conditions and buyer preferences, how to use international operations to improve overall competitiveness, and the unique characteristics of competing in emerging markets.

- Chapter 8 introduces the topic of corporate-level strategy—a topic of concern for multibusiness companies pursuing diversification. This chapter begins by explaining why successful diversification strategies must create shareholder value and lays out the three essential tests that a strategy must pass to achieve this goal (*the industry attractiveness, cost of entry, and better-off tests*). Corporate strategy topics covered in the chapter include methods of entering new businesses, related diversification, unrelated diversification, combined related and unrelated diversification approaches, and strategic options for improving the overall performance of an already diversified company. The chapter's analytical spotlight is trained on the techniques and procedures for assessing a diversified company's business portfolio—the relative attractiveness of the various businesses the company has diversified into, the company's competitive strength in each of its business lines, and the *strategic fit* and *resource fit* among a diversified company's different businesses. The chapter concludes with a brief survey of a company's four main postdiversification strategy alternatives: (1) sticking closely with the existing business lineup,

(2) broadening the diversification base, (3) divesting some businesses and retrenching to a narrower diversification base, and (4) restructuring the makeup of the company's business lineup.

- Although the topic of ethics and values comes up at various points in this textbook, Chapter 9 brings more direct attention to such issues and may be used as a stand-alone assignment in either the early, middle, or late part of a course. It concerns the themes of ethical standards in business, approaches to ensuring consistent ethical standards for companies with international operations, corporate social responsibility, and environmental sustainability. The contents of this chapter are sure to give students some things to ponder, rouse lively discussion, and help to make students more ethically aware and conscious of *why all companies should conduct their business in a socially responsible and sustainable manner.*

- Chapter 10 is anchored around a pragmatic, compelling conceptual framework: (1) building dynamic capabilities, core competencies, resources, and structure necessary for proficient strategy execution; (2) allocating ample resources to strategy-critical activities; (3) ensuring that policies and procedures facilitate rather than impede strategy execution; (4) pushing for continuous improvement in how value chain activities are performed; (5) installing information and operating systems that enable company personnel to better carry out essential activities; (6) tying rewards and incentives directly to the achievement of performance targets and good strategy execution; (7) shaping the work environment and corporate culture to fit the strategy; and (8) exerting the internal leadership needed to drive execution forward. The recurring theme throughout the chapter is that implementing and executing strategy entails figuring out the specific actions, behaviors, and conditions that are needed for a smooth strategy-supportive operation—the goal here is to ensure that students understand that the strategy-implementing/strategy-executing phase is a make-it-happen-right kind of managerial exercise that leads to operating excellence and good performance.

In this latest edition, we have put our utmost effort into ensuring that the 10 chapters are consistent with the latest and best thinking of academics and practitioners in the field of strategic management and hit the bull's-eye in topical coverage for senior- and MBA-level strategy courses. The ultimate test of the text, of course, is the positive pedagogical impact it has in the classroom. If this edition sets a more effective stage for your lectures and does a better job of helping you persuade students that the discipline of strategy merits their rapt attention, then it will have fulfilled its purpose.

The Case Collection

The 12-case lineup in this edition is flush with interesting companies and valuable lessons for students in the art and science of crafting and executing strategy. There's a good blend of cases from a length perspective—about one-third are under 12 pages, yet offer plenty for students to chew on; about a third are medium-length cases; and the remaining one-third are detail-rich cases that call for sweeping analysis.

At least 10 of the 12 cases involve companies, products, people, or activities that students will have heard of, know about from personal experience, or can easily identify with. The lineup includes at least four cases that will provide students with insight into the special demands of competing in industry environments where technological developments are an everyday event, product life cycles are short, and competitive maneuvering among rivals comes fast and furious. All of the cases involve situations where the role of company resources and competitive capabilities in the strategy formulation, strategy execution scheme is emphasized. Scattered throughout the lineup are eight cases concerning non-U.S. companies, globally competitive industries, and/or cross-cultural situations; these cases, in conjunction with the globalized content of the text chapters, provide abundant material for linking the study of strategic management tightly to the ongoing globalization of the world economy. You'll also find four cases dealing with the strategic problems of family-owned or relatively small entrepreneurial businesses and 10 cases involving public companies and situations where students can do further research on the Internet. A number of the cases have accompanying videotape segments.

The Two Strategy Simulation Supplements: *The Business Strategy Game* and *GLO-BUS*

The Business Strategy Game and *GLO-BUS: Developing Winning Competitive Strategies*—two competition-based strategy simulations that are delivered online and that feature automated processing and grading of performance—are being marketed by the publisher as companion supplements for use with the fourth edition (and other texts in the field). *The Business Strategy Game* is the world's most popular strategy simulation, having been used by nearly 2,000 instructors in courses involving over 700,000 students at 900 university campuses in 60 countries. *GLO-BUS*, a somewhat simpler strategy simulation introduced in 2004, has been used by more than 1,100 instructors at 500+ university campuses in 40 countries. Both simulations allow students to apply strategy-making and analysis concepts presented in the text and may be used as part of a comprehensive effort to assess undergraduate or graduate program learning objectives.

The Compelling Case for Incorporating Use of a Strategy Simulation

There are *three exceptionally important benefits* associated with using a competition-based simulation in strategy courses taken by seniors and MBA students:

- *A three-pronged text-case-simulation course model delivers significantly more teaching and learning power than the traditional text-case model.* Using *both* cases and a strategy simulation to drill students in thinking strategically and applying what they read in the text chapters is a stronger, more effective means of helping them connect theory with practice and develop better business judgment. What cases do that a simulation cannot is give class members broad exposure to a variety of companies and industry situations and insight into the kinds of strategy-related problems managers face. But what a competition-based strategy simulation does far better than case analysis is thrust class members squarely into *an active, hands-on managerial role* where they are totally responsible for assessing market conditions, determining how to respond to the actions of competitors, forging a long-term direction and strategy for their company, and making all kinds of operating decisions. Because they are held fully accountable for their decisions and their company's performance, *co-managers are strongly motivated* to dig deeply into company operations, probe for ways to be more cost-efficient and competitive, and ferret out strategic moves and decisions calculated to boost company performance. *Consequently, incorporating both case assignments and a strategy simulation to develop the skills of class members in thinking strategically and applying the concepts and tools of strategic analysis turns out to be more pedagogically powerful than relying solely on case assignments—there's stronger retention of the lessons learned and better achievement of course learning objectives.*

- *The competitive nature of a strategy simulation arouses positive energy and steps up the whole tempo of the course by a notch or two.* Nothing sparks class excitement quicker or better than the concerted efforts on the part of class members during each decision round to achieve a high industry ranking and avoid the perilous consequences of being outcompeted by other class members. Students really enjoy taking on the role of a manager, running their own company, crafting strategies, making all kinds of operating decisions, trying to outcompete rival companies, and getting immediate feedback on the resulting company performance. Co-managers become *emotionally invested* in running their company and figuring out what strategic moves to make to boost their company's performance. All this stimulates learning and causes students to see the practical relevance of the subject matter and the benefits of taking your course.

- *Use of a fully automated online simulation reduces the time instructors spend on course preparation, course administration, and grading.* Since the simulation exercise involves a 20- to 30-hour workload for student-teams (roughly 2 hours per decision round times 10-12 rounds, plus optional assignments), simulation adopters often compensate by trimming the number of assigned cases from, say, 10 to 12 to perhaps 4 to 6. This significantly reduces the time instructors spend reading cases, studying teaching notes, and otherwise getting ready to lead class discussion of a case or grade oral team presentations. Course preparation time is further cut because you can use several class days to have students meet in the computer lab to work on upcoming decision rounds or a three-year strategic plan (in lieu of lecturing on a chapter or covering an additional assigned case). Not only does use of a simulation permit assigning fewer cases, but it also permits you to eliminate at least one assignment that entails considerable grading on your part. Grading one less written case or essay exam or other written assignment saves enormous time. With *BSG* and *GLO-BUS*, grading is effortless and takes only minutes; once you enter percentage weights for each assignment in your online grade book, a suggested overall grade is calculated for you. You'll be pleasantly surprised—and quite pleased—at how little time it takes to gear up for and to administer *The Business Strategy Game* or *GLO-BUS*.

In sum, incorporating use of a strategy simulation turns out to be *a win-win proposition for both students and instructors.* Moreover, a very convincing argument can be made that a competition-based strategy simulation is *the single most effective teaching/learning tool that instructors can employ to teach the discipline of business and competitive strategy, to make learning more enjoyable, and to promote better achievement of course learning objectives.*

Administration and Operating Features of the Two Simulations

The Internet delivery and user-friendly designs of both *BSG* and *GLO-BUS* make them incredibly easy to administer, even for first-time users. And the menus and controls are so similar that you can readily switch between the two simulations or use one in your undergraduate class and the other in a graduate class. If you have not yet used either of the two simulations, you may find the following of particular interest:

- Setting up the simulation for your course is done online and takes about 10 to 15 minutes. Once setup is completed, no other administrative actions are required beyond that of moving participants to a different team (should the need arise) and monitoring the progress of the simulation (to whatever extent desired).

- Participant's Guides are delivered electronically to class members at the website—students can read it on their monitors or print out a copy, as they prefer.

- There are two- to four-minute Video Tutorials scattered throughout the software (including each decision screen and each page of each report) that provide on-demand guidance to class members who may be uncertain about how to proceed.

- Complementing the video tutorials are detailed and clearly written Help sections explaining "all there is to know" about (a) each decision entry and the relevant cause-effect relationships, (b) the information on each page of the Industry Reports, and (c) the numbers presented in the Company Reports. *The Video Tutorials and the Help screens allow company co-managers to figure things out for themselves, thereby curbing the need for students to ask the instructor "how things work."*

- Team members running the same company who are logged-in simultaneously on different computers at different locations can click a button to enter Collaboration Mode, enabling them to work collaboratively from the same screen in viewing reports and making decision entries, and click a second button to enter Audio Mode, letting them talk to one another.
    - When in "Collaboration Mode," each team member sees the same screen at the same time as all other team members who are logged in and have joined Collaboration Mode. If one team member chooses to view a particular decision screen, that same screen appears on the monitors for all team members in Collaboration Mode.

- Team members each control their own color-coded mouse pointer (with their first-name appearing in a color-coded box linked to their mouse pointer) and can make a decision entry or move the mouse to point to particular on-screen items.

- A decision entry change made by one team member is seen by all, in real time, and all team members can immediately view the on-screen calculations that result from the new decision entry.

- If one team member wishes to view a report page and clicks on the menu link to the desired report, that same report page will immediately appear for the other team members engaged in collaboration.

- Use of Audio Mode capability requires that team members work from a computer with a built-in microphone (if they want to be heard by their team members) and speakers (so they may hear their teammates) or else have a headset with a microphone that they can plug into their desktop or laptop. A headset is recommended for best results, but most laptops now are equipped with a built-in microphone and speakers that will support use of our new voice chat feature.

- Real-time VoIP audio chat capability among team members who have entered both the Audio Mode and the Collaboration Mode is a tremendous boost in functionality that enables team members to go online simultaneously on computers at different locations and conveniently and effectively collaborate in running their simulation company.

- In addition, instructors have the capability to join the online session of any company and speak with team members, thus circumventing the need for team members to arrange for and attend a meeting in the instructor's office. Using the standard menu for administering a particular industry, instructors can connect with the company desirous of assistance. Instructors who wish not only to talk but also enter Collaboration (highly recommended because all attendees are then viewing the same screen) have a red-colored mouse pointer linked to a red box labeled Instructor.

    Without a doubt, the Collaboration and Voice-Chat capabilities are hugely valuable for students enrolled in online and distance-learning courses where meeting face-to-face is impractical or time-consuming. Likewise, the instructors of online and distance-learning courses will appreciate having the capability to join the online meetings of particular company teams when their advice or assistance is requested.

- Both simulations are quite suitable for use in distance-learning or online courses (and are currently being used in such courses on numerous campuses).

- Participants and instructors are notified via e-mail when the results are ready (usually about 15 to 20 minutes after the decision round deadline specified by the instructor/game administrator).

- Following each decision round, participants are provided with a complete set of reports—a six-page Industry Report, a one-page Competitive Intelligence report for each geographic region that includes strategic group maps and bulleted lists of competitive strengths and weaknesses, and a set of Company Reports (income statement, balance sheet, cash flow statement, and assorted production, marketing, and cost statistics).

- Two "open-book" multiple-choice tests of 20 questions are built into each simulation. The quizzes, which you can require or not as you see fit, are taken online and automatically graded, with scores reported instantaneously to participants and automatically recorded in the instructor's electronic grade book. Students are automatically provided with three sample questions for each test.

- Both simulations contain a three-year strategic plan option that you can assign. Scores on the plan are automatically recorded in the instructor's online grade book.

- At the end of the simulation, you can have students complete online peer evaluations (again, the scores are automatically recorded in your online grade book).

- Both simulations have a Company Presentation feature that enables each team of company co-managers to easily prepare PowerPoint slides for use in describing their strategy and summarizing their company's performance in a presentation to either the class, the instructor, or an "outside" board of directors.

- *A Learning Assurance Report provides you with hard data concerning how well your students performed vis-à-vis students playing the simulation worldwide over the past 12 months.* The report is based on nine measures of student proficiency, business know-how, and decision-making skill and can also be used in evaluating the extent to which your school's academic curriculum produces the desired degree of student learning insofar as accreditation standards are concerned.

For more details on either simulation, please consult Section 2 of the Instructor's Manual accompanying this text or register as an instructor at the simulation websites (www.bsg-online.com and www.globus.com) to access even more comprehensive information. You should also consider signing up for one of the webinars that the simulation authors conduct several times each month (sometimes several times weekly) to demonstrate how the software works, walk you through the various features and menu options, and answer any questions. You have an open invitation to call the senior author of this text at (205) 722-9145 to arrange a personal demonstration or talk about how one of the simulations might work in one of your courses. We think you'll be quite impressed with the cutting-edge capabilities that have been programmed into *The Business Strategy Game* and *GLO-BUS*, the simplicity with which both simulations can be administered, and their exceptionally tight connection to the text chapters, core concepts, and standard analytical tools.

Resources and Support Materials for the Fourth Edition for Students

Key Points Summaries

At the end of each chapter is a synopsis of the core concepts, analytical tools, and other key points discussed in the chapter. These chapter-end synopses, along with the core concept definitions and margin notes scattered throughout each chapter, help students focus on basic strategy principles, digest the messages of each chapter, and prepare for tests.

Two Sets of Chapter-End Exercises

Each chapter concludes with two sets of exercises. The Assurance of Learning Exercises can be used as the basis for class discussion, oral presentation assignments, short written reports, and substitutes for case assignments. The Exercises for Simulation Participants are designed expressly for use by adopters who have incorporated use of a simulation and wish to go a step further in tightly and explicitly connecting the chapter content to the simulation company their students are running. The questions in both sets of exercises (along with those Concepts & Connections illustrations that qualify as "mini cases") can be used to round out the rest of a 75-minute class period should your lecture on a chapter only last for 50 minutes.

A Value-Added Website

The student version of the Online Learning Center (OLC) or website www. mhhe.com/gamble4e contains a number of helpful aids:

*   20-question self-scoring chapter tests that students can take to measure their grasp of the material presented in each of the 10 chapters.
*   A "Guide to Case Analysis" containing sections on what a case is, why cases are a standard part of courses in strategy, preparing a case for class discussion, doing a written case analysis, doing an oral presentation, and using financial ratio analysis to assess a company's financial condition. We suggest having students read this guide prior to the first class discussion of a case.
*   PowerPoint slides for each chapter.

The *Connect Management* Web-Based Assignment and Assessment Platform

We have taken advantage of the publisher's innovative *Connect Management* assignment and assessment platform and created several robust and valuable features that simplify the task of assigning and grading three types of exercises for students:

*   There are self-scoring chapter tests consisting of 20 multiple-choice questions that students can take to measure their grasp of the material presented in each of the 10 chapters.
*   *Connect Management* includes interactive versions of two Assurance of Learning Exercises for each chapter that drill students in the use and application of the concepts and tools of strategic analysis.
*   The *Connect Management* platform also includes fully autograded interactive application exercises for each of the 12 cases in this edition. The exercises require students to work through tutorials based upon the analysis set forth in the assignment questions for the case; these exercises have multiple components such as resource and capability analysis, financial

ratio analysis, identifcation of a company's strategy, or analysis of the five competitive forces. The content of these case exercises is tailored to match the circumstances presented in each case, calling upon students to do whatever strategic thinking and strategic analysis is called for to arrive at pragmatic, analysis-based action recommendations for improving company performance. The entire exercise is autograded, allowing instructors to focus on grading only the students' strategic recommendations.

All of the *Connect* exercises are automatically graded (with the exception of a few exercise components that entail student entry of essay answers), thereby simplifying the task of evaluating each class member's performance and monitoring the learning outcomes. The progress-tracking function built into the *Connect* system enables you to

- View scored work immediately and track individual or group performance with assignment and grade reports.
- Access an instant view of student or class performance relative to learning objectives.
- Collect data and generate reports required by many accreditation organizations, such as AACSB.

For Instructors

Online Learning Center (OLC)

In addition to the student resources, the instructor section of www.mhhe .com/gamble4e includes an Instructor's Manual and other support materials. Your McGraw-Hill representative can arrange delivery of instructor support materials in a format-ready Standard Cartridge for Blackboard, WebCT, and other web-based educational platforms.

Instructor's Manual

The accompanying IM contains:

- A section on suggestions for organizing and structuring your course.
- Sample syllabi and course outlines.
- A set of lecture notes on each chapter.
- Answers to the chapter-end Assurance of Learning Exercises.
- A comprehensive case teaching note for each of the 12 cases—these teaching notes are filled with suggestions for using the case effectively, have very thorough, analysis-based answers to the suggested assignment questions for the case, and contain an epilogue detailing any important developments since the case was written.

Test Bank and EZ Test Online

There is a test bank containing over 700 multiple-choice questions and short-answer/essay questions. It has been tagged with AACSB and Bloom's Taxonomy criteria. All of the test bank questions are also accessible within a computerized test bank powered by McGraw-Hill's flexible electronic testing program EZ Test Online (www.eztestonline.com). Using EZ Test Online allows you to create paper and online tests or quizzes. With EZ Test Online, instructors can select questions from multiple McGraw-Hill test banks or author their own, and then either print the test for paper distribution or give it online.

PowerPoint Slides

To facilitate delivery preparation of your lectures and to serve as chapter outlines, you'll have access to approximately 350 colorful and professional-looking slides displaying core concepts, analytical procedures, key points, and all the figures in the text chapters.

The Business Strategy Game and GLO-BUS Online Simulations

Using one of the two companion simulations is a powerful and constructive way of emotionally connecting students to the subject matter of the course. We know of no more effective way to arouse the competitive energy of students and prepare them for the challenges of real-world business decision making than to have them match strategic wits with classmates in running a company in head-to-head competition for global market leadership.

Acknowledgments

We heartily acknowledge the contributions of the case researchers whose case-writing efforts appear herein and the companies whose cooperation made the cases possible. To each one goes a very special thank-you. We cannot overstate the importance of timely, carefully researched cases in contributing to a substantive study of strategic management issues and practices. From a research standpoint, strategy-related cases are invaluable in exposing the generic kinds of strategic issues that companies face in forming hypotheses about strategic behavior and in drawing experienced-based generalizations about the practice of strategic management. From an instructional standpoint, strategy cases give students essential practice in diagnosing and evaluating the strategic situations of companies and organizations, in applying the concepts and tools of strategic analysis, in weighing strategic options and crafting strategies, and in tackling the challenges of successful strategy execution. Without a continuing stream of fresh, well-researched, and well-conceived cases, the discipline of strategic management would lose its close ties to the very institutions whose strategic actions and behavior it is aimed at explaining. There's no question, therefore, that first-class case research constitutes a valuable scholarly contribution to the theory and practice of strategic management.

A great number of colleagues and students at various universities, business acquaintances, and people at McGraw-Hill provided inspiration, encouragement, and counsel during the course of this project. Like all text authors in the strategy field, we are intellectually indebted to the many academics whose research and writing have blazed new trails and advanced the discipline of strategic management.

We also express our thanks to Todd M. Alessandri, Michael Anderson, Gerald D. Baumgardner, Edith C. Busija, Gerald E. Calvasina, Sam D. Cappel, Richard Churchman, John W. Collis, Connie Daniel, Christine DeLaTorre, Vickie Cox Edmondson, Diane D. Galbraith, Naomi A. Gardberg, Sanjay Goel, Les Jankovich, Jonatan Jelen, William Jiang, Bonnie Johnson, Roy Johnson, John J. Lawrence, Robert E. Ledman, Mark Lehrer, Fred Maidment, Frank Markham, Renata Mayrhofer, Simon Medcalfe, Elouise Mintz, Michael Monahan, Gerry Nkombo Muuka, Cori J. Myers, Jeryl L. Nelson, David Olson, John Perry, L. Jeff Seaton, Charles F. Seifert, Eugene S. Simko, Karen J. Smith, Susan Steiner, Troy V. Sullivan, Elisabeth J. Teal, Lori Tisher, Vincent Weaver, Jim Whitlock, and Beth Woodard. These reviewers provided valuable guidance in steering our efforts to improve earlier editions.

As always, we value your recommendations and thoughts about the book. Your comments regarding coverage and contents will be taken to heart, and we always are grateful for the time you take to call our attention to printing errors, deficiencies, and other shortcomings. Please e-mail us at john.gamble@tamucc.edu, or athompso@cba.ua.edu, or margaret.a.peteraf@ tuck.dartmouth.edu.

John E. Gamble
Margaret A. Peteraf
Arthur A. Thompson

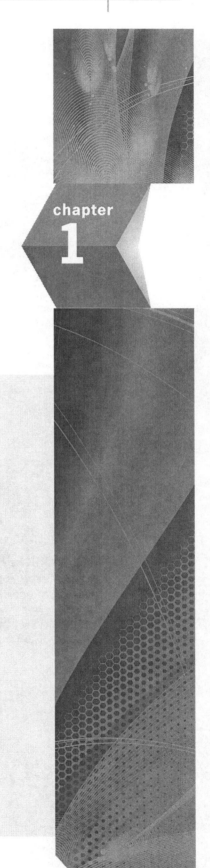

Strategy, Business Models, and Competitive Advantage

chapter

1

LEARNING OBJECTIVES

LO1 Understand why every company needs a distinctive strategy to compete successfully, manage its business operations, and strengthen its prospects for long-term success.

LO2 Learn why it is important for a company to have a viable business model that outlines the company's customer value proposition and its profit formula.

LO3 Develop an awareness of the five most dependable strategic approaches for setting a company apart from rivals and winning a sustainable competitive advantage.

LO4 Understand that a company's strategy tends to evolve over time because of changing circumstances and ongoing management efforts to improve the company's strategy.

LO5 Learn the three tests of a winning strategy.

In thinking strategically about a company, *managers of all types of businesses must develop a clear understanding of why a company exists and why the company matters in the marketplace.* Do the company's products or services offer customers value in ways that competitors cannot match? Is the company's approach to doing business different from that of rivals and thereby allows the company to offer superior customer value? What is it about the company's offering that is distinctive and makes it important in the minds of customers? How would customers be affected if the company did not exist? A company's **strategy** spells out why the company matters in the marketplace by defining its approach to creating superior value for customers and how capabilities and resources will be employed to deliver the desired value to customers. In effect, the crafting of a strategy represents a managerial commitment to pursuing an array of choices about how to compete. These include choices about:

- *How* to create products or services that attract and please customers.
- *How* to position the company in the industry.
- *How* to develop and deploy resources to build valuable competitive capabilities.
- *How* each functional piece of the business (R&D, supply chain activities, production, sales and marketing, distribution, finance, and human resources) will be operated.
- *How* to achieve the company's performance targets.

In most industries companies have considerable freedom in choosing the *hows* of strategy. Thus some rivals strive to create superior value for customers by achieving lower costs than rivals while others pursue product superiority or personalized customer service or the development of capabilities that rivals cannot match. Some competitors position themselves in only one part of the industry's chain of production/distribution activities, while others are partially or fully integrated, with operations ranging from components production to manufacturing and assembly to wholesale distribution or retailing. Some competitors deliberately confine their operations to local or regional markets; others opt to compete nationally, internationally (several countries), or globally. Some companies decide to operate in only one industry, while others diversify broadly or narrowly, into related or unrelated industries.

> **CORE CONCEPT**
>
> A company's **strategy** explains why the company matters in the marketplace by specifying an approach to creating superior value for customers and determining how capabilities and resources will be utilized to deliver the desired value to customers.

The role of this chapter is to define the concepts of strategy and competitive advantage, the relationship between a company's strategy and its business model, why strategies are partly proactive and partly reactive, and why company strategies evolve over time. Particular attention will be paid to what sets a winning strategy apart from a ho-hum or flawed strategy and why the caliber of a company's strategy determines whether it will enjoy a competitive advantage or be burdened by competitive disadvantage. By the end of this chapter, you will have a clear idea of why the tasks of crafting and executing strategy are core management functions and why excellent execution of an excellent strategy is the most reliable recipe for turning a company into a standout performer.

The Importance of Strategic Uniqueness

For a company to matter in the minds of customers, its strategy needs a distinctive element that sets it apart from rivals and produces a competitive edge. A strategy must tightly fit a company's own particular situation, but there is no shortage of opportunity to fashion a strategy that is discernibly different from the strategies of rivals. In fact, competitive success requires a company's managers to make strategic choices about the key building blocks of its strategy that differ from the choices made by competitors—not 100 percent different but at least different in several important respects. A strategy stands a chance of succeeding only when it is predicated on actions, business approaches, and competitive moves aimed at appealing to buyers *in ways that set a company apart from rivals.* Simply trying to mimic the strategies of the industry's successful companies rarely works. Rather, every company's strategy needs to have some distinctive element that draws in customers and produces a competitive edge. Strategy, at its essence, is about competing differently—doing what rival firms *don't* do or, better yet, what rival firms *can't* do.[1]

> **LO1** Understand why every company needs a distinctive strategy to compete successfully, manage its business operations, and strengthen its prospects for long-term success.

> Mimicking the strategies of successful industry rivals—with either copycat product offerings or efforts to stake out the same market position—rarely works. A creative, distinctive strategy that sets a company apart from rivals and yields a competitive advantage is a company's most reliable ticket for earning above-average profits.

Strategy and a Company's Business Model

Closely related to the concept of strategy is the concept of a company's **business model.** While the company's strategy sets forth an approach to offering superior value, a company's business model is management's blueprint for delivering a valuable product or service to customers in a manner that will yield an attractive profit.[2] The two elements of a company's business model are (1) its *customer value proposition* and (2) its *profit formula.* The customer value proposition is established by the company's overall strategy and lays out the company's approach to satisfying buyer wants and needs at a price customers will consider a good value. The greater the value provided and the lower the price, the more attractive the value proposition is to customers. The profit formula describes the company's approach to determining a cost structure that will allow for acceptable profits given the pricing tied to its customer value proposition. The lower the costs given the customer value proposition, the greater the ability of the business model to be a moneymaker. The nitty-gritty issue surrounding a company's business model is whether it can execute its customer value proposition profitably. Just because company managers have crafted a strategy for competing and running the business does not automatically mean the strategy will lead to profitability—it may or it may not.[3]

> **LO2** Learn why it is important for a company to have a viable business model that outlines the company's customer value proposition and its profit formula.

> **CORE CONCEPT**
> A company's **business model** sets forth how its strategy and operating approaches will create value for customers, while at the same time generate ample revenues to cover costs and realize a profit. The two elements of a company's business model are its (1) customer value proposition and (2) its profit formula.

Cable television providers utilize a business model, keyed to delivering news and entertainment that viewers will find valuable, to secure sufficient revenues from subscriptions and advertising to cover operating expenses and

CONCEPTS & CONNECTIONS 1.1

PANDORA, SIRIUS XM, AND OVER-THE-AIR BROADCAST RADIO: THREE CONTRASTING BUSINESS MODELS

The strategies of rival companies are often predicated on strikingly different business models. Consider, for example, the business models for over-the-air radio broadcasters, Sirius XM, and Pandora Media.

The business model of over-the-air broadcast radio—providing listeners with free programming and charging advertisers fees—is a proven moneymaker. Sirius XM's business model is proving to be viable with the company recording three consecutive years of profitability after recording losses for its first seven years. But the jury is still out on Pandora's business model of offering streaming Internet radio. Even though Pandora had established itself as the leading Internet radio service with more than 200 million users in the United States, the company ended fiscal 2013 with a $38 million loss.

	Pandora	**Sirius XM**	**Over-the-Air Radio Broadcasters**
Customer value proposition	Internet radio service that allowed PC, tablet computer, and smartphone users to create up to 100 personalized music and comedy stations. Users could create a new station by entering the name of a song, artist, or genre. Pandora utilized algorithms to generate playlists based upon the users' predicted music preferences. Programming for the free service was interrupted by brief, occasional ads, while advertising was eliminated for Pandora One subscribers.	Satellite-based music, news, sports, national and regional weather, traffic reports in limited areas, and talk radio programming provided for a monthly subscription fee. Programming was interrupted only by brief, occasional ads. The company also offered subscribers streaming Internet channels and the ability to create personalized commercial-free stations for online and mobile listening.	Free-of-charge music, national and local news, local traffic reports, national and local weather, and talk radio programming. Listeners could expect frequent programming interruption for ads.
Profit formula	*Revenue generation:* Display, audio, and video ads sold to local and national advertisers. Ads could be targeted to listeners based on age, gender, zip code, and content preferences. Subscription revenues were generated from an advertising-free option called Pandora One. *Cost structure:* Fixed costs associated with developing software for computers, smartphones, and tablet computers. Fixed and variable costs related to operating data centers to support streaming network, content royalties, marketing, and support activities. *Profit margin:* Pandora Media's profitability was dependent on generating sufficient advertising revenues and subscription revenues to cover its costs and provide attractive profits.	*Revenue generation:* Monthly subscription fees, sales of satellite radio equipment, and advertising revenues. *Cost structure:* Fixed costs associated with operating a satellite-based music delivery service and streaming Internet service. Fixed and variable costs related to programming and content royalties, marketing, and support activities. *Profit margin:* Sirius XM's profitability was dependent on attracting a sufficiently large number of subscribers to cover its costs and provide attractive profits.	*Revenue generation:* Advertising sales to national and local businesses. *Cost structure:* Fixed costs associated with terrestrial broadcasting operations. Fixed and variable costs related to local news reporting, advertising sales operations, network affiliate fees, programming and content royalties, commercial production activities, and support activities. *Profit margin:* The profitability of over-the-air radio stations was dependent on generating sufficient advertising revenues to cover costs and provide attractive profits.

Sources: Company documents, 10-Ks, and information posted on their websites.

allow for profits. The business model of automobile dealerships entails generating revenues from automobile sales and after-the-sale service. The cost structure of automobile dealerships allows for healthy profit margins as long as the dealership represents a brand that is valued by consumers and it is able to provide quality service during the warranty period and after warranties expire. Gillette's business model in razor blades involves achieving economies of scale in the production of its shaving products, selling razors at an attractively low price, and then making money on repeat purchases of razor blades. Printer manufacturers such as Hewlett-Packard, Lexmark, and Epson pursue much the same business model as Gillette—achieving economies of scale in production and selling printers at a low (virtually break-even) price and making large profit margins on the repeat purchases of printer supplies, especially ink cartridges. Concepts & Connections 1.1 discusses three contrasting business models in radio broadcasting.

Strategy and the Quest for Competitive Advantage

The heart and soul of any strategy is the actions and moves in the marketplace that managers are taking to gain a competitive edge over rivals.[4] Five of the most frequently used and dependable strategic approaches to setting a company apart from rivals and winning a sustainable competitive advantage are:

LO3 Develop an awareness of the five most dependable strategic approaches for setting a company apart from rivals and winning a sustainable competitive advantage.

1. *A low-cost provider strategy*—achieving a cost-based advantage over rivals. Walmart and Southwest Airlines have earned strong market positions because of the low-cost advantages they have achieved over their rivals. Low-cost provider strategies can produce a durable competitive edge when rivals find it hard to match the low-cost leader's approach to driving costs out of the business.

2. *A broad differentiation strategy*—seeking to differentiate the company's product or service from rivals' in ways that will appeal to a broad spectrum of buyers. Successful adopters of broad differentiation strategies include Johnson & Johnson in baby products (product reliability) and Apple (innovative products). Differentiation strategies can be powerful so long as a company is sufficiently innovative to thwart rivals' attempts to copy or closely imitate its product offering.

3. *A focused low-cost strategy*—concentrating on a narrow buyer segment (or market niche) and outcompeting rivals by having lower costs than rivals and thus being able to serve niche members at a lower price. Private-label manufacturers of food, health and beauty products, and nutritional supplements use their low-cost advantage to offer supermarket buyers lower prices than those demanded by producers of branded products.

4. *A focused differentiation strategy*—concentrating on a narrow buyer segment (or market niche) and outcompeting rivals by offering niche members customized attributes that meet their tastes and requirements better than rivals' products. Louis Vuitton and Rolex have sustained their advantage in the luxury goods industry through a focus on affluent consumers demanding luxury and prestige.

5. *A best-cost provider strategy*—giving customers more value for the money by satisfying buyers' expectations on key quality/features/performance/service attributes, while beating their price expectations. This approach is a hybrid strategy that blends elements of low-cost provider and differentiation strategies; the aim is to have the lowest (best) costs and prices among sellers offering products with comparable differentiating attributes. Target's best-cost advantage allows it to give discount store shoppers more value for the money by offering an attractive product lineup and an appealing shopping ambience at low prices.

In Concepts & Connections 1.2, it's evident that Starbucks has gained a competitive advantage over rivals through its efforts to offer the highest quality coffee-based beverages, create an emotional attachment with customers, expand its global presence, expand the product line, and ensure consistency in store operations. A creative, distinctive strategy such as that used by Starbucks is a company's most reliable ticket for developing a sustainable competitive advantage and earning above-average profits. A **sustainable competitive advantage** allows a company to attract sufficiently large numbers of buyers who have a lasting preference for its products or services over those offered by rivals, despite the efforts of competitors to offset that appeal and overcome the company's advantage. The bigger and more durable the competitive advantage, the better a company's prospects for winning in the marketplace and earning superior long-term profits relative to rivals.

> **CORE CONCEPT**
>
> A company achieves **sustainable competitive advantage** when an attractively large number of buyers develop a durable preference for its products or services over the offerings of competitors, despite the efforts of competitors to overcome or erode its advantage.

The Importance of Capabilities in Building and Sustaining Competitive Advantage

Winning a *sustainable* competitive edge over rivals with any of the above five strategies generally hinges as much on building competitively valuable capabilities that rivals cannot readily match as it does on having a distinctive product offering. Clever rivals can nearly always copy the attributes of a popular product or service, but it is substantially more difficult for rivals to match the know-how and specialized capabilities a company has developed and perfected over a long period. FedEx, for example, has superior capabilities in next-day delivery of small packages. And Hyundai has become the world's fastest-growing automaker as a result of its advanced manufacturing processes and unparalleled quality control system. The capabilities of both of these companies have proven difficult for competitors to imitate or best and have allowed each to build and sustain competitive advantage.

CONCEPTS & CONNECTIONS 1.2

STARBUCKS' STRATEGY IN THE SPECIALTY COFFEE MARKET

Since its founding in 1985 as a modest nine-store operation in Seattle, Washington, Starbucks had become the premier roaster and retailer of specialty coffees in the world, with over 18,800 store locations in more than 60 countries as of April 2013 and annual sales that were expected to exceed $15 billion in fiscal 2013. The sharp economic downturn that plagued much of the world's economy in late 2008 and all of 2009 hit Starbucks hard, but the strength of the company's strategy allowed it to rebound and set an earnings record in 2010. The company set new earnings records in 2011 and 2012 and was expected to record all-time high revenues and net earnings in fiscal 2013. The key elements of Starbucks' strategy in specialty coffees included:

- **Emphasis on store ambience and elevating the customer experience at Starbucks stores.** Starbucks management viewed each store as a billboard for the company and as a contributor to building the company's brand and image. Each detail was scrutinized to enhance the mood and ambience of the store, to make sure everything signaled "best-of-class" and reflected the personality of the community and the neighborhood. The thesis was "everything mattered." The company went to great lengths to make sure the store fixtures, the merchandise displays, the colors, the artwork, the banners, the music, and the aromas all blended to create a consistent, inviting, stimulating environment that evoked the romance of coffee, that signaled the company's passion for coffee, and that rewarded customers with ceremony, stories, and surprise.

- **Purchase and roast only top-quality coffee beans.** The company purchased only the highest quality arabica beans and carefully roasted coffee to exacting standards of quality and flavor. Starbucks did not use chemicals or artificial flavors when preparing its roasted coffees.

- **Commitment to corporate responsibility.** Starbucks was protective of the environment and contributed positively to the communities where Starbucks stores were located. In addition, Starbucks promoted fair trade practices and paid above-market prices for coffee beans

to provide its growers/suppliers with sufficient funding to sustain their operations and provide for their families.

- **Continue the drive to make Starbucks a global brand.** Starbucks had increased its store openings in Latin America, Europe, the Middle East, Africa, and Asia to expand its reach to more than 60 countries in 2013. Most of the company's international locations were operated by partners/licensees that had strong retail and restaurant experience and values that were compatible with Starbucks' corporate culture.

- **Expansion of the number of Starbucks stores domestically and internationally.** Starbucks operated stores in high-traffic, high-visibility locations in the United States and abroad. The company's ability to vary store size and format made it possible to locate stores in settings such as downtown and suburban shopping areas, office buildings, and university campuses. Starbucks added 161 new company-owned locations in the United States and another 237 company-owned stores internationally in fiscal 2012. Starbucks also added 101 licensed store locations in the United States and 275 licensed stores internationally in 2012. The company planned to open 1,650 new stores globally in fiscal 2013, which would include 350 Teavana tea emporiums selling premium loose-leaf teas and tea accessories.

- **Broaden and periodically refresh in-store product offerings.** Noncoffee products offered by Starbucks included teas, fresh pastries and other food items, candy, juice drinks, music CDs, and coffee mugs and coffee accessories.

- **Fully exploit the growing power of the Starbucks name and brand image with out-of-store sales.** Starbucks consumer packaged goods division included domestic and international sales of Frappuccino, coffee ice creams, and Starbucks coffees.

Sources: Company documents, 10-Ks, and information posted on Starbucks' website.

Why a Company's Strategy Evolves over Time

LO4 Understand that a company's strategy tends to evolve over time because of changing circumstances and ongoing management efforts to improve the company's strategy.

The appeal of a strategy that yields a sustainable competitive advantage is that it offers the potential for an enduring edge over rivals. However, managers of every company must be willing and ready to modify the strategy in response to the unexpected moves of competitors, shifting buyer needs and preferences, emerging market opportunities, new ideas for improving the strategy, and mounting evidence that the strategy is not working well. Most of the time, a company's strategy evolves incrementally as management fine-tunes various pieces of the strategy and adjusts the strategy to respond to unfolding events. However, on occasion, major strategy shifts are called for, such as when the strategy is clearly failing or when industry conditions change in dramatic ways.

Regardless of whether a company's strategy changes gradually or swiftly, the important point is that the task of crafting strategy is not a onetime event, but is always a work in progress.[5] The evolving nature of a company's strategy means the typical company strategy is a blend of (1) *proactive* moves to improve the company's financial performance and secure a competitive edge and (2) *adaptive* reactions to unanticipated developments and fresh market conditions—see Figure 1.1.[6] The biggest portion of a company's current strategy flows from ongoing actions that have proven themselves in the marketplace and newly launched initiatives aimed at building a larger lead over rivals and further boosting financial performance. This part of management's action plan for running the company is its proactive, **deliberate strategy**.

> Changing circumstances and ongoing management efforts to improve the strategy cause a company's strategy to evolve over time—a condition that makes the task of crafting a strategy a work in progress, not a onetime event.

At times, certain components of a company's deliberate strategy will fail in the marketplace and become **abandoned strategy elements**. Also, managers must always be willing to supplement or modify planned, deliberate strategy elements with as-needed reactions to unanticipated developments. Inevitably, there will be occasions when market and competitive conditions take unexpected turns that call for some kind of strategic reaction. Novel strategic moves

---

FIGURE 1.1   **A Company's Strategy Is a Blend of Planned Initiatives and Unplanned Reactive Adjustments**

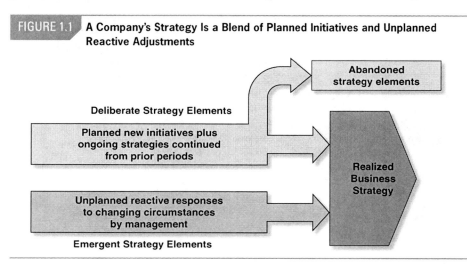

on the part of rival firms, unexpected shifts in customer preferences, fast-changing technological developments, and new market opportunities call for unplanned, reactive adjustments that form the company's **emergent strategy**. As shown in Figure 1.1, a company's **realized strategy** tends to be a *combination* of deliberate planned elements and unplanned, emergent elements.

> **CORE CONCEPT**
> A company's **realized strategy** is a combination of *deliberate planned elements* and *unplanned, emergent elements*. Some components of a company's deliberate strategy will fail in the marketplace and become *abandoned strategy elements*.

The Three Tests of a Winning Strategy

Three questions can be used to distinguish a winning strategy from a so-so or flawed strategy:

LO5 Learn the three tests of a winning strategy.

1. *How well does the strategy fit the company's situation?* To qualify as a winner, a strategy has to be well matched to the company's external and internal situations. The strategy must fit competitive conditions in the industry and other aspects of the enterprise's external environment. At the same time, it should be tailored to the company's collection of competitively important resources and capabilities. It's unwise to build a strategy upon the company's weaknesses or pursue a strategic approach that requires resources that are deficient in the company. Unless a strategy exhibits tight fit with both the external and internal aspects of a company's overall situation, it is unlikely to produce respectable first-rate business results.

    > A winning strategy must fit the company's external and internal situation, build sustainable competitive advantage, and improve company performance.

2. *Is the strategy helping the company achieve a sustainable competitive advantage?* Strategies that fail to achieve a durable competitive advantage over rivals are unlikely to produce superior performance for more than a brief period of time. Winning strategies enable a company to achieve a competitive advantage over key rivals that is long lasting. The bigger and more durable the competitive edge that the strategy helps build, the more powerful it is.

3. *Is the strategy producing good company performance?* The mark of a winning strategy is strong company performance. Two kinds of performance improvements tell the most about the caliber of a company's strategy: (1) gains in profitability and financial strength and (2) advances in the company's competitive strength and market standing.

Strategies that come up short on one or more of the above tests are plainly less appealing than strategies passing all three tests with flying colors. Managers should use the same questions when evaluating either proposed or existing strategies. New initiatives that don't seem to match the company's internal and external situation should be scrapped before they come to fruition, while existing strategies must be scrutinized on a regular basis to ensure they have good fit, offer a competitive advantage, and have contributed to above-average performance or performance improvements.

Why Crafting and Executing Strategy Are Important Tasks

High-achieving enterprises are nearly always the product of astute, creative, and proactive strategy making. Companies don't get to the top of the industry rankings or stay there with illogical strategies, copycat strategies, or timid attempts to try to do better. Among all the things managers do, nothing affects a company's ultimate success or failure more fundamentally than how well its management team charts the company's direction, develops competitively effective strategic moves and business approaches, and pursues what needs to be done internally to produce good day-in, day-out strategy execution and operating excellence. Indeed, *good strategy and good strategy execution are the most telling signs of good management.* The rationale for using the twin standards of good strategy making and good strategy execution to determine whether a company is well managed is therefore compelling: *The better conceived a company's strategy and the more competently it is executed, the more likely that the company will be a standout performer in the marketplace.* In stark contrast, a company that lacks clear-cut direction, has a flawed strategy, or can't execute its strategy competently is a company whose financial performance is probably suffering, whose business is at long-term risk, and whose management is sorely lacking.

> How well a company performs is directly attributable to the caliber of its strategy and the proficiency with which the strategy is executed.

The Road Ahead

Throughout the chapters to come and the accompanying case collection, the spotlight is trained on the foremost question in running a business enterprise: *What must managers do, and do well, to make a company a winner in the marketplace?* The answer that emerges is that doing a good job of managing inherently requires good strategic thinking and good management of the strategy formulation, strategy execution process.

The mission of this book is to provide a solid overview of what every business student and aspiring manager needs to know about crafting and executing strategy. We will explore what good strategic thinking entails, describe the core concepts and tools of strategic analysis, and examine the ins and outs of crafting and executing strategy. The accompanying cases will help build your skills in both diagnosing how well the strategy formulation, strategy execution task is being performed and prescribing actions for how the strategy in question or its execution can be improved. The strategic management course that you are enrolled in may also include a strategy simulation exercise where you will run a company in head-to-head competition with companies run by your classmates. Your mastery of the strategic management concepts presented in the following chapters will put you in a strong position to craft a winning strategy for your company and figure out how to execute it in a cost-effective and profitable manner. As you progress through the chapters of the text and the activities assigned during the term, we hope to convince you that first-rate capabilities in crafting and executing strategy are essential to good management.

KEY POINTS

1. A company's strategy is management's game plan to attract and please customers, compete successfully, conduct operations, and achieve targeted levels of performance. The essence of the strategy explains why the company matters to its customers. It outlines an approach to creating superior customer value and determining how capabilities and resources will be utilized to deliver the desired value to customers.

2. Closely related to the concept of strategy is the concept of a company's business model. A company's business model is management's blueprint for delivering customer value in a manner that will generate revenues sufficient to cover costs and yield an attractive profit. The two elements of a company's business model are its (1) customer value proposition and (2) its profit formula.

3. The central thrust of a company's strategy is undertaking moves to build and strengthen the company's long-term competitive position and financial performance by competing differently from rivals and gaining a sustainable competitive advantage over them.

4. A company's strategy typically evolves over time, arising from a blend of (1) proactive and deliberate actions on the part of company managers and (2) adaptive emergent responses to unanticipated developments and fresh market conditions.

5. A winning strategy fits the circumstances of a company's external and internal situations, builds competitive advantage, and boosts company performance.

ASSURANCE OF LEARNING EXERCISES

1. Based on your experiences as a coffee consumer, does Starbucks' strategy as described in Concepts & Connections 1.2 seem to set the company apart from rivals? Does the strategy seem to be keyed to a cost-based advantage, differentiating features, serving the unique needs of a niche, or some combination of these? What is there about Starbucks' strategy that can lead to sustainable competitive advantage?

    connect
    LO1, LO3

2. Go to www.nytco.com/investors and check whether *The New York Times'* recent financial reports indicate that its business model is working. Does the company's business model remain sound as more consumers go to the Internet to find general information and stay abreast of current events and news stories? Is its revenue stream from advertisements growing or declining? Are its subscription fees and circulation increasing or declining? Does its cost structure allow for acceptable profit margins?

    connect
    LO2

3. Elements of eBay's strategy have evolved in meaningful ways since the company's founding in 1995. After reviewing all of the links at the company's investor relations site, which can be found at investor.ebayinc.com, prepare a one-to two-page report that discusses how its strategy has evolved. Your report should also assess how well eBay's strategy passes the three tests of a winning strategy.

    LO4, LO5

EXERCISES FOR SIMULATION PARTICIPANTS

After you have read the Participant's Guide or Player's Manual for the strategy simulation exercise that you will participate in this academic term, you and your co-managers should come up with brief one- or two-paragraph answers to the questions that follow *before* entering your first set of decisions. While your answers to the first of the four questions can be developed from your reading of the manual, the remaining questions will require a collaborative discussion among the members of your company's management team about how you intend to manage the company you have been assigned to run.

LO5 1. What is your company's current situation? A substantive answer to this question should cover the following issues:

- Does your company appear to be in sound financial condition?
- What problems does your company have that need to be addressed?

LO1, LO3 2. Why will your company matter to customers? A complete answer to this question should say something about each of the following:

- How will you create customer value?
- What will be distinctive about the company's products or services?
- How will capabilities and resources be deployed to deliver customer value?

LO2 3. What are the primary elements of your company's business model?

- Describe your customer value proposition.
- Discuss the profit formula tied to your business model.
- What level of revenues is required for your company's business model to become a moneymaker?

LO3, LO4, LO5 4. How will you build and sustain competitive advantage?

- Which of the basic strategic and competitive approaches discussed in this chapter do you think makes the most sense to pursue?
- What kind of competitive advantage over rivals will you try to achieve?
- How do you envision that your strategy might evolve as you react to the competitive moves of rival firms?
- Does your strategy have the ability to pass the three tests of a winning strategy? Explain.

ENDNOTES

1. Michael E. Porter, "What Is Strategy?" *Harvard Business Review* 74, no. 6 (November–December 1996).
2. Mark W. Johnson, Clayton M. Christensen, and Henning Kagermann, "Reinventing Your Business Model," *Harvard Business Review* 86, no. 12 (December 2008); and Joan Magretta, "Why Business Models Matter," *Harvard Business Review* 80, no. 5 (May 2002).
3. W. Chan Kim and Renée Mauborgne, "How Strategy Shapes Structure," *Harvard Business Review* 87, no. 9 (September 2009).
4. Porter, "What Is Strategy?"
5. Cynthia A. Montgomery, "Putting Leadership Back Into Strategy," *Harvard Business Review* 86, no. 1 (January 2008).
6. Henry Mintzberg and Joseph Lampel, "Reflecting on the Strategy Process," *Sloan Management Review* 40, no. 3 (Spring 1999); Henry Mintzberg and J. A. Waters, "Of Strategies, Deliberate and Emergent," *Strategic Management Journal* 6 (1985); Costas Markides, "Strategy as Balance: From 'Either-Or' to 'And,'" *Business Strategy Review* 12, no. 3 (September 2001); Henry Mintzberg, Bruce Ahlstrand, and Joseph Lampel, *Strategy Safari: A Guided Tour through the Wilds of Strategic Management* (New York: Free Press, 1998); and C. K. Prahalad and Gary Hamel, "The Core Competence of the Corporation," *Harvard Business Review* 70, no. 3 (May–June 1990).

Charting a Company's Direction: Vision and Mission, Objectives, and Strategy

chapter

2

LEARNING OBJECTIVES

LO1 Grasp why it is critical for company managers to have a clear strategic vision of where a company needs to head and why.

LO2 Understand the importance of setting both strategic and financial objectives.

LO3 Understand why the strategic initiatives taken at various organizational levels must be tightly coordinated to achieve companywide performance targets.

LO4 Learn what a company must do to achieve operating excellence and to execute its strategy proficiently.

LO5 Become aware of the role and responsibility of a company's board of directors in overseeing the strategic management process.

Crafting and executing strategy are the heart and soul of managing a business enterprise. But exactly what is involved in developing a strategy and executing it proficiently? What are the various components of the strategy formulation, strategy execution process and to what extent are company personnel—aside from senior management—involved in the process? This chapter presents an overview of the ins and outs of crafting and executing company strategies. Special attention will be given to management's direction-setting responsibilities—charting a strategic course, setting performance targets, and choosing a strategy capable of producing the desired outcomes. We will also explain why strategy formulation is a task for a company's entire management team and discuss which kinds of strategic decisions tend to be made at which levels of management. The chapter concludes with a look at the roles and responsibilities of a company's board of directors and how good corporate governance protects shareholder interests and promotes good management.

What Does the Strategy Formulation, Strategy Execution Process Entail?

The managerial process of crafting and executing a company's strategy is an ongoing, continuous process consisting of five integrated stages:

1. *Developing a strategic vision* that charts the company's long-term direction, a *mission statement* that describes the company's business, and a set of *core values* to guide the pursuit of the strategic vision and mission.
2. *Setting objectives* for measuring the company's performance and tracking its progress in moving in the intended long-term direction.
3. *Crafting a strategy* for advancing the company along the path to management's envisioned future and achieving its performance objectives.
4. *Implementing and executing the chosen strategy* efficiently and effectively.
5. *Evaluating and analyzing the external environment and the company's internal situation and performance* to identify corrective adjustments that are needed in the company's long-term direction, objectives, strategy, or approach to strategy execution.

Figure 2.1 displays this five-stage process. The model illustrates the need for management to evaluate a number of external and internal factors in deciding upon a strategic direction, appropriate objectives, and approaches to crafting and executing strategy (see Table 2.1). Management's decisions that are made in the strategic management process must be shaped by the prevailing economic conditions and competitive environment and the company's own internal resources and competitive capabilities. These strategy-shaping conditions will be the focus of Chapters 3 and 4.

The model shown in Figure 2.1 also illustrates the need for management to evaluate the company's performance on an ongoing basis. Any indication that the company is failing to achieve its objectives calls for corrective adjustments in one of the first four stages of the process. The company's implementation efforts might have fallen short and new tactics must be devised to fully exploit

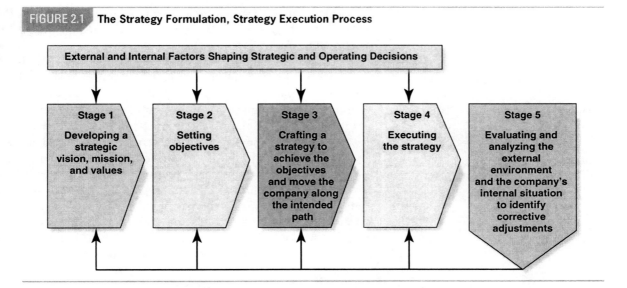

FIGURE 2.1   **The Strategy Formulation, Strategy Execution Process**

External and Internal Factors Shaping Strategic and Operating Decisions

Stage 1 — Developing a strategic vision, mission, and values

Stage 2 — Setting objectives

Stage 3 — Crafting a strategy to achieve the objectives and move the company along the intended path

Stage 4 — Executing the strategy

Stage 5 — Evaluating and analyzing the external environment and the company's internal situation to identify corrective adjustments

TABLE 2.1

Factors Shaping Decisions in the Strategy Formulation, Strategy Execution Process

External Considerations	Internal Considerations
• Does sticking with the company's present strategic course present attractive opportunities for growth and profitability?	• Does the company have an appealing customer value proposition?
• What kind of competitive forces are industry members facing and are they acting to enhance or weaken the company's prospects for growth and profitability?	• What are the company's competitively important resources and capabilities and are they potent enough to produce a sustainable competitive advantage?
• What factors are driving industry change and what impact on the company's prospects will they have?	• Does the company have sufficient business and competitive strength to seize market opportunities and nullify external threats?
• How are industry rivals positioned and what strategic moves are they likely to make next?	• Are the company's costs competitive with those of key rivals?
• What are the key factors of future competitive success and does the industry offer good prospects for attractive profits for companies possessing those capabilities?	• Is the company competitively stronger or weaker than key rivals?

the potential of the company's strategy. If management determines that the company's execution efforts are sufficient, it should challenge the assumptions underlying the company's business strategy and alter the strategy to better fit competitive conditions and the company's internal capabilities. If the company's strategic approach to competition is rated as sound, then perhaps management set overly ambitious targets for the company's performance.

The evaluation stage of the strategic management process shown in Figure 2.1 also allows for a change in the company's vision, but this should be necessary only when it becomes evident to management that the industry has changed in a significant way that renders its vision obsolete. Such occasions can be referred to as **strategic inflection points.** When a company reaches a strategic inflection point, management has tough decisions to make about the company's direction because abandoning an established course carries considerable risk. However, responding to unfolding changes in the marketplace in a timely fashion lessens a company's chances of becoming trapped in a stagnant or declining business or letting attractive new growth opportunities slip away.

> A company's **strategic plan** lays out its future direction, performance targets, and strategy.

The first three stages of the strategic management process make up a strategic plan. A **strategic plan** maps out where a company is headed, establishes strategic and financial targets, and outlines the competitive moves and approaches to be used in achieving the desired business results.[1]

Stage 1: Developing a Strategic Vision, a Mission, and Core Values

LO1 Grasp why it is critical for company managers to have a clear strategic vision of where a company needs to head and why.

At the outset of the strategy formulation, strategy execution process, a company's senior managers must wrestle with the issue of what directional path the company should take and whether its market positioning and future performance prospects could be improved by changing the company's product offerings and/or the markets in which it participates and/or the customers it caters to and/or the technologies it employs. Top management's views about the company's direction and future product-customer-market-technology focus constitute a **strategic vision** for the company. A clearly articulated strategic vision communicates management's aspirations to stakeholders about "where we are going" and helps steer the energies of company personnel in a common direction. For instance, Henry Ford's vision of a car in every garage had power because it captured the imagination of others, aided internal efforts to mobilize the Ford Motor Company's resources, and served as a reference point for gauging the merits of the company's strategic actions.

> **CORE CONCEPT**
> A **strategic vision** describes "where we are going"—the course and direction management has charted and the company's future product-customer-market-technology focus.

Well-conceived visions are *distinctive* and *specific* to a particular organization; they avoid generic, feel-good statements like "We will become a global leader and the first choice of customers in every market we choose to serve"—which could apply to any of hundreds of organizations.[2] And they are not the product of a committee charged with coming up with an innocuous but well-meaning one-sentence vision that wins consensus approval from various stakeholders. Nicely worded vision statements with no specifics about the company's product-market-customer-technology focus fall well short of what it takes for a vision to measure up.

For a strategic vision to function as a valuable managerial tool, it must provide understanding of what management wants its business to look like and provide managers with a reference point in making strategic decisions. It must say something definitive about how the company's leaders intend to position the company beyond where it is today. Table 2.2 lists some characteristics of effective vision statements.

A surprising number of the vision statements found on company websites and in annual reports are vague and unrevealing, saying very little about the company's future product-market-customer-technology focus. Some could apply to most any company in any industry. Many read like a public relations statement—lofty words that someone came up with because it is fashionable for companies to have an official vision statement.[3] Table 2.3

TABLE 2.2

Characteristics of Effectively Worded Vision Statements

Graphic—Paints a picture of the kind of company that management is trying to create and the market position(s) the company is striving to stake out.

Directional—Is forward-looking; describes the strategic course that management has charted and the kinds of product-market-customer-technology changes that will help the company prepare for the future.

Focused—Is specific enough to provide managers with guidance in making decisions and allocating resources.

Flexible—Is not so focused that it makes it difficult for management to adjust to changing circumstances in markets, customer preferences, or technology.

Feasible—Is within the realm of what the company can reasonably expect to achieve.

Desirable—Indicates why the directional path makes good business sense.

Easy to communicate—Is explainable in 5 to 10 minutes and, ideally, can be reduced to a simple, memorable "slogan" (like Henry Ford's famous vision of "a car in every garage").

Source: Based partly on John P. Kotter, *Leading Change* (Boston: Harvard Business School Press, 1996), p. 72.

TABLE 2.3

Common Shortcomings in Company Vision Statements

Vague or incomplete—Short on specifics about where the company is headed or what the company is doing to prepare for the future.

Not forward-looking—Doesn't indicate whether or how management intends to alter the company's current product-market-customer-technology focus.

Too broad—So all-inclusive that the company could head in most any direction, pursue most any opportunity, or enter most any business.

Bland or uninspiring—Lacks the power to motivate company personnel or inspire shareholder confidence about the company's direction.

Not distinctive—Provides no unique company identity; could apply to companies in any of several industries (including rivals operating in the same market arena).

Too reliant on superlatives—Doesn't say anything specific about the company's strategic course beyond the pursuit of such distinctions as being a recognized leader, a global or worldwide leader, or the first choice of customers.

Sources: Based on information in Hugh Davidson, *The Committed Enterprise* (Oxford: Butterworth Heinemann, 2002), chap. 2; and Michel Robert, *Strategy Pure and Simple II* (New York: McGraw-Hill, 1998), chaps. 2, 3, and 6.

provides a list of the most common shortcomings in company vision statements. Like any tool, vision statements can be used properly or improperly, either clearly conveying a company's strategic course or not. Concepts & Connections 2.1 provides a critique of the strategic visions of several prominent companies.

The Importance of Communicating the Strategic Vision

A strategic vision has little value to the organization unless it's effectively communicated down the line to lower-level managers and employees. It would be difficult for a vision statement to provide direction to decision makers and energize employees toward achieving long-term strategic intent unless they know of the vision and observe management's commitment to that vision. Communicating the vision to organization members nearly always means putting "where we are going and why" in writing, distributing the statement organization-wide, and having executives personally explain the vision and its rationale to as many people as feasible. Ideally, executives should present their vision for the company in a manner that reaches out and grabs people's attention. An engaging and convincing strategic vision has enormous motivational value—for the same reason that a stonemason is inspired by building a great cathedral for the ages. Therefore, an executive's ability to paint a convincing and inspiring picture of a company's journey to a future destination is an important element of effective strategic leadership.[4]

Expressing the Essence of the Vision in a Slogan   The task of effectively conveying the vision to company personnel is assisted when management can capture the vision of where to head in a catchy or easily remembered slogan. A number of organizations have summed up their vision in a brief phrase. Nike's vision slogan is "To bring innovation and inspiration to every athlete in the world." The Mayo Clinic's vision is to provide "The best care to every patient every day," while Greenpeace's envisioned future is "To halt environmental abuse and promote environmental solutions." Creating a short slogan to illuminate an organization's direction and then using it repeatedly as a reminder of "where we are headed and why" helps rally organization members to hurdle whatever obstacles lie in the company's path and maintain their focus.

> An effectively communicated vision is a valuable management tool for enlisting the commitment of company personnel to engage in actions that move the company in the intended direction.

Why a Sound, Well-Communicated Strategic Vision Matters   A well-thought-out, forcefully communicated strategic vision pays off in several respects: (1) it crystallizes senior executives' own views about the firm's long-term direction; (2) it reduces the risk of rudderless decision making by management at all levels; (3) it is a tool for winning the support of employees to help make the vision a reality; (4) it provides a beacon for lower-level managers in forming departmental missions; and (5) it helps an organization prepare for the future.

CONCEPTS & CONNECTIONS 2.1

EXAMPLES OF STRATEGIC VISIONS—HOW WELL DO THEY MEASURE UP?

Vision Statement	Effective Elements	Shortcomings
Coca-Cola Our vision serves as the framework for our roadmap and guides every aspect of our business by describing what we need to accomplish in order to continue achieving sustainable, quality growth. • People: Be a great place to work where people are inspired to be the best they can be. • Portfolio: Bring to the world a portfolio of quality beverage brands that anticipate and satisfy people's desires and needs. • Partners: Nurture a winning network of customers and suppliers; together we create mutual, enduring value. • Planet: Be a responsible citizen that makes a difference by helping build and support sustainable communities. • Profit: Maximize long-term return to shareowners while being mindful of our overall responsibilities. • Productivity: Be a highly effective, lean and fast-moving organization.	• Focused • Flexible • Feasible • Desirable	• Long • Not forward-looking
UBS We are determined to be the best global financial services company. We focus on wealth and asset management, and on investment banking and securities businesses. We continually earn recognition and trust from clients, shareholders, and staff through our ability to anticipate, learn and shape our future. We share a common ambition to succeed by delivering quality in what we do. Our purpose is to help our clients make financial decisions with confidence. We use our resources to develop effective solutions and services for our clients. We foster a distinctive, meritocratic culture of ambition, performance and learning as this attracts, retains and develops the best talent for our company. By growing both our client and our talent franchises, we add sustainable value for our shareholders.	• Focused • Feasible • Desirable	• Not forward-looking • Bland or uninspiring
Heinz We define a compelling, sustainable future and create the path to achieve it.	• Directional • Flexible	• Bland and uninspiring • Too broad • Vague • Not distinctive
Procter & Gamble We will provide branded products and services of superior quality and value that improve the lives of the world's consumers, now and for generations to come. As a result, consumers will reward us with leadership sales, profit and value creation, allowing our people, our shareholders, and the communities in which we live and work to prosper.	• Directional • Flexible • Desirable	• Too broad • Too reliant on superlatives

Sources: Company documents and websites.

Developing a Company Mission Statement

The defining characteristic of a well-conceived **strategic vision** is what it says about the company's *future strategic course*—*"where we are headed and what our future product-customer-market-technology focus will be."* The **mission statements** of most companies say much more about the enterprise's *present* business scope and purpose— "who we are, what we do, and why we are here." Very few mission statements are forward-looking in content or emphasis. Consider, for example, the mission statement of Trader Joe's (a specialty grocery chain):

> The distinction between a **strategic vision** and a **mission statement** is fairly clear-cut: A strategic vision portrays a company's *future business scope* ("where we are going") whereas a company's mission statement typically describes its *present business and purpose* ("who we are, what we do, and why we are here").

> The mission of Trader Joe's is to give our customers the best food and beverage values that they can find anywhere and to provide them with the information required for informed buying decisions. We provide these with a dedication to the highest quality of customer satisfaction delivered with a sense of warmth, friendliness, fun, individual pride, and company spirit.

Note that Trader Joe's mission statement does a good job of conveying "who we are, what we do, and why we are here," but it provides no sense of "where we are headed."

An example of a well-stated mission statement with ample specifics about what the organization does is that of the Occupational Safety and Health Administration (OSHA): "to assure the safety and health of America's workers by setting and enforcing standards; providing training, outreach, and education; establishing partnerships; and encouraging continual improvement in workplace safety and health." Google's mission statement, while short, still captures the essence of what the company is about: "to organize the world's information and make it universally accessible and useful." An example of a not-so-revealing mission statement is that of Microsoft. "To help people and businesses throughout the world realize their full potential" says nothing about its products or business makeup and could apply to many companies in many different industries. A well-conceived mission statement should employ language specific enough to give the company its own identity. A mission statement that provides scant indication of "who we are and what we do" has no apparent value.

CORE CONCEPT

A well-conceived **mission statement** conveys a company's purpose in language specific enough to give the company its own identity.

Ideally, a company mission statement is sufficiently descriptive to:

- Identify the company's products or services.
- Specify the buyer needs it seeks to satisfy.
- Specify the customer groups or markets it is endeavoring to serve.
- Specify its approach to pleasing customers.
- Give the company its own identity.

Occasionally, companies state that their mission is to simply earn a profit. This is misguided. Profit is more correctly an *objective* and a *result* of what a company does. Moreover, earning a profit is the obvious intent of every commercial enterprise. Such companies as BMW, Netflix, Shell Oil, Procter & Gamble, Google, and McDonald's are each striving to earn a profit for shareholders, but the fundamentals of their businesses are substantially different when it comes to "who we are and what we do."

Linking the Strategic Vision and Mission with Company Values

Many companies have developed a statement of **values** (sometimes called *core values*) to guide the actions and behavior of company personnel in conducting the company's business and pursuing its strategic vision and mission. These values are the designated beliefs and desired ways of doing things at the company and frequently relate to such things as fair treatment, honor and integrity, ethical behavior, innovativeness, teamwork, a passion for excellence, social responsibility, and community citizenship.

> **CORE CONCEPT**
>
> A company's **values** are the beliefs, traits, and behavioral norms that company personnel are expected to display in conducting the company's business and pursuing its strategic vision and mission.

Most companies normally have four to eight core values. At Kodak, the core values are respect for the dignity of the individual, uncompromising integrity, unquestioned trust, constant credibility, continual improvement and personal renewal, and open celebration of individual and team achievements. Home Depot embraces eight values—entrepreneurial spirit, excellent customer service, giving back to the community, respect for all people, doing the right thing, taking care of people, building strong relationships, and creating shareholder value—in its quest to be the world's leading home improvement retailer.

Do companies practice what they preach when it comes to their professed values? Sometimes no, sometimes yes—it runs the gamut. At one extreme are companies with window-dressing values; the professed values are given lip service by top executives but have little discernible impact on either how company personnel behave or how the company operates. At the other extreme are companies whose executives are committed to grounding company operations on sound values and principled ways of doing business. Executives at these companies deliberately seek to ingrain the designated core values into the corporate culture—the core values thus become an integral part of the company's DNA and what makes it tick. At such values-driven companies, executives "walk the talk" and company personnel are held accountable for displaying the stated values. Concepts & Connections 2.2 describes how core values drive the company's mission at Zappos, a widely known and quite successful online shoe and apparel retailer.

Stage 2: Setting Objectives

The managerial purpose of setting **objectives** is to convert the strategic vision into specific performance targets. Objectives reflect management's aspirations for company performance in light of the industry's prevailing economic and competitive conditions and the company's internal capabilities. Well-stated objectives are *quantifiable*, or *measurable*, and contain a *deadline for achievement*. Concrete, measurable objectives are managerially valuable because they serve

LO2 Understand the importance of setting both strategic and financial objectives.

CONCEPTS & CONNECTIONS 2.2

ZAPPOS MISSION AND CORE VALUES

We've been asked by a lot of people how we've grown so quickly, and the answer is actually really simple. . . . We've aligned the entire organization around one mission: *to provide* *the best customer service possible.* Internally, we call this our **WOW** philosophy.

These are the 10 core values that we live by:

Deliver Wow through Service. At Zappos, anything worth doing is worth doing with WOW. WOW is such a short, simple word, but it really encompasses a lot of things. To WOW, you must differentiate yourself, which means doing something a little unconventional and innovative. You must do something that's above and beyond what's expected. And whatever you do must have an emotional impact on the receiver. We are not an average company, our service is not average, and we don't want our people to be average. We expect every employee to deliver WOW.

Embrace and Drive Change. Part of being in a growing company is that change is constant. For some people, especially those who come from bigger companies, the constant change can be somewhat unsettling at first. If you are not prepared to deal with constant change, then you probably are not a good fit for the company.

Create Fun and a Little Weirdness. At Zappos, We're Always Creating Fun and A Little Weirdness! One of the things that makes Zappos different from a lot of other companies is that we value being fun and being a little weird. We don't want to become one of those big companies that feels corporate and boring. We want to be able to laugh at ourselves. We look for both fun and humor in our daily work.

Be Adventurous, Creative, and Open Minded. At Zappos, we think it's important for people and the company as a whole to be bold and daring (but not reckless). We do not want people to be afraid to take risks and make mistakes. We believe if people aren't making mistakes, then that means they're not taking enough risks. Over time, we want everyone to develop his/her gut about business decisions. We want people to develop and improve their decision-making skills. We encourage people to make mistakes as long as they learn from them.

Pursue Growth and Learning. At Zappos, we think it's important for employees to grow both personally and professionally. It's important to constantly challenge and stretch yourself and not be stuck in a job where you don't feel like you are growing or learning.

Build Open and Honest Relationships with Communication. Fundamentally, we believe that openness and honesty make for the best relationships because that leads to trust and faith. We value strong relationships in all areas: with managers, direct reports, customers (internal and external), vendors, business partners, team members, and co-workers.

Build a Positive Team and Family Spirit. At Zappos, we place a lot of emphasis on our culture because we are both a team and a family. We want to create an environment that is friendly, warm, and exciting. We encourage diversity in ideas, opinions, and points of view.

Do More with Less. Zappos has always been about being able to do more with less. While we may be casual in our interactions with each other, we are focused and serious about the operations of our business. We believe in working hard and putting in the extra effort to get things done.

Be Passionate and Determined. Passion is the fuel that drives us and our company forward. We value passion, determination, perseverance, and the sense of urgency. We are inspired because we believe in what we are doing and where we are going. We don't take "no" or "that'll never work" for an answer because if we had, then Zappos would have never started in the first place.

Be Humble. While we have grown quickly in the past, we recognize that there are always challenges ahead to tackle. We believe that no matter what happens we should always be respectful of everyone.

Source: Information posted at www.zappos.com, accessed June 6, 2010.

as yardsticks for tracking a company's performance and progress toward its vision. Vague targets such as "maximize profits," "reduce costs," "become more efficient," or "increase sales," which specify neither how much nor when, offer little value as a management tool to improve company performance. Ideally, managers should develop *challenging,* yet *achievable* objectives that *stretch an organization to perform at its full potential.* As Mitchell Leibovitz, former CEO of the auto parts and service retailer Pep Boys, once said, "If you want to have ho-hum results, have ho-hum objectives."

> **CORE CONCEPT**
>
> **Objectives** are an organization's performance targets—the results management wants to achieve.

What Kinds of Objectives to Set

Two very distinct types of performance yardsticks are required: those relating to financial performance and those relating to strategic performance. **Financial objectives** communicate management's targets for financial performance. Common financial objectives relate to revenue growth, profitability, and return on investment. **Strategic objectives** are related to a company's marketing standing and competitive vitality. The importance of attaining financial objectives is intuitive. Without adequate profitability and financial strength, a company's long-term health and ultimate survival is jeopardized. Furthermore, subpar earnings and a weak balance sheet alarm shareholders and creditors and put the jobs of senior executives at risk. However, good financial performance, by itself, is not enough.

> **CORE CONCEPT**
>
> **Financial objectives** relate to the financial performance targets management has established for the organization to achieve.
>
> **Strategic objectives** relate to target outcomes that indicate a company is strengthening its market standing, competitive vitality, and future business prospects.

A company's financial objectives are really *lagging indicators* that reflect the results of past decisions and organizational activities.[5] The results of past decisions and organizational activities are not reliable indicators of a company's future prospects. Companies that have been poor financial performers are sometimes able to turn things around, and good financial performers on occasion fall upon hard times. Hence, the best and most reliable predictors of a company's success in the marketplace and future financial performance are strategic objectives. Strategic outcomes are *leading indicators* of a company's future financial performance and business prospects. The accomplishment of strategic objectives signals the company is well positioned to sustain or improve its performance. For instance, if a company is achieving ambitious strategic objectives, then there's reason to expect that its *future* financial performance will be better than its current or past performance. If a company begins to lose competitive strength and fails to achieve important strategic objectives, then its ability to maintain its present profitability is highly suspect.

Consequently, utilizing a performance measurement system that strikes a *balance* between financial objectives and strategic objectives is optimal.[6] Just tracking a company's financial performance overlooks the fact that what ultimately enables a company to deliver better financial results is the achievement of strategic objectives that improve its competitiveness and market strength.

TABLE 2.4

The Balanced Scorecard Approach to Performance Measurement

Financial Objectives	Strategic Objectives	
• An *x* percent increase in annual revenues	• Win an *x* percent market share	• Increase percentage of sales coming from new products to *x* percent
• Annual increases in earnings per share of *x* percent	• Achieve customer satisfaction rates of *x* percent	• Improve information systems capabilities to give frontline managers defect information in *x* minutes
• An *x* percent return on capital employed (ROCE) or shareholder investment (ROE)	• Achieve a customer retention rate of *x* percent	
• Bond and credit ratings of *x*	• Acquire *x* number of new customers	
• Internal cash flows of *x* to fund new capital investment	• Introduce *x* number of new products in the next three years	• Improve teamwork by increasing the number of projects involving more than one business unit to *x*
	• Reduce product development times to *x* months	

Representative examples of financial and strategic objectives that companies often include in a **balanced scorecard** approach to measuring their performance are displayed in Table 2.4.[7]

CORE CONCEPT

The **balanced scorecard** is a widely used method for combining the use of both strategic and financial objectives, tracking their achievement, and giving management a more complete and balanced view of how well an organization is performing.

In 2010, nearly 50 percent of global companies used a balanced scorecard approach to measuring strategic and financial performance.[8] Examples of organizations that have adopted a balanced scorecard approach to setting objectives and measuring performance include SAS Institute, UPS, Ann Taylor Stores, Fort Bragg Army Garrison, Caterpillar, Daimler AG, Hilton Hotels, Susan G. Komen for the Cure, and Siemens AG.[9] Concepts & Connections 2.3 provides selected strategic and financial objectives of three prominent companies.

Short-Term and Long-Term Objectives A company's set of financial and strategic objectives should include both near-term and long-term performance targets. Short-term objectives focus attention on delivering performance improvements in the current period, while long-term targets force the organization to consider how actions currently under way will affect the company later. Specifically, long-term objectives stand as a barrier to an undue focus on short-term results by nearsighted management. When trade-offs have to be made between achieving long-run and short-run objectives, long-run objectives should take precedence (unless the achievement of one or more short-run performance targets has unique importance).

The Need for Objectives at All Organizational Levels Objective setting should not stop with the establishment of companywide performance targets. Company objectives need to be broken into performance targets for each of the organization's separate businesses, product lines, functional departments, and individual work units. Employees within various functional areas

CONCEPTS & CONNECTIONS 2.3

EXAMPLES OF COMPANY OBJECTIVES

PEPSICO

Accelerate top-line growth; build and expand our better-for-your snacks and beverages and nutrition businesses; improve our water use efficiency by 20 percent per unit of production by 2015; improve our electricity use efficiency by 20 percent per unit of production by 2015; maintain appropriate financial flexibility with ready access to global capital and credit markets at favorable interest rates.

WALGREENS

Increase revenues from $72 billion in 2012 to more than $130 billion in 2016; increase operating income from $3.5 billion in 2012 to $8.5 billion to $9.0 billion by 2016; increase operating cash flow from $4.4 billion in 2012 to approximately $8 billion in 2016; generate $1 billion in cost savings from combined pharmacy and general merchandise purchasing synergies by 2016.

YUM! BRANDS (KFC, PIZZA HUT, TACO BELL, LONG JOHN SILVER'S)

Increase operating profit derived from operations in emerging markets from 48 percent in 2010 to 57 percent in 2015; increase number of KFC units in Africa from 655 in 2010 to 2,100 in 2020; increase KFC revenues in Africa from $865 million in 2010 to $1.94 billion in 2014; increase number of KFC units in India from 101 in 2010 to 1,250 in 2020; increase number of KFC units in Vietnam from 87 in 2010 to 500 in 2020; increase number of KFC units in Russia from 150 in 2010 to 500 in 2020; open 100+ new Taco Bell units in international markets in 2015; increase annual cash flows from operations from $1.5 billion in 2010 to $2+ billion in 2015.

Source: Information posted on company websites.

and operating levels will be guided much better by narrow objectives relating directly to their departmental activities than broad organizational-level goals. Objective setting is thus a top-down process that must extend to the lowest organizational levels. And it means that each organizational unit must take care to set performance targets that support—rather than conflict with or negate—the achievement of companywide strategic and financial objectives.

Stage 3: Crafting a Strategy

As indicated earlier, the task of stitching a strategy together entails addressing a series of *hows: how* to attract and please customers, *how* to compete against rivals, *how* to position the company in the marketplace and capitalize on attractive opportunities to grow the business, *how* best to respond to changing economic and market conditions, *how* to manage each functional piece of the business, and *how* to achieve the company's performance targets. It also means choosing among the various strategic alternatives and proactively searching for opportunities to do new things or to do existing things in new or better ways.[10]

LO3 Understand why the strategic initiatives taken at various organizational levels must be tightly coordinated to achieve companywide performance targets.

Strategy Formulation Involves Managers at All Organizational Levels

In some enterprises, the CEO or owner functions as strategic visionary and chief architect of the strategy, personally deciding what the key elements of the company's strategy will be, although the CEO may seek the advice of key subordinates in fashioning an overall strategy and deciding on important strategic moves. However, it is a mistake to view strategy making as a *top* management function—the exclusive province of owner-entrepreneurs, CEOs, high-ranking executives, and board members. The more a company's operations cut across different products, industries, and geographical areas, the more that headquarters executives have little option but to delegate considerable strategy-making authority to down-the-line managers. On-the-scene managers who oversee specific operating units are likely to have a more detailed command of the strategic issues and choices for the particular operating unit under their supervision—knowing the prevailing market and competitive conditions, customer requirements and expectations, and all the other relevant aspects affecting the several strategic options available.

> In most companies, crafting strategy is a *collaborative team effort* that includes managers in various positions and at various organizational levels. Crafting strategy is rarely something only high-level executives do.

A Company's Strategy-Making Hierarchy

The larger and more diverse the operations of an enterprise, the more points of strategic initiative it will have and the more managers at different organizational levels will have a relevant strategy-making role. In diversified companies, where multiple and sometimes strikingly different businesses have to be managed, crafting a full-fledged strategy involves four distinct types of strategic actions and initiatives, each undertaken at different levels of the organization and partially or wholly crafted by managers at different organizational levels, as shown in Figure 2.2. A company's overall strategy is therefore *a collection of strategic initiatives and actions* devised by managers up and down the whole organizational hierarchy. Ideally, the pieces of a company's strategy up and down the strategy hierarchy should be cohesive and mutually reinforcing, fitting together like a jigsaw puzzle.

> **Corporate strategy** establishes an overall game plan for managing a *set of businesses* in a diversified, multibusiness company.
>
> **Business strategy** is primarily concerned with strengthening the company's market position and building competitive advantage in a single business company or a single business unit of a diversified multibusiness corporation.

As shown in Figure 2.2, **corporate strategy** is orchestrated by the CEO and other senior executives and establishes an overall game plan for managing a *set of businesses* in a diversified, multibusiness company. Corporate strategy addresses the questions of how to capture cross-business synergies, what businesses to hold or divest, which new markets to enter, and how to best enter new markets—by acquisition, by creation of a strategic alliance, or through internal development. Corporate strategy and business diversification are the subject of Chapter 8, where they are discussed in detail.

Business strategy is primarily concerned with building competitive advantage in a single business unit of a diversified company or strengthening the market position of a nondiversified single business company. Business strategy is also the responsibility of the CEO and other senior executives, but key business-unit heads may also be influential, especially in strategic decisions

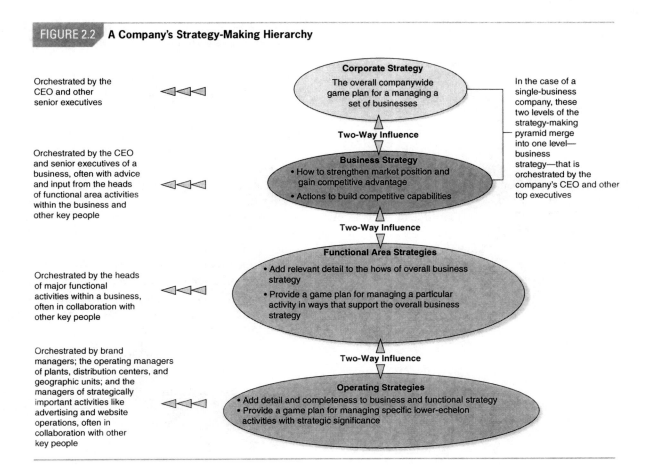

FIGURE 2.2   **A Company's Strategy-Making Hierarchy**

Orchestrated by the CEO and other senior executives

Corporate Strategy
The overall companywide game plan for a managing a set of businesses

Two-Way Influence

In the case of a single-business company, these two levels of the strategy-making pyramid merge into one level—business strategy—that is orchestrated by the company's CEO and other top executives

Orchestrated by the CEO and senior executives of a business, often with advice and input from the heads of functional area activities within the business and other key people

Business Strategy
• How to strengthen market position and gain competitive advantage
• Actions to build competitive capabilities

Two-Way Influence

Orchestrated by the heads of major functional activities within a business, often in collaboration with other key people

Functional Area Strategies
• Add relevant detail to the hows of overall business strategy
• Provide a game plan for managing a particular activity in ways that support the overall business strategy

Two-Way Influence

Orchestrated by brand managers; the operating managers of plants, distribution centers, and geographic units; and the managers of strategically important activities like advertising and website operations, often in collaboration with other key people

Operating Strategies
• Add detail and completeness to business and functional strategy
• Provide a game plan for managing specific lower-echelon activities with strategic significance

affecting the businesses they lead. *In single-business companies, the corporate and business levels of the strategy-making hierarchy merge into a single level—business strategy*—because the strategy for the entire enterprise involves only one distinct business. So, a single-business company has three levels of strategy: business strategy, functional-area strategies, and operating strategies.

Functional-area strategies concern the actions related to particular functions or processes within a business. A company's product development strategy, for example, represents the managerial game plan for creating new products that are in tune with what buyers are looking for. Lead responsibility for functional strategies within a business is normally delegated to the heads of the respective functions, with the general manager of the business having final approval over functional strategies. For the overall business strategy to have maximum impact, a company's marketing strategy, production strategy, finance strategy, customer service strategy, product development strategy, and human resources strategy should be compatible and mutually reinforcing rather than each serving its own narrower purpose.

Operating strategies concern the relatively narrow strategic initiatives and approaches for managing key operating units (plants, distribution centers, geographic units) and specific operating activities such as materials purchasing or Internet sales. Operating strategies are limited in scope, but add further detail to functional-area strategies and the overall business strategy. Lead responsibility for operating strategies is usually delegated to frontline managers, subject to review and approval by higher-ranking managers.

Stage 4: Implementing and Executing the Chosen Strategy

LO4 Learn what a company must do to achieve operating excellence and to execute its strategy proficiently.

Managing the implementation and execution of strategy is easily the most demanding and time-consuming part of the strategic management process. Good strategy execution entails that managers pay careful attention to how key internal business processes are performed and see to it that employees' efforts are directed toward the accomplishment of desired operational outcomes. The task of implementing and executing the strategy also necessitates an ongoing analysis of the efficiency and effectiveness of a company's internal activities and a managerial awareness of new technological developments that might improve business processes. In most situations, managing the strategy execution process includes the following principal aspects:

- Staffing the organization to provide needed skills and expertise.
- Allocating ample resources to activities critical to good strategy execution.
- Ensuring that policies and procedures facilitate rather than impede effective execution.
- Installing information and operating systems that enable company personnel to perform essential activities.
- Pushing for continuous improvement in how value chain activities are performed.
- Tying rewards and incentives directly to the achievement of performance objectives.
- Creating a company culture and work climate conducive to successful strategy execution.
- Exerting the internal leadership needed to propel implementation forward.

Stage 5: Evaluating Performance and Initiating Corrective Adjustments

The fifth stage of the strategy management process—evaluating and analyzing the external environment and the company's internal situation and performance to identify needed corrective adjustments—is the trigger point for deciding whether to continue or change the company's vision, objectives, strategy, and/or strategy execution methods. So long as the company's direction and strategy seem well matched to industry and competitive conditions and performance targets are being met, company executives may well decide to stay the course. Simply fine-tuning the strategic plan and continuing with efforts to improve strategy execution are sufficient.

But whenever a company encounters disruptive changes in its environment, questions need to be raised about the appropriateness of its direction and strategy. If a company experiences a downturn in its market position or persistent shortfalls in performance, then company managers are obligated to ferret out the causes—do they relate to poor strategy, poor strategy execution, or both?—and take timely corrective action. A company's direction, objectives, and strategy have to be revisited any time external or internal conditions warrant.

> A company's vision, objectives, strategy, and approach to strategy execution are never final; managing strategy is an ongoing process, not an every-now-and-then task.

Also, it is not unusual for a company to find that one or more aspects of its strategy implementation and execution are not going as well as intended. Proficient strategy execution is always the product of much organizational learning. It is achieved unevenly—coming quickly in some areas and proving nettlesome in others. Successful strategy execution entails vigilantly searching for ways to improve and then making corrective adjustments whenever and wherever it is useful to do so.

Corporate Governance: The Role of the Board of Directors in the Strategy Formulation, Strategy Execution Process

Although senior managers have *lead responsibility* for crafting and executing a company's strategy, it is the duty of the board of directors to exercise strong oversight and see that the five tasks of strategic management are done in a manner that benefits shareholders (in the case of investor-owned enterprises) or stakeholders (in the case of not-for-profit organizations). In watching over management's strategy formulation, strategy execution actions, a company's board of directors has four important corporate governance obligations to fulfill:

LO5 Become aware of the role and responsibility of a company's board of directors in overseeing the strategic management process.

1. *Oversee the company's financial accounting and financial reporting practices.* While top management, particularly the company's CEO and CFO (chief financial officer), is primarily responsible for seeing that the company's financial statements accurately report the results of the company's operations, board members have a fiduciary duty to protect shareholders by exercising oversight of the company's financial practices. In addition, corporate boards must ensure that generally acceptable accounting principles (GAAP) are properly used in preparing the company's financial statements and determine whether proper financial controls are in place to prevent fraud and misuse of funds. Virtually all boards of directors monitor the financial reporting activities by appointing an audit committee, always composed entirely of *outside directors* (*inside directors* hold management positions in the company and either directly or indirectly report to the CEO). The members of the audit committee have lead responsibility

for overseeing the decisions of the company's financial officers and consulting with both internal and external auditors to ensure that financial reports are accurate and adequate financial controls are in place. Faulty oversight of corporate accounting and financial reporting practices by audit committees and corporate boards during the early 2000s resulted in the federal investigation of more than 20 major corporations between 2000 and 2002. The investigations of such well-known companies as AOL Time Warner, Global Crossing, Enron, Qwest Communications, and WorldCom found that upper management had employed fraudulent or unsound accounting practices to artificially inflate revenues, overstate assets, and reduce expenses. The scandals resulted in the conviction of a number of corporate executives and the passage of the Sarbanes-Oxley Act of 2002, which tightened financial reporting standards and created additional compliance requirements for public boards.

2. *Diligently critique and oversee the company's direction, strategy, and business approaches.* Even though board members have a legal obligation to warrant the accuracy of the company's financial reports, directors must set aside time to guide management in choosing a strategic direction and to make independent judgments about the validity and wisdom of management's proposed strategic actions. Many boards have found that meeting agendas become consumed by compliance matters and little time is left to discuss matters of strategic importance. The board of directors and management at Philips Electronics hold annual two- to three-day retreats devoted to evaluating the company's long-term direction and various strategic proposals. The company's exit from the semiconductor business and its increased focus on medical technology and home health care resulted from management–board discussions during such retreats.[11]

3. *Evaluate the caliber of senior executives' strategy formulation and strategy execution skills.* The board is always responsible for determining whether the current CEO is doing a good job of strategic leadership and whether senior management is actively creating a pool of potential successors to the CEO and other top executives.[12] Evaluation of senior executives' strategy formulation and strategy execution skills is enhanced when outside directors go into the field to personally evaluate how well the strategy is being executed. Independent board members at GE visit operating executives at each major business unit once per year to assess the company's talent pool and stay abreast of emerging strategic and operating issues affecting the company's divisions. Home Depot board members visit a store once per quarter to determine the health of the company's operations.[13]

4. *Institute a compensation plan for top executives that rewards them for actions and results that serve shareholder interests.* A basic principle of corporate governance is that the owners of a corporation delegate operating authority and managerial control to top management in return for compensation. In their role as an *agent* of shareholders, top executives have a clear and unequivocal duty to make decisions and operate the company in

CONCEPTS & CONNECTIONS 2.4

CORPORATE GOVERNANCE FAILURES AT FANNIE MAE AND FREDDIE MAC

Executive compensation in the financial services industry during the mid-2000s ranks high among examples of failed corporate governance. Corporate governance at the government-sponsored mortgage giants Fannie Mae and Freddie Mac was particularly weak. The politically appointed boards at both enterprises failed to understand the risks of the subprime loan strategies being employed, did not adequately monitor the decisions of the CEO, did not exercise effective oversight of the accounting principles being employed (which led to inflated earnings), and approved executive compensation systems that allowed management to manipulate earnings to receive lucrative performance bonuses. The audit and compensation committees at Fannie Mae were particularly ineffective in protecting shareholder interests, with the audit committee allowing the government-sponsored enterprise's financial officers to audit reports prepared under their direction and used to determine performance bonuses. Fannie Mae's audit committee also was aware of management's use of questionable accounting practices that reduced losses and recorded onetime gains to achieve EPS targets linked to bonuses. In addition, the audit committee failed to investigate formal charges of accounting improprieties filed by a manager in the Office of the Controller.

Fannie Mae's compensation committee was equally ineffective. The committee allowed the company's CEO, Franklin Raines, to select the consultant employed to design the mortgage firm's executive compensation plan and agreed to a tiered bonus plan that would permit Raines and other senior managers to receive maximum bonuses without great difficulty. The compensation plan allowed Raines to earn performance-based bonuses of $52 million and total compensation of $90 million between 1999 and 2004. Raines was forced to resign in December 2004 when the Office of Federal Housing Enterprise Oversight found that Fannie Mae

executives had fraudulently inflated earnings to receive bonuses linked to financial performance. Securities and Exchange Commission investigators also found evidence of improper accounting at Fannie Mae and required it to restate its earnings between 2002 and 2004 by $6.3 billion.

Poor governance at Freddie Mac allowed its CEO and senior management to manipulate financial data to receive performance-based compensation as well. Freddie Mac CEO Richard Syron received 2007 compensation of $19.8 million while the mortgage company's share price declined from a high of $70 in 2005 to $25 at year-end 2007. During Syron's tenure as CEO the company became embroiled in a multibillion-dollar accounting scandal, and Syron personally disregarded internal reports dating to 2004 that warned of an impending financial crisis at the company. Forewarnings within Freddie Mac and by federal regulators and outside industry observers proved to be correct, with loan underwriting policies at Freddie Mac and Fannie Mae leading to combined losses at the two firms in 2008 of more than $100 billion. The price of Freddie Mac's shares had fallen to below $1 by Syron's resignation in September 2008.

Both organizations were placed into a conservatorship under the direction of the U.S. government in September 2008 and were provided bailout funds of nearly $200 billion by 2013.

Sources: Chris Isidore, "Fannie, Freddie Bailout: $153 Billion . . . and Counting," *CNNMoney*, February 11, 2011; "Adding Up the Government's Total Bailout Tab," *The New York Times Online*, February 4, 2009; Eric Dash, "Fannie Mae to Restate Results by $6.3 Billion Because of Accounting," *The New York Times Online*, www.nytimes.com, December 7, 2006; Annys Shin, "Fannie Mae Sets Executive Salaries," *The Washington Post*, February 9, 2006, p. D4; and Scott DeCarlo, Eric Weiss, Mark Jickling, and James R. Cristie, *Fannie Mae and Freddie Mac: Scandal in U.S. Housing.* (Hauppauge, NY: Nova Publishers, 2006), pp. 266–86.

accord with shareholder interests (but this does not mean disregarding the interests of other stakeholders, particularly those of employees, with whom they also have an agency relationship). Most boards of directors have a compensation committee, composed entirely of directors from outside the company, to develop a salary and incentive compensation plan that rewards senior executives for boosting the company's *long-term* performance and growing the economic value of the enterprise on behalf of shareholders; the compensation committee's recommendations are presented to the full board for approval. But during the past 10 to 15 years, many boards of directors have done a poor job of ensuring that executive salary increases, bonuses, and stock option awards are tied tightly to performance measures that are truly in the long-term interests of shareholders. Rather, compensation packages at many companies have increasingly rewarded executives for short-term performance improvements—most notably, achieving quarterly and annual earnings targets and boosting the stock price by specified percentages. This has had the perverse effect of causing company managers to become preoccupied with actions to improve a company's near-term performance, often motivating them to take unwise business risks to boost short-term earnings by amounts sufficient to qualify for multimillion-dollar bonuses and stock option awards (that, in the view of many people, were obscenely large). The greater weight being placed on short-term performance improvements has worked against shareholders since, in many cases, the excessive risk-taking has proved damaging to long-term company performance—witness the huge loss of shareholder wealth that occurred at many financial institutions in 2008–2009 because of executive risk-taking in subprime loans, credit default swaps, and collateralized mortgage securities in 2006–2007. As a consequence, the need to overhaul and reform executive compensation has become a hot topic in both public circles and corporate boardrooms. Concepts & Connections 2.4 discusses how weak governance at Fannie Mae and Freddie Mac allowed opportunistic senior managers to secure exorbitant bonuses, while making decisions that imperiled the futures of the companies they managed.

Every corporation should have a strong, independent board of directors that (1) is well informed about the company's performance, (2) guides and judges the CEO and other top executives, (3) has the courage to curb management actions it believes are inappropriate or unduly risky, (4) certifies to shareholders that the CEO is doing what the board expects, (5) provides insight and advice to management, and (6) is intensely involved in debating the pros and cons of key decisions and actions.[14] Boards of directors that lack the backbone to challenge a strong-willed or "imperial" CEO or that rubber-stamp most anything the CEO recommends without probing inquiry and debate abandon their duty to represent and protect shareholder interests.

KEY POINTS

The strategic management process consists of five interrelated and integrated stages:

1. *Developing a strategic vision* of where the company needs to head and what its future product-customer-market-technology focus should be. This managerial step provides long-term direction, infuses the organization with a sense of purposeful action, and communicates to stakeholders management's aspirations for the company.

2. *Setting objectives* and using the targeted results as yardsticks for measuring the company's performance. Objectives need to spell out *how much* of *what kind* of performance *by when*. A *balanced scorecard* approach for measuring company performance entails setting both *financial objectives and strategic objectives.*

3. *Crafting a strategy to achieve the objectives* and move the company along the strategic course that management has charted. The total strategy that emerges is really a collection of strategic actions and business approaches initiated partly by senior company executives, partly by the heads of major business divisions, partly by functional-area managers, and partly by operating managers on the frontlines. A single business enterprise has three levels of strategy—business strategy for the company as a whole, functional-area strategies for each main area within the business, and operating strategies undertaken by lower-echelon managers. In diversified, multibusiness companies, the strategy-making task involves four distinct types or levels of strategy: corporate strategy for the company as a whole, business strategy (one for each business the company has diversified into), functional-area strategies within each business, and operating strategies. Typically, the strategy-making task is more top-down than bottom-up, with higher-level strategies serving as the guide for developing lower-level strategies.

4. *Implementing and executing the chosen strategy efficiently and effectively.* Managing the implementation and execution of strategy is an operations-oriented, make-things-happen activity aimed at shaping the performance of core business activities in a strategy supportive manner. Management's handling of the strategy implementation process can be considered successful if things go smoothly enough that the company meets or beats its strategic and financial performance targets and shows good progress in achieving management's strategic vision.

5. *Evaluating and analyzing the external environment and the company's internal situation and performance to identify corrective adjustments* in vision, objectives, strategy, or execution. This stage of the strategy management process is the trigger point for deciding whether to continue or change the company's vision, objectives, strategy, and/or strategy execution methods.

The sum of a company's strategic vision, objectives, and strategy constitutes a *strategic plan*.

Boards of directors have a duty to shareholders to play a vigilant role in overseeing management's handling of a company's strategy formulation, strategy execution process. A company's board is obligated to (1) ensure that the company issues accurate financial reports and has adequate financial controls, (2) critically appraise and ultimately approve strategic action plans, (3) evaluate the strategic leadership skills of the CEO, and (4) institute a compensation plan for top executives that rewards them for actions and results that serve stakeholder interests, most especially those of shareholders.

ASSURANCE OF LEARNING EXERCISES

1. Using the information in Tables 2.2 and 2.3, critique the adequacy and merit of the following vision statements, listing effective elements and shortcomings. Rank the vision statements from best to worst once you complete your evaluation.

LO1

VISION STATEMENT	EFFECTIVE ELEMENTS	SHORTCOMINGS

Wells Fargo

We want to satisfy all of our customers' financial needs, help them succeed financially, be the premier provider of financial services in every one of our markets, and be known as one of America's great companies.

Hilton Hotels Corporation

Our vision is to be the first choice of the world's travelers. Hilton intends to build on the rich heritage and strength of our brands by:
- Consistently delighting our customers
- Investing in our team members
- Delivering innovative products and services
- Continuously improving performance
- Increasing shareholder value
- Creating a culture of pride
- Strengthening the loyalty of our constituents

BASF

We are "The Chemical Company" successfully operating in all major markets.
- Our customers view BASF as their partner of choice.
- Our innovative products, intelligent solutions and services make us the most competent worldwide supplier in the chemical industry.
- We generate a high return on assets.
- We strive for sustainable development.
- We welcome change as an opportunity.
- We, the employees of BASF, together ensure our success.

Source: Company websites and annual reports.

LO2   2. Go to the company investor relations websites for ExxonMobil (ir.exxonmobil.com), Pfizer (www.pfizer.com/investors), and Intel (www.intc.com) to find examples of strategic and financial objectives. List four objectives for each company and indicate which of these are strategic and which are financial.

LO3   3. American Airlines' Chapter 11 reorganization plan filed in 2012 involved the company reducing operating expenses by $2 billion, while increasing revenues by $1 billion. The company's strategy to increase revenues included expanding the number of international flights and destinations and increasing daily departures for its five largest markets by 20 percent. The company also intended to upgrade its fleet by spending $2 billion to purchase new aircraft and refurbish the first-class cabins for planes not replaced. A final component of the restructuring plan included a merger with US Airways to create a global airline with more than 56,700 daily flights to 336 destinations in 56 countries. The merger was expected to produce cost savings from synergies of more than $1 billion and result in a stronger airline capable of paying creditors and rewarding employees and shareholders. Explain why the strategic initiatives at various organizational levels and functions require tight coordination to achieve the results desired by American Airlines.

4. Go to the investor relations website for Wal-Mart Stores, Inc., (http://investors. walmartstores.com) and review past presentations it has made during various investor conferences by clicking on the Events option in the navigation bar. Prepare a one- to two-page report that outlines what Wal-Mart has said to investors about its approach to strategy execution. Specifically, what has management discussed concerning staffing, resource allocation, policies and procedures, information and operating systems, continuous improvement, rewards and incentives, corporate culture, and internal leadership at the company?   LO4

5. Based on the information provided in Concepts & Connections 2.4, explain how corporate governance at Freddie Mac failed the enterprise's shareholders and other stakeholders. Which important obligations to shareholders were fulfilled by Fannie Mae's board of directors? What is your assessment of how well Fannie Mae's compensation committee handled executive compensation at the government-sponsored mortgage giant?   LO5

 EXERCISES FOR SIMULATION PARTICIPANTS

1. Meet with your co-managers and prepare a strategic vision statement for your company. It should be at least one sentence long and no longer than a brief paragraph. When you are finished, check to see if your vision statement meets the conditions for an effectively worded strategic vision set forth in Table 2.2 and avoids the shortcomings set forth in Table 2.3. If not, then revise it accordingly. What would be a good slogan that captures the essence of your strategic vision and that could be used to help communicate the vision to company personnel, shareholders, and other stakeholders?   LO1

2. What are your company's financial objectives? What are your company's strategic objectives?   LO2

3. What are the three or four key elements of your company's strategy?   LO3

 ENDNOTES

1. Gordon Shaw, Robert Brown, and Philip Bromiley, "Strategic Stories: How 3M Is Rewriting Business Planning," *Harvard Business Review* 76, no. 3 (May–June 1998); and David J. Collins and Michael G. Rukstad, "Can You Say What Your Strategy Is?" *Harvard Business Review* 86, no. 4 (April 2008).

2. Hugh Davidson, *The Committed Enterprise: How to Make Vision and Values Work* (Oxford: Butterworth Heinemann, 2002); W. Chan Kim and Renée Mauborgne, "Charting

Your Company's Future," *Harvard Business Review* 80, no. 6 (June 2002); James C. Collins and Jerry I. Porras, "Building Your Company's Vision," *Harvard Business Review* 74, no. 5 (September–October 1996); Jim Collins and Jerry Porras, *Built to Last: Successful Habits of Visionary Companies* (New York: HarperCollins, 1994); Michel Robert, *Strategy Pure and Simple II: How Winning Companies Dominate Their Competitors* (New York: McGraw-Hill, 1998).

3. Hugh Davidson, *The Committed Enterprise* (Oxford: Butterworth Heinemann, 2002).

4. Ibid.

5. Robert S. Kaplan and David P. Norton, *The Strategy-Focused Organization* (Boston: Harvard Business School Press, 2001).

6. Ibid. Also, see Robert S. Kaplan and David P. Norton, *The Balanced Scorecard: Translating Strategy into Action* (Boston: Harvard Business School Press, 1996); Kevin B. Hendricks,

Larry Menor, and Christine Wiedman, "The Balanced Scorecard: To Adopt or Not to Adopt," *Ivey Business Journal* 69, no. 2 (November–December 2004); and Sandy Richardson, "The Key Elements of Balanced Scorecard Success," *Ivey Business Journal* 69, no. 2 (November–December 2004).

7. Kaplan and Norton, *The Balanced Scorecard: Translating Strategy into Action*, pp. 25—29. Kaplan and Norton classify strategic objectives under the categories of customer-related, business processes, and learning and growth. In practice, companies using the balanced scorecard may choose categories of strategic objectives that best reflect the organization's value-creating activities and processes.

8. Information posted on the website of Bain and Company, www.bain. com, accessed May 27, 2011.

9. Information posted on the website of Balanced Scorecard Institute, accessed May 27, 2011.

10. Henry Mintzberg, Bruce Ahlstrand, and Joseph Lampel, *Strategy Safari: A Guided Tour through the Wilds of Strategic Management* (New York: Free Press, 1998); Bruce Barringer and Allen C. Bluedorn, "The Relationship between Corporate Entrepreneurship and Strategic Management," *Strategic Management Journal* 20 (1999); Jeffrey G. Covin and Morgan P. Miles, "Corporate Entrepreneurship and the Pursuit of Competitive Advantage," *Entrepreneurship: Theory and Practice* 23, no. 3 (Spring 1999); and David A. Garvin and Lynne C. Levesque, "Meeting the Challenge of Corporate Entrepreneurship," *Harvard Business Review* 84, no. 10 (October 2006).

11. Jay W. Lorsch and Robert C. Clark, "Leading from the Boardroom," *Harvard Business Review* 86, no. 4 (April 2008).

12. Ibid., p. 110.

13. Stephen P. Kaufman, "Evaluating the CEO," *Harvard Business Review* 86, no. 10 (October 2008).

14. David A. Nadler, "Building Better Boards," *Harvard Business Review* 82, no. 5 (May 2004); Cynthia A. Montgomery and Rhonda Kaufman, "The Board's Missing Link," *Harvard Business Review* 81, no. 3 (March 2003); John Carver, "What Continues to Be Wrong with Corporate Governance and How to Fix It," *Ivey Business Journal* 68, no. 1 (September/October 2003); and Gordon Donaldson, "A New Tool for Boards: The Strategic Audit," *Harvard Business Review* 73, no. 4 (July–August 1995).

Evaluating a Company's External Environment

LEARNING OBJECTIVES

LO1 Identify factors in a company's broad macro-environment that may have strategic significance.

LO2 Recognize the factors that cause competition in an industry to be fierce, more or less normal, or relatively weak.

LO3 Become adept at mapping the market positions of key groups of industry rivals.

LO4 Learn how to determine whether an industry's outlook presents a company with sufficiently attractive opportunities for growth and profitability.

In Chapter 2, we learned that the strategy formulation, strategy execution process begins with an appraisal of the company's present situation. The company's situation includes two facets: (1) the competitive conditions in the industry in which the company operates—its external environment; and (2) its resources and organizational capabilities—its internal environment.

Charting a company's long-term direction, conceiving its customer value proposition, setting objectives, or crafting a strategy without first gaining an understanding of the company's external and internal environments hamstrings attempts to build competitive advantage and boost company performance. Indeed, the first test of a winning strategy inquires, *"How well does the strategy fit the company's situation?"*

This chapter presents the concepts and analytical tools for zeroing in on a single-business company's external environment. Attention centers on the competitive arena in which the company operates, the drivers of market change, the market positions of rival companies, and the factors that determine competitive success. Chapter 4 explores the methods of evaluating a company's internal circumstances and competitiveness.

Evaluating the Strategically Relevant Components of a Company's Macro-Environment

LO1 Identify factors in a company's broad macro-environment that may have strategic significance.

A company's external environment includes the immediate industry and competitive environment and broader macro-environmental factors such as general economic conditions, societal values and cultural norms, political factors, the legal and regulatory environment, ecological considerations, and technological factors. These two levels of a company's external environment—the broad outer ring macro-environment and immediate inner ring industry and competitive environment—are illustrated in Figure 3.1. Strictly speaking, a company's **macro-environment** encompasses all of the *relevant factors* making up the broad environmental context in which a company operates; by *relevant*, we mean the factors are important enough that they should shape management's decisions regarding the company's long-term direction, objectives, strategy, and business model. The relevance of macro-environmental factors can be evaluated using **PESTEL analysis,** an acronym for the six principal components of the macro-environment: political factors, economic conditions in the firm's general environment, sociocultural forces, technological factors, environmental forces, and legal/regulatory factors. Table 3.1 provides a description of each of the six PESTEL components of the macro-environment.

> **CORE CONCEPT**
>
> The **macro-environment** encompasses the broad environmental context in which a company is situated and is comprised of six principal components: political factors, economic conditions, sociocultural forces, technological factors, environmental factors, and legal/regulatory conditions.
>
> **PESTEL analysis** can be used to assess the strategic relevance of the six principal components of the macro-environment: political, economic, social, technological, environmental, and legal forces.

The impact of outer ring macro-environmental factors on a company's choice of strategy can be big or small. But even if the factors of the macro-environment change slowly or are likely to have a low impact on the company's

FIGURE 3.1 **The Components of a Company's External Environment**

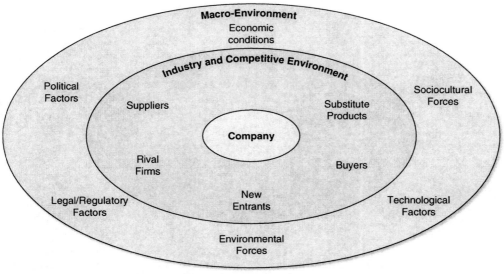
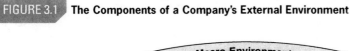

TABLE 3.1

The Six Components of the Macro-Environment Included in a PESTEL Analysis

Component	Description
Political factors	These factors include political policies and processes, including the extent to which a government intervenes in the economy. They include such matters as tax policy, fiscal policy, tariffs, the political climate, and the strength of institutions such as the federal banking system. Some political factors, such as bailouts, are industry-specific. Others, such as energy policy, affect certain types of industries (energy producers and heavy users of energy) more than others.
Economic conditions	Economic conditions include the general economic climate and specific factors such as interest rates, exchange rates, the inflation rate, the unemployment rate, the rate of economic growth, trade deficits or surpluses, savings rates, and per capita domestic product. Economic factors also include conditions in the markets for stocks and bonds, which can affect consumer confidence and discretionary income. Some industries, such as construction, are particularly vulnerable to economic downturns but are positively affected by factors such as low interest rates. Others, such as discount retailing, may benefit when general economic conditions weaken, as consumers become more price-conscious.
Sociocultural forces	Sociocultural forces include the societal values, attitudes, cultural factors, and lifestyles that impact businesses, as well as demographic factors such as the population size, growth rate, and age distribution. Sociocultural forces vary by locale and change over time. An example is the trend toward healthier lifestyles, which can shift spending toward exercise equipment and health clubs and away from alcohol and snack foods. Population demographics can have large implications for industries such as health care, where costs and service needs vary with demographic factors such as age and income distribution.
Technological factors	Technological factors include the pace of technological change and technical developments that have the potential for wide-ranging effects on society, such as genetic engineering and nanotechnology. They include institutions involved in creating knowledge and controlling the use of technology, such as R&D consortia, university-sponsored technology incubators, patent and copyright laws, and government control over the Internet. Technological change can encourage the birth of new industries, such as those based on nanotechnology, and disrupt others, such as the recording industry.

(continued)

TABLE 3.1   *(continued)*

Component	Description
Environmental forces	These include ecological and environmental forces such as weather, climate, climate change, and associated factors like water shortages. These factors can directly impact industries such as insurance, farming, energy production, and tourism. They may have an indirect but substantial effect on other industries such as transportation and utilities.
Legal and regulatory factors	These factors include the regulations and laws with which companies must comply such as consumer laws, labor laws, antitrust laws, and occupational health and safety regulation. Some factors, such as banking deregulation, are industry-specific. Others, such as minimum wage legislation, affect certain types of industries (low-wage, labor-intensive industries) more than others.

business situation, they still merit a watchful eye. Motor vehicle companies must adapt their strategies to customer concerns about carbon emissions and high gasoline prices. Changes in lifestyles, attitudes toward nutrition and fitness, and leisure preferences have begun to have strategy-shaping effects on companies competing in the processed food, restaurant, and fitness industries. As company managers scan the external environment, they must be alert for potentially important outer ring developments, assess their impact and influence, and adapt the company's direction and strategy as needed.

However, the factors and forces in a company's macro-environment that have the *biggest* strategy-shaping impact typically pertain to the company's immediate inner ring industry and competitive environment—competitive pressures, the actions of rival firms, buyer behavior, supplier-related considerations, and so on. Consequently, this chapter concentrates on a company's industry and competitive environment.

Assessing the Company's Industry and Competitive Environment

Thinking strategically about a company's industry and competitive environment entails using some well-validated concepts and analytical tools to get clear answers to seven questions:

1. Do the dominant economic characteristics of the industry offer sellers opportunities for growth and attractive profits?
2. What kinds of competitive forces are industry members facing, and how strong is each force?
3. What forces are driving industry change, and what impact will these changes have on competitive intensity and industry profitability?
4. What market positions do industry rivals occupy—who is strongly positioned and who is not?
5. What strategic moves are rivals likely to make next?
6. What are the key factors of competitive success?
7. Does the industry outlook offer good prospects for profitability?

Analysis-based answers to these questions are prerequisites for a strategy offering good fit with the external situation. The remainder of this chapter is devoted to describing the methods of obtaining solid answers to the seven questions above.

Question 1: What Are the Industry's Dominant Economic Characteristics?

Analyzing a company's industry and competitive environment begins with identifying the industry's dominant economic characteristics. While the general economic conditions of the macro-environment identified through PESTEL analysis may prove to be strategically relevant, it is the economic characteristics of the industry that will have a greater bearing on the industry's prospects for growth and attractive profits. An industry's dominant economic characteristics include such factors as market size and growth rate, the geographic boundaries of the market (which can extend from local to worldwide), market demand-supply conditions, market segmentation, and the pace of technological change. Table 3.2 summarizes analytical questions that define the industry's dominant economic features.

Getting a handle on an industry's distinguishing economic features not only provides a broad overview of the attractiveness of the industry, but also

TABLE 3.2

What to Consider in Identifying an Industry's Dominant Economic Features

Economic Characteristic	Questions to Answer
Market size and growth rate	• How big is the industry and how fast is it growing? • What does the industry's position in the life cycle (early development, rapid growth and takeoff, early maturity and slowing growth, saturation and stagnation, decline) reveal about the industry's growth prospects?
Scope of competitive rivalry	• Is the geographic area over which most companies compete local, regional, national, multinational, or global?
Demand-supply conditions	• Is a surplus of capacity pushing prices and profit margins down? • Is the industry overcrowded with too many competitors?
Market segmentation	• Is the industry characterized by various product characteristics or customer wants, needs, or preferences that divide the market into distinct segments?
Pace of technological change	• What role does advancing technology play in this industry? • Do most industry members have or need strong technological capabilities? Why?

promotes understanding of the kinds of strategic moves that industry members are likely to employ. For example, industries that are characterized by rapid technological change may require substantial investments in R&D and the development of strong product innovation capabilities—continuous product innovation is primarily a survival strategy in such industries as video games, computers, and pharmaceuticals.

Question 2: How Strong Are the Industry's Competitive Forces?

LO2 Recognize the factors that cause competition in an industry to be fierce, more or less normal, or relatively weak.

After gaining an understanding of the industry's general economic characteristics, industry and competitive analysis should focus on the competitive dynamics of the industry. The nature and subtleties of competitive forces are never the same from one industry to another and must be wholly understood to accurately assess the company's current situation. Far and away the most powerful and widely used tool for assessing the strength of the industry's competitive forces is the *five-forces model of competition*.[1] This model, as depicted in Figure 3.2, holds that competitive forces affecting industry attractiveness go beyond rivalry among competing sellers and include pressures stemming from four coexisting sources. The five competitive forces affecting industry attractiveness are listed below.

1. Competitive pressures stemming from *buyer* bargaining power.
2. Competitive pressures coming from companies in other industries to win buyers over to *substitute products*.
3. Competitive pressures stemming from *supplier* bargaining power.
4. Competitive pressures associated with the threat of *new entrants* into the market.
5. Competitive pressures associated with *rivalry among competing sellers* to attract customers. This is usually the strongest of the five competitive forces.

The Competitive Force of Buyer Bargaining Power

Whether seller-buyer relationships represent a minor or significant competitive force depends on (1) whether some or many buyers have sufficient bargaining leverage to obtain price concessions and other favorable terms, and (2) the extent to which buyers are price sensitive. Buyers with strong bargaining power can limit industry profitability by demanding price concessions, better payment terms, or additional features and services that increase industry members' costs. Buyer price sensitivity limits the profit potential of industry members by restricting the ability of sellers to raise prices without losing volume or unit sales.

The leverage that buyers have in negotiating favorable terms of the sale can range from weak to strong. Individual consumers, for example, rarely have much bargaining power in negotiating price concessions or other favorable terms with sellers. The primary exceptions involve situations in which price

FIGURE 3.2   **The Five-Forces Model of Competition**

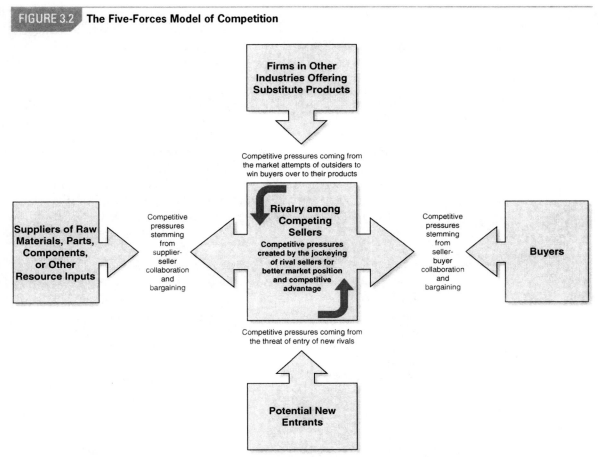

Sources: Based on Michael E. Porter, "How Competitive Forces Shape Strategy," *Harvard Business Review* 57, no. 2 (March–April 1979), pp. 137–45; and Michael E. Porter, "The Five Competitive Forces That Shape Strategy," *Harvard Business Review* 86, no. 1 (January 2008), pp. 80–86.

haggling is customary, such as the purchase of new and used motor vehicles, homes, and other big-ticket items such as jewelry and pleasure boats. For most consumer goods and services, individual buyers have no bargaining leverage—their option is to pay the seller's posted price, delay their purchase until prices and terms improve, or take their business elsewhere.

In contrast, large retail chains such as Walmart, Best Buy, Staples, and Home Depot typically have considerable negotiating leverage in purchasing products from manufacturers because retailers usually stock just two or three competing brands of a product and rarely carry all competing brands. In addition, the strong bargaining power of major supermarket chains such as Kroger, Safeway, and Albertsons allows them to demand promotional allowances and lump-sum payments (called slotting fees) from food products manufacturers in return for stocking certain brands or putting them in the best shelf locations. Motor vehicle manufacturers have strong bargaining power in negotiating to buy original equipment tires from Goodyear, Michelin, Bridgestone/Firestone, Continental, and Pirelli not only because they buy in large quantities, but also because tire makers have judged original equipment tires to be important contributors to brand awareness and brand loyalty.

Even if buyers do not purchase in large quantities or offer a seller important market exposure or prestige, they gain a degree of bargaining leverage in the following circumstances:

- *If buyers' costs of switching to competing brands or substitutes are relatively low.* Buyers who can readily switch between several sellers have more negotiating leverage than buyers who have high switching costs. When the products of rival sellers are virtually identical, it is relatively easy for buyers to switch from seller to seller at little or no cost. For example, the screws, rivets, steel, and capacitors used in the production of large home appliances such as washers and dryers are all commodity-like and available from many sellers. The potential for buyers to easily switch from one seller to another encourages sellers to make concessions to win or retain a buyer's business.

- *If the number of buyers is small or if a customer is particularly important to a seller.* The smaller the number of buyers, the less easy it is for sellers to find alternative buyers when a customer is lost to a competitor. The prospect of losing a customer who is not easily replaced often makes a seller more willing to grant concessions of one kind or another. Because of the relatively small number of digital camera brands, the sellers of lenses and other components used in the manufacture of digital cameras are in a weak bargaining position in their negotiations with buyers of their components.

- *If buyer demand is weak.* Weak or declining demand creates a "buyers' market"; conversely, strong or rapidly growing demand creates a "sellers' market" and shifts bargaining power to sellers.

- *If buyers are well informed about sellers' products, prices, and costs.* The more information buyers have, the better bargaining position they are in. The mushrooming availability of product information on the Internet is giving added bargaining power to individuals. It has become common for automobile shoppers to arrive at dealerships armed with invoice prices, dealer holdback information, a summary of incentives, and manufacturers' financing terms.

- *If buyers pose a credible threat of integrating backward into the business of sellers.* Companies such as Anheuser-Busch, Coors, and Heinz have integrated backward into metal can manufacturing to gain bargaining power in obtaining the balance of their can requirements from otherwise powerful metal can manufacturers.

Figure 3.3 summarizes factors causing buyer bargaining power to be strong or weak.

Not all buyers of an industry's product have equal degrees of bargaining power with sellers, and some may be less sensitive than others to price, quality, or service differences. For example, apparel manufacturers confront significant bargaining power when selling to big retailers such as Macy's, T. J. Maxx, or Target, but they can command much better prices selling to small owner-managed apparel boutiques.

| FIGURE 3.3 | **Factors Affecting the Strength of Buyer Bargaining Power** |

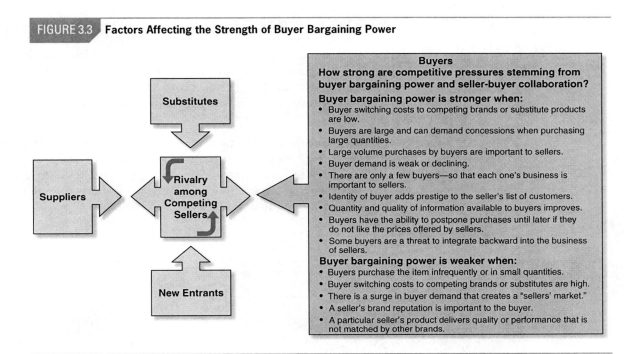

Buyers
How strong are competitive pressures stemming from buyer bargaining power and seller-buyer collaboration?

Buyer bargaining power is stronger when:
- Buyer switching costs to competing brands or substitute products are low.
- Buyers are large and can demand concessions when purchasing large quantities.
- Large volume purchases by buyers are important to sellers.
- Buyer demand is weak or declining.
- There are only a few buyers—so that each one's business is important to sellers.
- Identity of buyer adds prestige to the seller's list of customers.
- Quantity and quality of information available to buyers improves.
- Buyers have the ability to postpone purchases until later if they do not like the prices offered by sellers.
- Some buyers are a threat to integrate backward into the business of sellers.

Buyer bargaining power is weaker when:
- Buyers purchase the item infrequently or in small quantities.
- Buyer switching costs to competing brands or substitutes are high.
- There is a surge in buyer demand that creates a "sellers' market."
- A seller's brand reputation is important to the buyer.
- A particular seller's product delivers quality or performance that is not matched by other brands.

The Competitive Force of Substitute Products

Companies in one industry are vulnerable to competitive pressure from the actions of companies in another industry whenever buyers view the products of the two industries as good substitutes. For instance, the producers of sugar experience competitive pressures from the sales and marketing efforts of the makers of Equal, Splenda, and Sweet'N Low. Newspapers are struggling to maintain their relevance to subscribers who can watch the news on numerous television channels or go to the Internet for updates, blogs, and articles. Similarly, the producers of eyeglasses and contact lenses face competitive pressures from doctors who do corrective laser surgery.

Just how strong the competitive pressures are from the sellers of substitute products depends on three factors:

1. *Whether substitutes are readily available and attractively priced.* The presence of readily available and attractively priced substitutes creates competitive pressure by placing a ceiling on the prices industry members can charge. When substitutes are cheaper than an industry's product, industry members come under heavy competitive pressure to reduce their prices and find ways to absorb the price cuts with cost reductions.

2. *Whether buyers view the substitutes as comparable or better in terms of quality, performance, and other relevant attributes.* Customers are prone to compare performance and other attributes as well as price. For example, consumers have found digital cameras to be a superior substitute to film cameras because of the superior ease of use, the ability to download images to a home computer, and the ability to delete bad shots without paying for film developing.

3. *Whether the costs that buyers incur in switching to the substitutes are high or low.* High switching costs deter switching to substitutes while low switching costs make it easier for the sellers of attractive substitutes to lure buyers to their products. Typical switching costs include the inconvenience of switching to a substitute, the costs of additional equipment, the psychological costs of severing old supplier relationships, and employee retraining costs.

Figure 3.4 summarizes the conditions that determine whether the competitive pressures from substitute products are strong, moderate, or weak. As a rule, the lower the price of substitutes, the higher their quality and performance, and the lower the user's switching costs, the more intense the competitive pressures posed by substitute products.

FIGURE 3.4   **Factors Affecting Competition from Substitute Products**

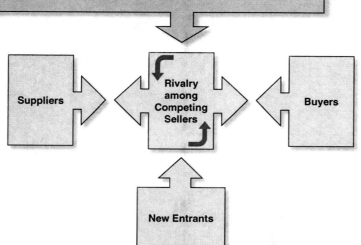

Firms in Other Industries Offering Substitute Products

How strong are competitive pressures coming from substitute products from outside the industry?

Competitive pressures from substitutes are stronger when:
• Good substitutes are readily available or new ones are emerging.
• Substitutes are attractively priced.
• Substitutes have comparable or better performance features.
• End users have low costs in switching to substitutes.
• End users grow more comfortable with using substitutes.

Competitive pressures from substitutes are weaker when:
• Good substitutes are not readily available or don't exist.
• Substitutes are higher priced relative to the performance they deliver.
• End users have high costs in switching to substitutes.

Signs That Competition from Substitutes Is Strong
• Sales of substitutes are growing faster than sales of the industry being analyzed (an indication that the sellers of substitutes are drawing customers away from the industry in question).
• Producers of substitutes are moving to add new capacity.
• Profits of the producers of substitutes are on the rise.

Suppliers

Rivalry among Competing Sellers

Buyers

New Entrants

The Competitive Force of Supplier Bargaining Power

Whether the suppliers of industry members represent a weak or strong competitive force depends on the degree to which suppliers have sufficient *bargaining power* to influence the terms and conditions of supply in their favor. Suppliers with strong bargaining power can erode industry profitability by charging industry members higher prices, passing costs on to them, and limiting their opportunities to find better deals. For instance, Microsoft and Intel, both of which supply PC makers with essential components, have been known to use their dominant market status not only to charge PC makers premium prices but also to leverage PC makers in other ways. The bargaining power possessed by Microsoft and Intel when negotiating with customers is so great that both companies have faced antitrust charges on numerous occasions. Before a legal agreement ending the practice, Microsoft pressured PC makers to load only Microsoft products on the PCs they shipped. Intel has also defended against antitrust charges resulting from its bargaining strength, but continues to give PC makers that use the biggest percentages of Intel chips in their PC models top priority in filling orders for newly introduced Intel chips. Being on Intel's list of preferred customers helps a PC maker get an early allocation of Intel's latest chips and thus allows a PC maker to get new models to market ahead of rivals.

The factors that determine whether any of the industry suppliers are in a position to exert substantial bargaining power or leverage are fairly clear-cut:

- *If the item being supplied is a commodity that is readily available from many suppliers.* Suppliers have little or no bargaining power or leverage whenever industry members have the ability to source from any of several alternative and eager suppliers.

- *The ability of industry members to switch their purchases from one supplier to another or to switch to attractive substitutes.* High switching costs increase supplier bargaining power, whereas low switching costs and the ready availability of good substitute inputs weaken supplier bargaining power.

- *If certain inputs are in short supply.* Suppliers of items in short supply have some degree of pricing power.

- *If certain suppliers provide a differentiated input that enhances the performance, quality, or image of the industry's product.* The greater the ability of a particular input to enhance a product's performance, quality, or image, the more bargaining leverage its suppliers are likely to possess.

- *Whether certain suppliers provide equipment or services that deliver cost savings to industry members in conducting their operations.* Suppliers who provide cost-saving equipment or services are likely to possess some degree of bargaining leverage.

- *The fraction of the costs of the industry's product accounted for by the cost of a particular input.* The bigger the cost of a specific part or component, the more opportunity for competition in the marketplace to be affected by the actions of suppliers to raise or lower their prices.

- *If industry members are major customers of suppliers.* As a rule, suppliers have less bargaining leverage when their sales to members of this one industry

---

FIGURE 3.5 Factors Affecting the Strength of Supplier Bargaining Power

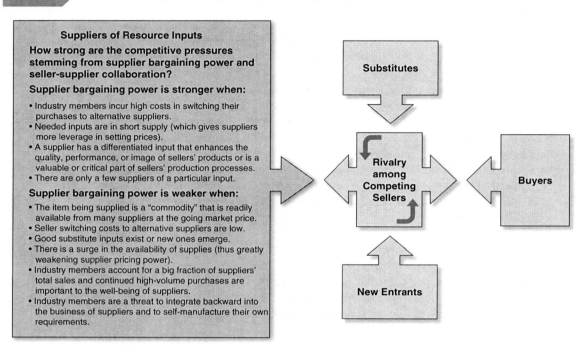

Suppliers of Resource Inputs

How strong are the competitive pressures stemming from supplier bargaining power and seller-supplier collaboration?

Supplier bargaining power is stronger when:

• Industry members incur high costs in switching their purchases to alternative suppliers.
• Needed inputs are in short supply (which gives suppliers more leverage in setting prices).
• A supplier has a differentiated input that enhances the quality, performance, or image of sellers' products or is a valuable or critical part of sellers' production processes.
• There are only a few suppliers of a particular input.

Supplier bargaining power is weaker when:

• The item being supplied is a "commodity" that is readily available from many suppliers at the going market price.
• Seller switching costs to alternative suppliers are low.
• Good substitute inputs exist or new ones emerge.
• There is a surge in the availability of supplies (thus greatly weakening supplier pricing power).
• Industry members account for a big fraction of suppliers' total sales and continued high-volume purchases are important to the well-being of suppliers.
• Industry members are a threat to integrate backward into the business of suppliers and to self-manufacture their own requirements.

Substitutes → Rivalry among Competing Sellers ← Buyers ← New Entrants

---

constitute a big percentage of their total sales. In such cases, the well-being of suppliers is closely tied to the well-being of their major customers.

• *Whether it makes good economic sense for industry members to vertically integrate backward.* The make-or-buy decision generally boils down to whether suppliers are able to supply a particular component at a lower cost than industry members could achieve if they were to integrate backward.

Figure 3.5 summarizes the conditions that tend to make supplier bargaining power strong or weak.

The Competitive Force of Potential New Entrants

Several factors determine whether the threat of new companies entering the marketplace presents a significant competitive pressure. One factor relates to the size of the pool of likely entry candidates and the resources at their command. As a rule, the bigger the pool of entry candidates, the stronger the threat of potential entry. This is especially true when some of the likely entry candidates have ample resources to support entry into a new line of business. Frequently, the strongest competitive pressures associated with potential entry come not from outsiders but from current industry participants looking for growth opportunities. *Existing industry members are often strong candidates to enter market segments or geographic areas where they currently do not have a market presence.*

A second factor concerns whether the likely entry candidates face high or low entry barriers. High barriers reduce the competitive threat of potential entry, while low barriers make entry more likely, especially if the industry is growing and offers attractive profit opportunities. The most widely encountered barriers that entry candidates must hurdle include:[2]

- *The presence of sizable economies of scale in production or other areas of operation.* When incumbent companies enjoy cost advantages associated with large-scale operations, outsiders must either enter on a large scale (a costly and perhaps risky move) or accept a cost disadvantage and consequently lower profitability.

- *Cost and resource disadvantages not related to scale of operation.* Aside from enjoying economies of scale, industry incumbents can have cost advantages that stem from the possession of proprietary technology, partnerships with the best and cheapest suppliers, low fixed costs (because they have older facilities that have been mostly depreciated), and experience/learning curve effects. The microprocessor industry is an excellent example of how learning/experience curves put new entrants at a substantial cost disadvantage. Manufacturing unit costs for microprocessors tend to decline about 20 percent each time *cumulative* production volume doubles. With a 20 percent experience curve effect, if the first 1 million chips cost $100 each, once production volume reaches 2 million the unit cost would fall to $80 (80 percent of $100), and by a production volume of 4 million the unit cost would be $64 (80 percent of $80).[3] The bigger the learning or experience curve effect, the bigger the cost advantage of the company with the largest *cumulative* production volume.

- *Strong brand preferences and high degrees of customer loyalty.* The stronger the attachment of buyers to established brands, the harder it is for a newcomer to break into the marketplace.

- *High capital requirements.* The larger the total dollar investment needed to enter the market successfully, the more limited the pool of potential entrants. The most obvious capital requirements for new entrants relate to manufacturing facilities and equipment, introductory advertising and sales promotion campaigns, working capital to finance inventories and customer credit, and sufficient cash to cover start-up costs.

- *The difficulties of building a network of distributors-retailers and securing adequate space on retailers' shelves.* A potential entrant can face numerous distribution channel challenges. Wholesale distributors may be reluctant to take on a product that lacks buyer recognition. Retailers have to be recruited and convinced to give a new brand ample display space and an adequate trial period. Potential entrants sometimes have to "buy" their way into wholesale or retail channels by cutting their prices to provide dealers and distributors with higher markups and profit margins or by giving them big advertising and promotional allowances.

- *Restrictive regulatory policies.* Government agencies can limit or even bar entry by requiring licenses and permits. Regulated industries such as cable TV, telecommunications, electric and gas utilities, and radio and television broadcasting entail government-controlled entry.

- *Tariffs and international trade restrictions.* National governments commonly use tariffs and trade restrictions (antidumping rules, local content requirements, local ownership requirements, quotas, etc.) to raise entry barriers for foreign firms and protect domestic producers from outside competition.

- *The ability and willingness of industry incumbents to launch vigorous initiatives to block a newcomer's successful entry.* Even if a potential entrant has or can acquire the needed competencies and resources to attempt entry, it must still worry about the reaction of existing firms.[4] Sometimes, there's little that incumbents can do to throw obstacles in an entrant's path. But there are times when incumbents use price cuts, increase advertising, introduce product improvements, and launch legal attacks to prevent the entrant from building a clientele. Cable TV companies have vigorously fought the entry of satellite TV into the industry by seeking government intervention to delay satellite providers in offering local stations, offering satellite customers discounts to switch back to cable, and charging satellite customers high monthly rates for cable Internet access.

Figure 3.6 summarizes conditions making the threat of entry strong or weak.

FIGURE 3.6   **Factors Affecting the Threat of Entry**

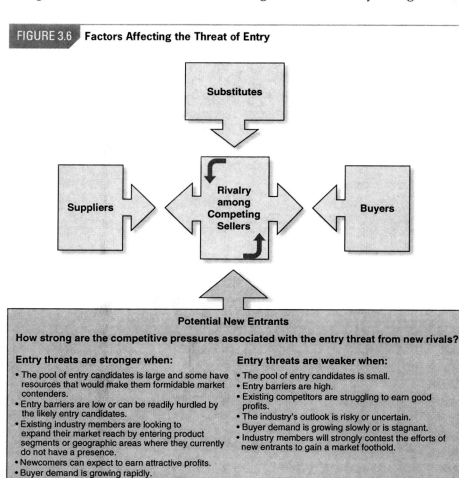

The Competitive Force of Rivalry among Competing Sellers

The strongest of the five competitive forces is nearly always the rivalry among competing sellers of a product or service. In effect, *a market is a competitive battlefield* where there's no end to the campaign for buyer patronage. Rival sellers are prone to employ whatever weapons they have in their business arsenal to improve their market positions, strengthen their market position with buyers, and earn good profits. The strategy formulation challenge is to craft a competitive strategy that, at the very least, allows a company to hold its own against rivals and that, ideally, *produces a competitive edge over rivals.* But competitive contests are ongoing and dynamic. When one firm makes a strategic move that produces good results, its rivals typically respond with offensive or defensive countermoves of their own. This pattern of action and reaction produces a continually evolving competitive landscape where the market battle ebbs and flows and produces winners and losers. But the current market leaders have no guarantees of continued leadership. In every industry, the ongoing jockeying of rivals leads to one or more companies gaining or losing momentum in the marketplace according to whether their latest strategic maneuvers succeed or fail.[5]

Figure 3.7 shows a sampling of competitive weapons that firms can deploy in battling rivals and indicates the factors that influence the intensity of their rivalry. Some factors that influence the tempo of rivalry among industry competitors include:

- *Rivalry intensifies when competing sellers regularly launch fresh actions to boost their market standing and business performance.* Normally, competitive jockeying among rival sellers is fairly intense. Indicators of strong competitive rivalry include lively price competition, the rapid introduction of next-generation products, and moves to differentiate products by offering better performance features, higher quality, improved customer service, or a wider product selection. Other common tactics used to temporarily boost sales include special sales promotions, heavy advertising, rebates, or low-interest-rate financing.

- *Rivalry is stronger in industries where competitors are equal in size and capability.* Competitive rivalry in the quick-service restaurant industry is particularly strong where there are numerous relatively equal-sized hamburger, deli sandwich, chicken, and taco chains. For the most part, McDonald's, Burger King, Taco Bell, KFC, Arby's, and other national fast-food chains have comparable capabilities and are required to compete aggressively to hold their own in the industry.

- *Rivalry is usually stronger in slow-growing markets and weaker in fast-growing markets.* Rapidly expanding buyer demand produces enough new business for all industry members to grow. But in markets where growth is sluggish or where buyer demand drops off unexpectedly, it is not uncommon for competitive rivalry to intensify significantly as rivals battle for market share and volume gains.

- *Rivalry is usually weaker in industries comprised of vast numbers of small rivals; likewise, it is often weak when there are fewer than five competitors.*

FIGURE 3.7 Factors Affecting the Strength of Competitive Rivalry

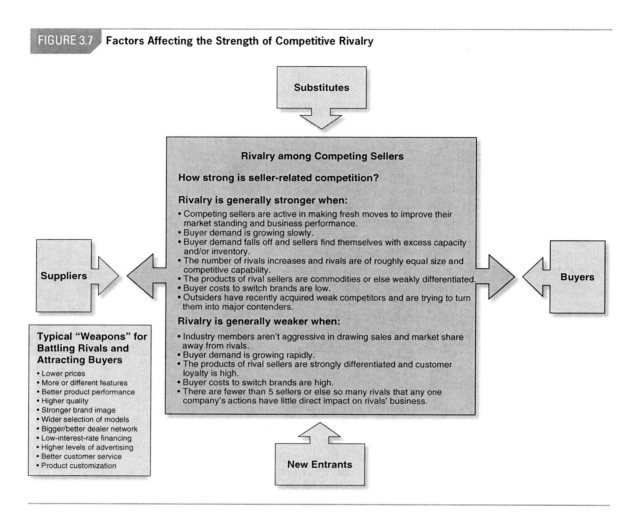

Head-to-head rivalry tends to be weak once an industry becomes populated with so many rivals that the strategic moves of any one competitor have little discernible impact on the success of rivals. Rivalry also *tends* to be weak if an industry consists of just two to four sellers. In a market with few rivals, each competitor soon learns that aggressive moves to grow its sales and market share can have an immediate adverse impact on rivals' businesses, almost certainly provoking vigorous retaliation. However, some caution must be exercised in concluding that rivalry is weak just because there are only a few competitors. The fierceness of the current battle between Google and Microsoft and the decades-long war between Coca-Cola and Pepsi are prime examples.

- *Rivalry increases when buyer demand falls off and sellers find themselves with excess capacity and/or inventory.* Excess supply conditions create a "buyers' market," putting added competitive pressure on industry rivals to scramble for profitable sales levels (often by price discounting).

- *Rivalry increases as it becomes less costly for buyers to switch brands.* The less expensive it is for buyers to switch their purchases from the seller of one brand to the seller of another brand, the easier it is for sellers to steal customers away from rivals.

- *Rivalry increases as the products of rival sellers become more standardized and diminishes as the products of industry rivals become more differentiated.* When the offerings of rivals are identical or weakly differentiated, buyers have less reason to be brand loyal—a condition that makes it easier for rivals to persuade buyers to switch to their offering. On the other hand, strongly differentiated product offerings among rivals breed high brand loyalty on the part of buyers.

- *Rivalry is more intense when industry conditions tempt competitors to use price cuts or other competitive weapons to boost unit volume.* When a product is perishable, seasonal, or costly to hold in inventory, competitive pressures build quickly any time one or more firms decide to cut prices and dump supplies on the market. Likewise, whenever fixed costs account for a large fraction of total cost, so that unit costs tend to be lowest at or near full capacity, firms come under significant pressure to cut prices or otherwise try to boost sales whenever they are operating below full capacity.

- *Rivalry increases when one or more competitors become dissatisfied with their market position.* Firms that are losing ground or are in financial trouble often pursue aggressive (or perhaps desperate) turnaround strategies that can involve price discounts, greater advertising, or merger with other rivals. Such strategies can turn competitive pressures up a notch.

- *Rivalry increases when strong companies outside the industry acquire weak firms in the industry and launch aggressive, well-funded moves to build market share.* A concerted effort to turn a weak rival into a market leader nearly always entails launching well-financed strategic initiatives to dramatically improve the competitor's product offering, excite buyer interest, and win a much bigger market share—actions that, if successful, put added pressure on rivals to counter with fresh strategic moves of their own.

Rivalry can be characterized as *cutthroat* or *brutal* when competitors engage in protracted price wars or habitually employ other aggressive tactics that are mutually destructive to profitability. Rivalry can be considered *fierce* to *strong* when the battle for market share is so vigorous that the profit margins of most industry members are squeezed to bare-bones levels. Rivalry can be characterized as *moderate* or *normal* when the maneuvering among industry members, while lively and healthy, still allows most industry members to earn acceptable profits. Rivalry is *weak* when most companies in the industry are relatively well satisfied with their sales growth and market share and rarely undertake offensives to steal customers away from one another.

The Collective Strengths of the Five Competitive Forces and Industry Profitability

Scrutinizing each of the five competitive forces one by one provides a powerful diagnosis of what competition is like in a given market. Once the strategist has gained an understanding of the competitive pressures associated with each of the five forces, the next step is to evaluate the collective strength of the five forces and determine if companies in this industry should reasonably expect to earn decent profits.

As a rule, the stronger the collective impact of the five competitive forces, the lower the combined profitability of industry participants. The most extreme case of a "competitively unattractive" industry is when all five forces are producing strong competitive pressures: Rivalry among sellers is vigorous, low entry barriers allow new rivals to gain a market foothold, competition from substitutes is intense, and both suppliers and customers are able to exercise considerable bargaining leverage. Fierce to strong competitive pressures coming from all five directions nearly always drive industry profitability to unacceptably low levels, frequently producing losses for many industry members and forcing some out of business. But an industry can be competitively unattractive without all five competitive forces being strong. Fierce competitive pressures from just one of the five forces, such as brutal price competition among rival sellers, may suffice to destroy the conditions for good profitability.

> The stronger the forces of competition, the harder it becomes for industry members to earn attractive profits.

In contrast, when the collective impact of the five competitive forces is moderate to weak, an industry is competitively attractive in the sense that industry members can reasonably expect to earn good profits and a nice return on investment. The ideal competitive environment for earning superior profits is one in which both suppliers and customers are in weak bargaining positions, there are no good substitutes, high barriers block further entry, and rivalry among present sellers generates only moderate competitive pressures. Weak competition is the best of all possible worlds for companies with mediocre strategies and second-rate implementation because even they can expect a decent profit.

Question 3: What Are the Industry's Driving Forces of Change and What Impact Will They Have?

The intensity of competitive forces and the level of industry attractiveness are almost always fluid and subject to change. It is essential for strategy makers to understand the current competitive dynamics of the industry, but it is equally important for strategy makers to consider how the industry is changing and the effect of industry changes that are under way. Any strategies devised by management will play out in a dynamic industry environment, so it's imperative that such plans consider what the industry environment might look like during the near term.

The Concept of Industry Driving Forces

Industry and competitive conditions change because forces are enticing or pressuring certain industry participants (competitors, customers, suppliers) to alter their actions in important ways. The most powerful of the change agents are called **driving forces** because they have the biggest influences in reshaping the industry landscape and altering competitive conditions. Some driving forces originate in the outer ring of the company's macro-environment (see Figure 3.1), but most originate in the company's more immediate industry and competitive environment.

> ### CORE CONCEPT
> **Driving forces** are the major underlying causes of change in industry and competitive conditions.

Driving forces analysis has three steps: (1) identifying what the driving forces are, (2) assessing whether the drivers of change are, individually or collectively, acting to make the industry more or less attractive, and (3) determining what strategy changes are needed to prepare for the impact of the driving forces.

Identifying an Industry's Driving Forces

Many developments can affect an industry powerfully enough to qualify as driving forces, but most drivers of industry and competitive change fall into one of the following categories:

- *Changes in an industry's long-term growth rate.* Shifts in industry growth have the potential to affect the balance between industry supply and buyer demand, entry and exit, and the character and strength of competition. An upsurge in buyer demand triggers a race among established firms and newcomers to capture the new sales opportunities. A slowdown in the growth of demand nearly always brings an increase in rivalry and increased efforts by some firms to maintain their high rates of growth by taking sales and market share away from rivals.

- *Increasing globalization.* Competition begins to shift from primarily a regional or national focus to an international or global focus when industry members begin seeking customers in foreign markets or when production activities begin to migrate to countries where costs are lowest. The forces of globalization are sometimes such a strong driver that companies find it highly advantageous, if not necessary, to spread their operating reach into more and more country markets. Globalization is very much a driver of industry change in such industries as credit cards, mobile phones, digital cameras, motor vehicles, steel, petroleum, personal computers, and video games.

- *Changes in who buys the product and how they use it.* Shifts in buyer demographics and the ways products are used can alter competition by affecting how customers perceive value, how customers make purchasing decisions, and where customers purchase the product. The burgeoning popularity of streaming video has affected broadband providers, wireless phone carriers, and television broadcasters and created opportunities for such new entertainment businesses as Hulu and Netflix.

- *Product innovation.* An ongoing stream of product innovations tends to alter the pattern of competition in an industry by attracting more first-time buyers, rejuvenating industry growth, and/or creating wider or narrower product differentiation among rival sellers. Product innovation has been a key driving force in such industries as computers, digital cameras, televisions, video games, and prescription drugs.

- *Technological change and manufacturing process innovation.* Advances in technology can dramatically alter an industry's landscape, making it possible to produce new and better products at lower cost and opening new industry frontiers. For instance, Voice over Internet Protocol technology (VoIP) has spawned low-cost, Internet-based phone networks that have begun competing with traditional telephone companies worldwide (whose higher-cost technology depends on hard-wire connections via overhead and underground telephone lines).

- *Marketing innovation.* When firms are successful in introducing *new ways* to market their products, they can spark a burst of buyer interest, widen industry demand, increase product differentiation, and lower unit costs—any or all of which can alter the competitive positions of rival firms and force strategy revisions.

- *Entry or exit of major firms.* The entry of one or more foreign companies into a geographic market once dominated by domestic firms nearly always shakes up competitive conditions. Likewise, when an established domestic firm from another industry attempts entry either by acquisition or by launching its own start-up venture, it usually pushes competition in new directions.

- *Diffusion of technical know-how across more companies and more countries.* As knowledge about how to perform a particular activity or execute a particular manufacturing technology spreads, the competitive advantage held by firms originally possessing this know-how erodes. Knowledge diffusion can occur through scientific journals, trade publications, on-site plant tours, word of mouth among suppliers and customers, employee migration, and Internet sources.

- *Changes in cost and efficiency.* Widening or shrinking differences in the costs among key competitors tend to dramatically alter the state of competition. Declining costs to produce PCs have enabled price cuts and spurred PC sales (especially lower-priced models) by making them more affordable to lower-income households worldwide.

- *Growing buyer preferences for differentiated products instead of a commodity product (or for a more standardized product instead of strongly differentiated products).* When a shift from standardized to differentiated products occurs, rivals must adopt strategies to outdifferentiate one another. However, buyers sometimes decide that a standardized, budget-priced product suits their requirements as well as a premium-priced product with lots of snappy features and personalized services.

- *Regulatory influences and government policy changes.* Government regulatory actions can often force significant changes in industry practices and strategic approaches. New rules and regulations pertaining to government-sponsored health insurance programs are driving changes in the health care industry. In international markets, host governments can drive competitive changes by opening their domestic markets to foreign participation or closing them.

TABLE 3.3

Common Driving Forces

1. Changes in the long-term industry growth rate.
2. Increasing globalization.
3. Emerging new Internet capabilities and applications.
4. Changes in who buys the product and how they use it.
5. Product innovation.
6. Technological change and manufacturing process innovation.
7. Marketing innovation.
8. Entry or exit of major firms.
9. Diffusion of technical know-how across more companies and more countries.
10. Changes in cost and efficiency.
11. Growing buyer preferences for differentiated products instead of a standardized commodity product (or for a more standardized product instead of strongly differentiated products).
12. Regulatory influences and government policy changes.
13. Changing societal concerns, attitudes, and lifestyles.

- *Changing societal concerns, attitudes, and lifestyles.* Emerging social issues and changing attitudes and lifestyles can be powerful instigators of industry change. Consumer concerns about the use of chemical additives and the nutritional content of food products have forced food producers to revamp food-processing techniques, redirect R&D efforts into the use of healthier ingredients, and compete in developing nutritious, good-tasting products.

While many forces of change may be at work in a given industry, *no more than three or four* are likely to be true driving forces powerful enough to qualify as the *major determinants* of why and how the industry is changing. Thus, company strategists must resist the temptation to label every change they see as a driving force. Table 3.3 lists the most common driving forces.

Assessing the Impact of the Industry Driving Forces

The second step in driving forces analysis is to determine whether the prevailing driving forces are acting to make the industry environment more or less attractive. Getting a handle on the collective impact of the driving forces usually requires looking at the likely effects of each force separately, because the driving forces may not all be pushing change in the same direction. For example, two driving forces may be acting to spur demand for the industry's product while one driving force may be working to curtail demand. Whether the net effect on industry demand is up or down hinges on which driving forces are the more powerful.

> An important part of driving forces analysis is to determine whether the individual or collective impact of the driving forces will be to increase or decrease market demand, make competition more or less intense, and lead to higher or lower industry profitability.

Determining Strategy Changes Needed to Prepare for the Impact of Driving Forces

The third step of driving forces analysis—where the real payoff for strategy making comes—is for managers to draw some conclusions about what

> The real payoff of driving forces analysis is to help managers understand what strategy changes are needed to prepare for the impacts of the driving forces.

strategy adjustments will be needed to deal with the impact of the driving forces. Without understanding the forces driving industry change and the impacts these forces will have on the industry environment over the next one to three years, managers are ill prepared to craft a strategy tightly matched to emerging conditions. Similarly, if managers are uncertain about the implications of one or more driving forces, or if their views are off-base, it will be difficult for them to craft a strategy that is responsive to the consequences of driving forces. So driving forces analysis is not something to take lightly; it has practical value and is basic to the task of thinking strategically about where the industry is headed and how to prepare for the changes ahead.

LO3 Become adept at mapping the market positions of key groups of industry rivals.

Question 4: How Are Industry Rivals Positioned?

The nature of competitive strategy inherently positions companies competing in an industry into strategic groups with diverse price/quality ranges, different distribution channels, varying product features, and different geographic coverages. The best technique for revealing the market positions of industry competitors is **strategic group mapping**. This analytical tool is useful for comparing the market positions of industry competitors or for grouping industry combatants into like positions.

CORE CONCEPT

Strategic group mapping is a technique for displaying the different market or competitive positions that rival firms occupy in the industry.

Using Strategic Group Maps to Assess the Positioning of Key Competitors

A **strategic group** consists of those industry members with similar competitive approaches and positions in the market. Companies in the same strategic group can resemble one another in any of several ways—they may have comparable product-line breadth, sell in the same price/quality range, emphasize the same distribution channels, use essentially the same product attributes to appeal to similar types of buyers, depend on identical technological approaches, or offer buyers similar services and technical assistance.[6] An industry with a commodity-like product may contain only one strategic group whereby all sellers pursue essentially identical strategies and have comparable market positions. But even with commodity products, there is likely some attempt at differentiation occurring in the form of varying delivery times, financing terms, or levels of customer service. Most industries offer a host of competitive approaches that allow companies to find unique industry positioning and avoid fierce competition in a crowded strategic group. Evaluating strategy options entails examining what strategic groups exist, identifying which companies exist within each group, and determining if a

CORE CONCEPT

A **strategic group** is a cluster of industry rivals that have similar competitive approaches and market positions.

competitive "white space" exists where industry competitors are able to create and capture altogether new demand.

The procedure for constructing a *strategic group map* is straightforward:

- Identify the competitive characteristics that delineate strategic approaches used in the industry. Typical variables used in creating strategic group maps are the price/quality range (high, medium, low), geographic coverage (local, regional, national, global), degree of vertical integration (none, partial, full), product-line breadth (wide, narrow), choice of distribution channels (retail, wholesale, Internet, multiple channels), and degree of service offered (no-frills, limited, full).

- Plot firms on a two-variable map based upon their strategic approaches.

- Assign firms occupying the same map location to a common strategic group.

- Draw circles around each strategic group, making the circles proportional to the size of the group's share of total industry sales revenues.

This produces a two-dimensional diagram like the one for the retail chain store industry in Concepts & Connections 3.1.

Several guidelines need to be observed in creating strategic group maps. First, the two variables selected as axes for the map should *not* be highly correlated; if they are, the circles on the map will fall along a diagonal and strategy makers will learn nothing more about the relative positions of competitors than they would by considering just one of the variables. For instance, if companies with broad product lines use multiple distribution channels while companies with narrow lines use a single distribution channel, then looking at product line-breadth reveals just as much about industry positioning as looking at the two competitive variables. Second, the variables chosen as axes for the map should reflect key approaches to offering value to customers and expose big differences in how rivals position themselves in the marketplace. Third, the variables used as axes don't have to be either quantitative or continuous; rather, they can be discrete variables or defined in terms of distinct classes and combinations. Fourth, drawing the sizes of the circles on the map proportional to the combined sales of the firms in each strategic group allows the map to reflect the relative sizes of each strategic group. Fifth, if more than two good competitive variables can be used as axes for the map, multiple maps can be drawn to give different exposures to the competitive positioning in the industry. Because there is not necessarily one best map for portraying how competing firms are positioned in the market, it is advisable to experiment with different pairs of competitive variables.

The Value of Strategic Group Maps

Strategic group maps are revealing in several respects. The *most important* has to do with identifying which rivals are similarly positioned and are thus close rivals and which are distant rivals. Generally, *the closer strategic groups are to each other on the map, the stronger the cross-group competitive rivalry tends to be.* Although firms in the same strategic group are the closest rivals, the next closest rivals are in the immediately adjacent groups.[7] Often, firms in strategic groups

CONCEPTS & CONNECTIONS 3.1

COMPARATIVE MARKET POSITIONS OF SELECTED RETAIL CHAINS: A STRATEGIC GROUP MAP APPLICATION

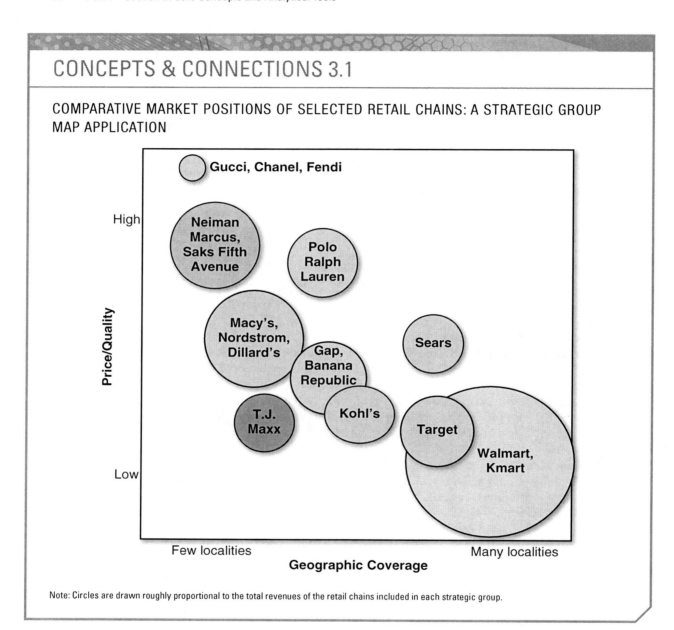

Note: Circles are drawn roughly proportional to the total revenues of the retail chains included in each strategic group.

Some strategic groups are more favorably positioned than others because they confront weaker competitive forces and/or because they are more favorably impacted by industry driving forces.

that are far apart on the map hardly compete. For instance, Walmart's clientele, merchandise selection, and pricing points are much too different to justify calling them close competitors of Neiman Marcus or Saks Fifth Avenue in retailing. For the same reason, Timex is not a meaningful competitive rival of Rolex, and Kia is not a close competitor of Porsche or Lexus.

The second thing to be gleaned from strategic group mapping is that *not all positions on the map are equally attractive.* Two reasons account for why some positions can be more attractive than others:

1. *Industry driving forces may favor some strategic groups and hurt others.* Driving forces in an industry may be acting to grow the demand for the products of firms in some strategic groups and shrink the demand for the products of firms in other strategic groups—as is the case in the news industry where Internet news services and cable news networks are gaining ground at the expense of newspapers and network television. The industry driving forces of emerging Internet capabilities and applications, changes in who buys the product and how they use it, and changing societal concerns, attitudes, and lifestyles are making it increasingly difficult for traditional media to increase audiences and attract new advertisers.

2. *Competitive pressures may cause the profit potential of different strategic groups to vary.* The profit prospects of firms in different strategic groups can vary from good to poor because of differing degrees of competitive rivalry within strategic groups, differing degrees of exposure to competition from substitute products outside the industry, and differing degrees of supplier or customer bargaining power from group to group. For instance, the competitive battle between Walmart and Target is more intense (with consequently smaller profit margins) than the rivalry among Versace, Chanel, Fendi, and other high-end fashion retailers.

Thus, part of strategic group analysis always entails drawing conclusions about where on the map is the "best" place to be and why. Which companies or strategic groups are in the best positions to prosper and which might be expected to struggle? And equally important, how might firms in poorly positioned strategic groups reposition themselves to improve their prospects for good financial performance?

Question 5: What Strategic Moves Are Rivals Likely to Make Next?

As in sports, scouting the business opposition is an essential part of game plan development. **Competitive intelligence** about rivals' strategies, their latest actions and announcements, their resources and organizational capabilities, and the thinking and leadership styles of their executives is valuable for predicting the strategic moves competitors are likely to make next. Having good information to predict the likely moves of key competitors allows a company to prepare defensive countermoves and to exploit any openings that arise from competitors' missteps.

Considerations in trying to predict what strategic moves rivals are likely to make next include the following:

- What executives are saying about where the industry is headed, the firm's situation, and their past actions and leadership styles.
- Identifying trends in the timing of product launches or new marketing promotions.
- Determining which rivals badly need to increase unit sales and market share.
- Considering which rivals have a strong incentive, along with the resources, to make major strategic changes.

CONCEPTS & CONNECTIONS 3.2

BUSINESS ETHICS AND COMPETITIVE INTELLIGENCE

Those who gather competitive intelligence on rivals can sometimes cross the fine line between honest inquiry and unethical or even illegal behavior. For example, calling rivals to get information about prices, the dates of new-product introductions, or wage and salary levels is legal, but misrepresenting one's company affiliation during such calls is unethical. Pumping rivals' representatives at trade shows is ethical only if one wears a name tag with accurate company affiliation indicated. Avon Products at one point secured information about its biggest rival, Mary Kay Cosmetics (MKC), by having its personnel search through the garbage bins outside MKC's headquarters.[8] When MKC officials learned of the action and sued, Avon claimed it did nothing illegal because a 1988 Supreme Court ruling declared that trash left on public property (in this case, a sidewalk) was anyone's for the taking. Avon even produced a videotape of its removal of the trash at the MKC site. Avon won the lawsuit—but Avon's action, while legal, scarcely qualifies as ethical.

- Knowing which rivals are likely to enter new geographic markets.
- Deciding which rivals are strong candidates to expand their product offerings and enter new product segments.

To succeed in predicting a competitor's next moves, company strategists need to have a good understanding of each rival's situation, its pattern of behavior and preferences in responding to prior strategic attacks, what its best strategic options are, and how rival management measures success. Doing the necessary detective work can be tedious and time-consuming, but scouting competitors well enough to anticipate their next moves allows managers to prepare effective countermoves and to take rivals' probable actions into account in crafting their own offensive strategies.[9] Concepts & Connections 3.2 discusses the ethical limits to gathering competitive intelligence.

> Studying competitors' past behavior and preferences provides a valuable assist in anticipating what moves rivals are likely to make next and outmaneuvering them in the marketplace.

Question 6: What Are the Industry Key Success Factors?

An industry's **key success factors (KSFs)** are those competitive factors that most affect industry members' ability to prosper in the marketplace. Key success factors may include particular strategy elements, product attributes, resources, competitive capabilities, or intangible assets. KSFs by their very nature are so important to future competitive success that *all firms* in the industry must pay close attention to them or risk an eventual exit from the industry.

CORE CONCEPT

Key success factors are the strategy elements, product attributes, competitive capabilities, or intangible assets with the greatest impact on future success in the marketplace.

In the ready-to-wear apparel industry, the KSFs are appealing designs and color combinations, low-cost manufacturing, a strong network of retailers or company-owned stores, distribution capabilities that allow stores to keep the best-selling items in stock, and advertisements that effectively convey the brand's image. These attributes and capabilities apply to all brands of apparel ranging from private-label brands sold by discounters to premium-priced ready-to-wear brands sold by upscale department stores. Table 3.4 lists the most common types of industry key success factors.

TABLE 3.4
Common Types of Industry Key Success Factors

Technology-related KSFs	• Expertise in a particular technology or in scientific research (important in pharmaceuticals, Internet applications, mobile communications, and most high-tech industries)
	• Proven ability to improve production processes (important in industries where advancing technology opens the way for higher manufacturing efficiency and lower production costs)
Manufacturing-related KSFs	• Ability to achieve scale economies and/or capture experience curve effects (important to achieving low production costs)
	• Quality control know-how (important in industries where customers insist on product reliability)
	• High utilization of fixed assets (important in capital-intensive/high-fixed-cost industries)
	• Access to attractive supplies of skilled labor
	• High labor productivity (important for items with high labor content)
	• Low-cost product design and engineering (reduces manufacturing costs)
	• Ability to manufacture or assemble products that are customized to buyer specifications
Distribution-related KSFs	• A strong network of wholesale distributors/dealers
	• Strong direct sales capabilities via the Internet and/or having company-owned retail outlets
	• Ability to secure favorable display space on retailer shelves
Marketing-related KSFs	• Breadth of product line and product selection
	• A well-known and well-respected brand name
	• Fast, accurate technical assistance
	• Courteous, personalized customer service
	• Accurate filling of buyer orders (few back orders or mistakes)
	• Customer guarantees and warranties (important in mail-order and online retailing, big-ticket purchases, and new-product introductions)
	• Clever advertising
Skills- and capability-related KSFs	• A talented workforce (superior talent is important in professional services such as accounting and investment banking)
	• National or global distribution capabilities
	• Product innovation capabilities (important in industries where rivals are racing to be first to market with new product attributes or performance features)
	• Design expertise (important in fashion and apparel industries)
	• Short delivery time capability
	• Supply chain management capabilities
	• Strong e-commerce capabilities—a user-friendly website and/or skills in using Internet technology applications to streamline internal operations
Other types of KSFs	• Overall low costs (not just in manufacturing) to be able to meet low-price expectations of customers
	• Convenient locations (important in many retailing businesses)
	• Ability to provide fast, convenient, after-the-sale repairs and service
	• A strong balance sheet and access to financial capital (important in newly emerging industries with high degrees of business risk and in capital-intensive industries)
	• Patent protection

An industry's key success factors can usually be deduced through identifying the industry's dominant characteristics, assessing the five competitive forces, considering the impacts of the driving forces, comparing the market positions of industry members, and forecasting the likely next moves of key rivals. In addition, the answers to the following three questions help identify an industry's key success factors:

1. On what basis do buyers of the industry's product choose between the competing brands of sellers? That is, what product attributes are crucial?

2. Given the nature of the competitive forces prevailing in the marketplace, what resources and competitive capabilities does a company need to have to be competitively successful?

3. What shortcomings are almost certain to put a company at a significant competitive disadvantage?

Only rarely are there more than five or six key factors for future competitive success. Managers should therefore resist the temptation to label a factor that has only minor importance a KSF. To compile a list of every factor that matters even a little bit defeats the purpose of concentrating management attention on the factors truly critical to long-term competitive success.

Question 7: Does the Industry Offer Good Prospects for Attractive Profits?

LO4 Learn how to determine whether an industry's outlook presents a company with sufficiently attractive opportunities for growth and profitability.

The final step in evaluating the industry and competitive environment is boiling down the results of the analyses performed in Questions 1–6 to determine if the industry offers a company strong prospects for attractive profits.

The important factors on which to base such a conclusion include:

- The industry's growth potential.
- Whether powerful competitive forces are squeezing industry profitability to subpar levels and whether competition appears destined to grow stronger or weaker.
- Whether industry profitability will be favorably or unfavorably affected by the prevailing driving forces.
- The company's competitive position in the industry vis-à-vis rivals. (Well-entrenched leaders or strongly positioned contenders have a much better chance of earning attractive margins than those fighting a steep uphill battle.)
- How competently the company performs industry key success factors.

The degree to which an industry is attractive or unattractive is not the same for all industry participants and potential new entrants. The attractiveness of an industry depends on the degree of fit between a company's competitive capabilities and industry key success factors.

It is a mistake to think of a particular industry as being equally attractive or unattractive to all industry participants and all potential entrants. Conclusions have to be drawn from the perspective of a particular company. Industries attractive to insiders may be unattractive to outsiders. Industry environments unattractive to weak competitors may be attractive to strong competitors. A favorably positioned company may survey a business environment and see a host of opportunities that weak competitors cannot capture.

When a company decides an industry is fundamentally attractive, a strong case can be made that it should invest aggressively to capture the opportunities it sees. When a strong competitor concludes an industry is relatively unattractive, it may elect to simply protect its present position, investing cautiously if at all, and begin looking for opportunities in other industries. A competitively weak company in an unattractive industry may see its best option as finding a buyer, perhaps a rival, to acquire its business.

 KEY POINTS

Thinking strategically about a company's external situation involves probing for answers to the following eight questions:

1. *What are the strategically relevant factors in the macro-environment?* Industries differ as to how they are affected by conditions in the broad macro-environment. PESTEL analysis of the political, economic, sociocultural, technological, environmental/ecological, and legal/regulatory factors provides a framework for approaching this issue systematically.

2. *What are the industry's dominant economic features?* Industries may also differ significantly on such factors as market size and growth rate, the number and relative sizes of both buyers and sellers, the geographic scope of competitive rivalry, the degree of product differentiation, the speed of product innovation, demand-supply conditions, the extent of vertical integration, and the extent of scale economies and learning curve effects.

3. *What kinds of competitive forces are industry members facing, and how strong is each force?* The strength of competition is a composite of five forces: (1) competitive pressures stemming from buyer bargaining power and seller-buyer collaboration, (2) competitive pressures associated with the sellers of substitutes, (3) competitive pressures stemming from supplier bargaining power and supplier-seller collaboration, (4) competitive pressures associated with the threat of new entrants into the market, and (5) competitive pressures stemming from the competitive jockeying among industry rivals.

4. *What forces are driving changes in the industry, and what impact will these changes have on competitive intensity and industry profitability?* Industry and competitive conditions change because forces are in motion that create incentives or pressures for change. The first phase is to identify the forces that are driving industry change. The second phase of driving forces analysis is to determine whether the driving forces, taken together, are acting to make the industry environment more or less attractive.

5. *What market positions do industry rivals occupy—who is strongly positioned and who is not?* Strategic group mapping is a valuable tool for understanding the similarities and differences inherent in the market positions of rival companies. Rivals in the same or nearby strategic groups are close competitors, whereas companies in distant strategic groups usually pose little or no immediate threat. Some strategic groups are more favorable than others. The profit potential of different strategic

groups may not be the same because industry driving forces and competitive forces likely have varying effects on the industry's distinct strategic groups.

6. *What strategic moves are rivals likely to make next?* Scouting competitors well enough to anticipate their actions can help a company prepare effective countermoves (perhaps even beating a rival to the punch) and allows managers to take rivals' probable actions into account in designing their own company's best course of action.

7. *What are the key factors for competitive success?* An industry's key success factors (KSFs) are the particular product attributes, competitive capabilities, and intangible assets that spell the difference between being a strong competitor and a weak competitor—and sometimes between profit and loss. KSFs by their very nature are so important to competitive success that *all firms* in the industry must pay close attention to them or risk being driven out of the industry.

8. *Does the outlook for the industry present the company with sufficiently attractive prospects for profitability?* Conclusions regarding industry attractiveness are a major driver of company strategy. When a company decides an industry is fundamentally attractive and presents good opportunities, a strong case can be made that it should invest aggressively to capture the opportunities it sees. When a strong competitor concludes an industry is relatively unattractive and lacking in opportunity, it may elect to simply protect its present position, investing cautiously if at all and looking for opportunities in other industries. A competitively weak company in an unattractive industry may see its best option as finding a buyer, perhaps a rival, to acquire its business. On occasion, an industry that is unattractive overall is still very attractive to a favorably situated company with the skills and resources to take business away from weaker rivals.

ASSURANCE OF LEARNING EXERCISES

LO2   1. Prepare a brief analysis of the coffee industry using the information provided on industry trade association websites. Based upon information provided on the websites of these associations, draw a five-forces diagram for the coffee industry and briefly discuss the nature and strength of each of the five competitive forces.

LO3   2. Based on the strategic group map in Concepts & Connections 3.1, who are Nordstrom's closest competitors? Between which two strategic groups is competition the strongest? Why do you think no retail chains are positioned in the upper-right corner of the map? Which company/strategic group faces the weakest competition from the members of other strategic groups?

LO1, LO4   3. The National Restaurant Association publishes an annual industry factbook that can be found at www.restaurant.org. Based on information in the latest report, does it appear that macro-environmental factors and the economic characteristics of the industry will present industry participants with attractive opportunities for growth and profitability? Explain.

EXERCISES FOR SIMULATION PARTICIPANTS

LO1, LO2, LO3, LO4

1. Which of the five competitive forces is creating the strongest competitive pressures for your company?

2. What are the "weapons of competition" that rival companies in your industry can use to gain sales and market share? See Figure 3.7 to help you identify the various competitive factors.

3. What are the factors affecting the intensity of rivalry in the industry in which your company is competing? Use Figure 3.7 and the accompanying discussion to help you in pinpointing the specific factors most affecting competitive intensity. Would you characterize the rivalry and jockeying for better market position, increased sales, and market share among the companies in your industry as fierce, very strong, strong, moderate, or relatively weak? Why?

4. Are there any driving forces in the industry in which your company is competing? What impact will these driving forces have? Will they cause competition to be more or less intense? Will they act to boost or squeeze profit margins? List at least two actions your company should consider taking to combat any negative impacts of the driving forces.

5. Draw a strategic group map showing the market positions of the companies in your industry. Which companies do you believe are in the most attractive position on the map? Which companies are the most weakly positioned? Which companies do you believe are likely to try to move to a different position on the strategic group map?

6. What do you see as the key factors for being a successful competitor in your industry? List at least three.

7. Does your overall assessment of the industry suggest that industry rivals have sufficiently attractive opportunities for growth and profitability? Explain.

ENDNOTES

1. Michael E. Porter, *Competitive Strategy: Techniques for Analyzing Industries and Competitors* (New York: Free Press, 1980), chap. 1; Michael E. Porter, "The Five Competitive Forces That Shape Strategy," *Harvard Business Review* 86, no. 1 (January 2008).

2. J. S. Bain, *Barriers to New Competition* (Cambridge, MA: Harvard University Press, 1956); F. M. Scherer, *Industrial Market Structure and Economic Performance* (Chicago: Rand McNally & Co., 1971).

3. Pankaj Ghemawat, "Building Strategy on the Experience Curve," *Harvard Business Review* 64, no. 2 (March–April 1985).

4. Michael E. Porter, "How Competitive Forces Shape Strategy," *Harvard Business Review* 57, no. 2 (March–April 1979).

5. Pamela J. Derfus, Patrick G. Maggitti, Curtis M. Grimm, and Ken G. Smith, "The Red Queen Effect: Competitive Actions and Firm Performance," *Academy of Management Journal* 51, no. 1 (February 2008).

6. Mary Ellen Gordon and George R. Milne, "Selecting the Dimensions That Define Strategic Groups: A Novel Market-Driven Approach," *Journal of Managerial Issues* 11, no. 2 (Summer 1999).

7. Avi Fiegenbaum and Howard Thomas, "Strategic Groups as Reference Groups: Theory, Modeling and Empirical Examination of Industry and Competitive Strategy," *Strategic Management Journal* 16 (1995); and S. Ade Olusoga, Michael P. Mokwa, and Charles H. Noble, "Strategic Groups, Mobility Barriers, and Competitive Advantage," *Journal of Business Research* 33 (1995).

8. Larry Kahaner, *Competitive Intelligence* (New York: Simon and Schuster, 1996).

9. Kevin P. Coyne and John Horn, "Predicting Your Competitor's Reaction," *Harvard Business Review* 87, no. 4 (April 2009).

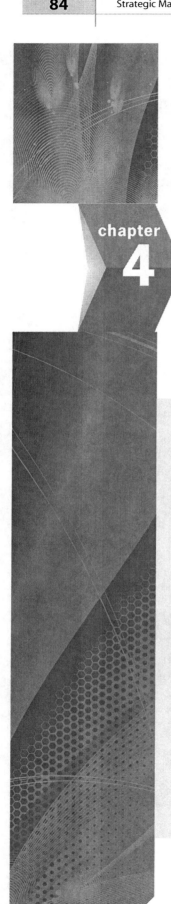

Evaluating a Company's Resources, Capabilities, and Competitiveness

LEARNING OBJECTIVES

LO1 Learn how to assess how well a company's strategy is working.

LO2 Understand why a company's resources and capabilities are central to its strategic approach and how to evaluate their potential for giving the company a competitive edge over rivals.

LO3 Grasp how a company's value chain activities can affect the company's cost structure and customer value proposition.

LO4 Learn how to evaluate a company's competitive strength relative to key rivals.

LO5 Understand how a comprehensive evaluation of a company's external and internal situations can assist managers in making critical decisions about their next strategic moves.

Chapter 3 described how to use the tools of industry and competitive analysis to assess a company's external environment and lay the groundwork for matching a company's strategy to its external situation. This chapter discusses the techniques of evaluating a company's internal situation, including its collection of resources and capabilities, its cost structure and customer value proposition, and its competitive strength versus its rivals. The analytical spotlight will be trained on five questions:

1. How well is the company's strategy working?
2. What are the company's competitively important resources and capabilities?
3. Are the company's cost structure and customer value proposition competitive?
4. Is the company competitively stronger or weaker than key rivals?
5. What strategic issues and problems merit front-burner managerial attention?

The answers to these five questions complete management's understanding of the company's overall situation and position the company for a good strategy-situation fit required by the "The Three Tests of a Winning Strategy" (see Chapter 1, page 9).

Question 1: How Well Is the Company's Strategy Working?

The two best indicators of how well a company's strategy is working are (1) whether the company is recording gains in financial strength and profitability and (2) whether the company's competitive strength and market standing are improving. Persistent shortfalls in meeting company financial performance targets and weak performance relative to rivals are reliable warning signs that the company suffers from poor strategy making, less-than-competent strategy execution, or both. Other indicators of how well a company's strategy is working include:

LO1 Learn how to assess how well a company's strategy is working.

- Trends in the company's sales and earnings growth.
- Trends in the company's stock price.
- The company's overall financial strength.
- The company's customer retention rate.
- The rate at which new customers are acquired.
- Changes in the company's image and reputation with customers.
- Evidence of improvement in internal processes such as defect rate, order fulfillment, delivery times, days of inventory, and employee productivity.

The stronger a company's current overall performance, the less likely the need for radical changes in strategy. The weaker a company's financial performance and market standing, the more its current strategy must be questioned. (A compilation of financial ratios most commonly used to evaluate a company's financial performance and balance sheet strength is presented in the Appendix on pages 240–241.)

Question 2: What Are the Company's Competitively Important Resources and Capabilities?

LO2 Understand why a company's resources and capabilities are central to its strategic approach and how to evaluate their potential for giving the company a competitive edge over rivals.

As discussed in Chapter 1, a company's business model and strategy must be well matched to its collection of resources and capabilities. An attempt to create and deliver customer value in a manner that depends on resources or capabilities that are deficient and cannot be readily acquired or developed is unwise and positions the company for failure. A company's competitive approach requires a tight fit with a company's internal situation and is strengthened when it exploits resources that are competitively valuable, rare, hard to copy, and not easily trumped by rivals' substitute resources. In addition, long-term competitive advantage requires the ongoing development and expansion of resources and capabilities to pursue emerging market opportunities and defend against future threats to its market standing and profitability.[1]

Sizing up the company's collection of resources and capabilities and determining whether they can provide the foundation for competitive success can be achieved through **resource and capability analysis.** This is a two-step process: (1) identify the company's resources and capabilities, and (2) examine them more closely to ascertain which are the most competitively important and whether they can support a sustainable competitive advantage over rival firms.[2] This second step involves applying the *four tests of a resource's competitive power.*

Resource and capability analysis is a powerful tool for sizing up a company's competitive assets and determining if the assets can support a sustainable competitive advantage over market rivals.

Identifying Competitively Important Resources and Capabilities

A company's **resources** are competitive assets that are owned or controlled by the company and may either be *tangible resources* such as plants, distribution centers, manufacturing equipment, patents, information systems, and capital reserves or creditworthiness or *intangible assets* such as a well-known brand or a results-oriented organizational culture. Table 4.1 lists the common types of tangible and intangible resources that a company may possess.

A **capability** is the capacity of a firm to competently perform some internal activity. A capability may also be referred to as a **competence.** Capabilities or competences also vary in form, quality, and competitive importance, with some being more competitively valuable than others. *Organizational capabilities are developed and enabled through the deployment of a company's resources or some combination of its resources.*[3] Some capabilities rely heavily on a company's intangible

CORE CONCEPT

A **resource** is a competitive asset that is owned or controlled by a company; a **capability** is the capacity of a company to competently perform some internal activity. Capabilities are developed and enabled through the deployment of a company's resources.

TABLE 4.1

Common Types of Tangible and Intangible Resources

Tangible Resources

- *Physical resources*—state-of-the-art manufacturing plants and equipment, efficient distribution facilities, attractive real estate locations, or ownership of valuable natural resource deposits.
- *Financial resources*—cash and cash equivalents, marketable securities, and other financial assets such as a company's credit rating and borrowing capacity.
- *Technological assets*—patents, copyrights, superior production technology, and technologies that enable activities.
- *Organizational resources*—information and communication systems (servers, workstations, etc.), proven quality control systems, and strong network of distributors or retail dealers.

Intangible Resources

- *Human assets and intellectual capital*—an experienced and capable workforce, talented employees in key areas, collective learning embedded in the organization, or proven managerial know-how.
- *Brand, image, and reputational assets*—brand names, trademarks, product or company image, buyer loyalty, and reputation for quality, superior service.
- *Relationships*—alliances or joint ventures that provide access to technologies, specialized know-how, or geographic markets, and trust established with various partners.
- *Company culture*—the norms of behavior, business principles, and ingrained beliefs within the company.

resources, such as human assets and intellectual capital. For example, General Mills' brand management capabilities draw upon the knowledge of the company's brand managers, the expertise of its marketing department, and the company's relationships with retailers. Electronic Arts' video game design capabilities result from the creative talents and technological expertise of its game developers and the company's culture that encourages creative thinking.

Determining the Competitive Power of a Company's Resources and Capabilities

What is most telling about a company's aggregation of resources and capabilities is how powerful they are in the marketplace. The competitive power of a resource or capability is measured by how many of the following four tests it can pass.[4]

The tests are often referred to as the **VRIN tests for sustainable competitive advantage**—an acronym for *valuable, rare, inimitable,* and *nonsubstitutable.* The first two tests determine whether the resource or capability may contribute to a competitive advantage. The last two determine the degree to which the competitive advantage potential can be sustained.

> **CORE CONCEPT**
>
> The **VRIN tests for sustainable competitive advantage** ask if a resource or capability is *valuable, rare, inimitable,* and *nonsubstitutable.*

1. *Is the resource or capability competitively **valuable**?* All companies possess a collection of resources and capabilities—some have the potential

to contribute to a competitive advantage while others may not. Apple's operating system for its personal computers by some accounts is superior to Windows 8, but Apple has failed in converting its resources devoted to operating system design into anything more than moderate competitive success in the global PC market.

> **CORE CONCEPT**
>
> A **core competence** is a proficiently performed internal activity that is *central* to a company's strategy and competitiveness. A core competence that is performed with a very high level of proficiency is referred to as a **distinctive competence.**

A capability that passes the "competitively valuable" test and is *central* to a company's strategy and competitiveness is frequently referred to as a **core competence.** A competitively valuable capability that is performed with a very high level of proficiency is sometimes known as a **distinctive competence.** Most often, *a core competence or distinctive competence is knowledge-based, residing in people and in a company's intellectual capital and not in its assets on the balance sheet.*

2. *Is the resource or capability **rare**—is it something rivals lack?* Resources and capabilities that are common among firms and widely available cannot be a source of competitive advantage. All makers of branded cookies and sweet snacks have valuable marketing capabilities and brands. Therefore, these skills are not rare or unique in the industry. However, the brand strength of Oreo is uncommon and has provided Kraft Foods with greater market share as well as the opportunity to benefit from brand extensions such as Double Stuf Oreo cookies and Mini Oreo cookies.

3. *Is the resource or capability **inimitable** or hard to copy?* The more difficult and more expensive it is to imitate a company's resource or capability, the more likely that it can also provide a *sustainable* competitive advantage. Resources tend to be difficult to copy when they are unique (a fantastic real estate location, patent protection), when they must be built over time (a brand name, a strategy-supportive organizational culture), and when they carry big capital requirements (a cost-effective plant to manufacture cutting-edge microprocessors). Imitation by rivals is most challenging when capabilities reflect a high level of *social complexity* (for example, a stellar team-oriented culture or unique trust-based relationships with employees, suppliers, or customers) and *causal ambiguity,* a term that signifies the hard-to-disentangle nature of complex processes, such as the web of intricate activities enabling a new drug discovery.

4. *Is the resource or capability **nonsubstitutable** or is it vulnerable to the threat of substitution from different types of resources and capabilities?* Resources that are competitively valuable, rare, and costly to imitate may lose much of their ability to offer competitive advantage if rivals possess equivalent substitute resources. For example, manufacturers relying on automation to gain a cost-based advantage in production activities may find their technology-based advantage nullified by rivals' use of low-wage offshore manufacturing. Resources can contribute to a competitive advantage only when resource substitutes don't exist.

Understanding the nature of competitively important resources allows managers to identify resources or capabilities that should be further developed to play an important role in the company's future strategies. In addition, management may determine that it doesn't possess a resource that independently passes all four tests listed here with high marks, but that it does have a **bundle of resources** that can pass the tests. Although Nike's resources dedicated to research and development, marketing research, and product design are matched relatively well by rival Adidas, its cross-functional design process allows it to set the pace for innovation in athletic apparel and footwear and consistently outperform Adidas and other rivals in the marketplace. Nike's footwear designers get ideas for new performance features from the professional athletes who endorse its products and then work alongside footwear materials researchers, consumer trend analysts, color designers, and marketers to design new models that are presented to a review committee. Nike's review committee is made up of hundreds of individuals who evaluate prototype details such as shoe proportions and color designs, the size of the swoosh, stitching patterns, sole color and tread pattern, and insole design. About 400 models are approved by the committee each year, which are sourced from contract manufacturers and marketed in more than 180 countries. The bundling of Nike's professional endorsements, R&D activities, marketing research efforts, styling expertise, and managerial know-how has become an important source of the company's competitive advantage and has allowed it to remain number one in the athletic footwear and apparel industry for more than 20 years.

> **CORE CONCEPT**
> Companies that lack a stand-alone resource that is competitively powerful may nonetheless develop a competitive advantage through **resource bundles** that enable the superior performance of important cross-functional capabilities.

Companies lacking certain resources needed for competitive success in an industry may be able to adopt strategies directed at eroding or at least neutralizing the competitive potency of a particular rival's resources and capabilities by identifying and developing **substitute resources** to accomplish the same purpose. For example, Amazon.com lacks a big network of retail stores to compete with those operated by rival Barnes & Noble, but Amazon's much larger, readily accessible, and searchable book inventory—coupled with its short delivery times and free shipping on orders over $25—are more attractive to many busy consumers than visiting a big-box bookstore. In other words, Amazon has carefully and consciously developed a set of competitively valuable resources that are proving to be effective substitutes for competing head-to-head against Barnes & Noble without having to invest in hundreds of brick-and-mortar retail stores.[5]

> Rather than try to match the resources possessed by a rival company, a company may develop entirely different resources that substitute for the strengths of the rival.

The Importance of Dynamic Capabilities in Sustaining Competitive Advantage

Resources and capabilities must be continually strengthened and nurtured to sustain their competitive power and, at times, may need to be broadened and deepened to allow the company to position itself to pursue emerging market opportunities.[6] Organizational resources and capabilities that grow stale can impair competitiveness unless they are refreshed, modified, or even phased out and replaced in response to ongoing market changes and shifts in company strategy. In addition, disruptive environmental change may destroy the value of key strategic assets, turning *static* resources and capabilities "from diamonds to rust."[7] Management's organization-building challenge has two elements: (1) attending to ongoing recalibration of existing capabilities and resources, and (2) casting a watchful eye for opportunities to develop totally new capabilities for delivering better customer value and/or outcompeting rivals. Companies that know the importance of recalibrating and upgrading resources and capabilities make it a routine management function to build new resource configurations and capabilities. Such a managerial approach allows a company to prepare for market changes and pursue emerging opportunities. This ability to build and integrate new competitive assets becomes a capability in itself—a **dynamic capability.** A dynamic capability is the ability to modify, deepen, or reconfigure the company's existing resources and capabilities in response to its changing environment or market opportunities.[8]

Management at Toyota has aggressively upgraded the company's capabilities in fuel-efficient hybrid engine technology and constantly fine-tuned the famed Toyota Production System to enhance the company's already proficient

> ### CORE CONCEPT
> A **dynamic capability** is the ability to modify, deepen, or reconfigure the company's existing resources and capabilities in response to its changing environment or market opportunities.

> A company requires a dynamically evolving portfolio of resources and capabilities in order to sustain its competitiveness and position itself to pursue future market opportunities.

capabilities in manufacturing top-quality vehicles at relatively low costs. Likewise, management at Honda has recently accelerated the company's efforts to broaden its expertise and capabilities in hybrid engines to stay close to Toyota. Resources and capabilities can also be built and augmented through alliances and acquisitions.[9] Cisco Systems has greatly expanded its engineering capabilities and its ability to enter new product categories through frequent acquisitions. Strategic alliances are a commonly used approach to developing and reconfiguring capabilities in the biotech and pharmaceutical industries.

Is the Company Able to Seize Market Opportunities and Nullify External Threats?

An essential element in evaluating a company's overall situation entails examining the company's resources and competitive capabilities in terms of the degree to which they enable it to pursue its best market opportunities and defend against the external threats to its future well-being. The simplest and

> ### CORE CONCEPT
> **SWOT analysis** is a simple but powerful tool for sizing up a company's internal strengths and competitive deficiencies, its market opportunities, and the external threats to its future well-being.

most easily applied tool for conducting this examination is widely known as *SWOT analysis,* so named because it zeros in on a company's internal **S**trengths and **W**eaknesses, market **O**pportunities, and external **T**hreats. *A company's internal strengths should always serve as the basis of its strategy— placing heavy reliance on a company's best competitive* *assets is the soundest route to attracting customers and competing successfully against rivals.*[10] As a rule, strategies that place heavy demands on areas where the company is weakest or has unproven competencies should be avoided. Plainly, managers must look toward correcting competitive weaknesses that make the company vulnerable, hold down profitability, or disqualify it from pursuing an attractive opportunity. Furthermore, a company's strategy should be aimed squarely at capturing those market opportunities that are most attractive and suited to the company's collection of capabilities. How much attention to devote to defending against external threats to the company's future performance hinges on how vulnerable the company is, whether defensive moves can be taken to lessen their impact, and whether the costs of undertaking such moves represent the best use of company resources. A first-rate SWOT analysis provides the basis for crafting a strategy that capitalizes on the company's strengths, aims squarely at capturing the company's best opportunities, and defends against the threats to its well-being. Table 4.2 lists the kinds of factors to consider in compiling a company's resource strengths and weaknesses.

> Basing a company's strategy on its strengths resulting from most competitively valuable resources and capabilities gives the company its best chance for market success.

The Value of a SWOT Analysis   A SWOT analysis involves more than making four lists. The most important parts of SWOT analysis are:

1. Drawing conclusions from the SWOT listings about the company's overall situation.

2. Translating these conclusions into strategic actions to better match the company's strategy to its strengths and market opportunities, correcting problematic weaknesses, and defending against worrisome external threats.

> Simply listing a company's strengths, weaknesses, opportunities, and threats is not enough; the payoff from SWOT analysis comes from the conclusions about a company's situation and the implications for strategy improvement that flow from the four lists.

Question 3: Are the Company's Cost Structure and Customer Value Proposition Competitive?

Company managers are often stunned when a competitor cuts its prices to "unbelievably low" levels or when a new market entrant comes on strong with a great new product offered at a surprisingly low price. Such competitors may not, however, be buying market positions with prices that are below costs. They may simply have substantially lower costs and therefore are able to offer prices that result in more appealing customer value propositions. One of the most telling signs of whether a company's business position is strong or precarious is whether its cost structure and customer value proposition are competitive with industry rivals.

LO3 Grasp how a company's value chain activities can affect the company's cost structure and customer value proposition.

Cost comparisons are especially critical in industries where price competition is typically the ruling market force. But even in industries where products are differentiated, rival companies have to keep their costs in line with rivals offering value propositions based upon a similar mix of differentiating features.

TABLE 4.2

Factors to Consider When Identifying a Company's Strengths, Weaknesses, Opportunities, and Threats

Potential Internal Strengths and Competitive Capabilities

- Core competencies in _____.
- A strong financial condition; ample financial resources to grow the business.
- Strong brand-name image/company reputation.
- Economies of scale and/or learning and experience curve advantages over rivals.
- Proprietary technology/superior technological skills/important patents.
- Cost advantages over rivals.
- Product innovation capabilities.
- Proven capabilities in improving production processes.
- Good supply chain management capabilities.
- Good customer service capabilities.
- Better product quality relative to rivals.
- Wide geographic coverage and/or strong global distribution capability.
- Alliances/joint ventures with other firms that provide access to valuable technology, competencies, and/or attractive geographic markets.

Potential Internal Weaknesses and Competitive Deficiencies

- No clear strategic direction.
- No well-developed or proven core competencies.
- A weak balance sheet; burdened with too much debt.
- Higher overall unit costs relative to key competitors.
- A product/service with features and attributes that are inferior to those of rivals.
- Too narrow a product line relative to rivals.
- Weak brand image or reputation.
- Weaker dealer network than key rivals.
- Behind on product quality, R&D, and/or technological know-how.
- Lack of management depth.
- Short on financial resources to grow the business and pursue promising initiatives.

Potential Market Opportunities

- Serving additional customer groups or market segments.
- Expanding into new geographic markets.
- Expanding the company's product line to meet a broader range of customer needs.
- Utilizing existing company skills or technological know-how to enter new product lines or new businesses.
- Falling trade barriers in attractive foreign markets.
- Acquiring rival firms or companies with attractive technological expertise or capabilities.

Potential External Threats to a Company's Future Prospects

- Increasing intensity of competition among industry rivals—may squeeze profit margins.
- Slowdowns in market growth.
- Likely entry of potent new competitors.
- Growing bargaining power of customers or suppliers.
- A shift in buyer needs and tastes away from the industry's product.
- Adverse demographic changes that threaten to curtail demand for the industry's product.
- Vulnerability to unfavorable industry driving forces.
- Restrictive trade policies on the part of foreign governments.
- Costly new regulatory requirements.

But a company must also remain competitive in terms of its customer value proposition. Tiffany's value proposition, for example, remains attractive to people who want customer service, the assurance of quality, and a high-status brand despite the availability of cut-rate diamond jewelry online. Target's customer value proposition has withstood the Walmart low-price juggernaut by attention to product design, image, and attractive store layouts in addition to efficiency. The key for managers is to keep close track of how *cost effectively* the company can deliver value to customers relative to its competitors. *If the company can deliver the same amount of value with lower expenditures (or more value at a similar cost), it will maintain a competitive edge.* Two analytical tools are particularly useful in determining whether a company's value proposition and costs are competitive: value chain analysis and benchmarking.

> Competitive advantage hinges on how cost effectively a company can execute its customer value proposition.

Company Value Chains

Every company's business consists of a collection of activities undertaken in the course of designing, producing, marketing, delivering, and supporting its product or service. All of the various activities that a company performs internally combine to form a **value chain,** so called because the underlying intent of a company's activities is to do things that ultimately *create value for buyers.*

As shown in Figure 4.1, a company's value chain consists of two broad categories of activities that drive costs and create customer value: the *primary activities* that are foremost in creating value for customers and the requisite *support activities* that facilitate and enhance the performance of the primary activities.[11] For example, the primary activities and cost drivers for a big-box retailer such as Target include merchandise selection and buying, store layout and product display, advertising, and customer service; its support activities that affect customer value and costs include site selection, hiring and training, store maintenance, plus the usual assortment of administrative activities. A hotel chain's primary activities and costs are mainly comprised of reservations and hotel operations (check-in and check-out, maintenance and housekeeping, dining and room service, and conventions and meetings); principal support activities that drive costs and impact customer value include accounting, hiring and training hotel staff, and general administration. Supply chain management is a crucial activity for Nissan or Amazon.com but is not a value chain component at Google or CBS. Sales and marketing are dominant activities at Procter & Gamble and Sony but have minor roles at oil-drilling companies and natural gas pipeline companies. With its focus on value-creating activities, the value chain is an ideal tool for examining how a company delivers on its customer value proposition. It permits a deep look at the company's cost structure and ability to offer low prices. It reveals the emphasis that a company places on activities that enhance differentiation and support higher prices, such as service and marketing.

> **CORE CONCEPT**
>
> A company's **value chain** identifies the primary activities that create customer value and related support activities.

The value chain also includes a profit margin component; profits are necessary to compensate the company's owners/shareholders and investors,

---

FIGURE 4.1   **A Representative Company Value Chain**

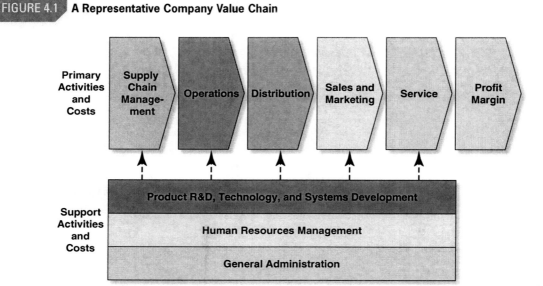

PRIMARY ACTIVITIES

- **Supply Chain Management**—Activities, costs, and assets associated with purchasing fuel, energy, raw materials, parts and components, merchandise, and consumable items from vendors; receiving, storing, and disseminating inputs from suppliers; inspection; and inventory management.

- **Operations**—Activities, costs, and assets associated with converting inputs into final product form (production, assembly, packaging, equipment maintenance, facilities, operations, quality assurance, environmental protection).

- **Distribution**—Activities, costs, and assets dealing with physically distributing the product to buyers (finished goods warehousing, order processing, order picking and packing, shipping, delivery vehicle operations, establishing and maintaining a network of dealers and distributors).

- **Sales and Marketing**—Activities, costs, and assets related to sales force efforts, advertising and promotion, market research and planning, and dealer/distributor support.

- **Service**—Activities, costs, and assets associated with providing assistance to buyers, such as installation, spare parts delivery, maintenance and repair, technical assistance, buyer inquiries, and complaints.

SUPPORT ACTIVITIES

- **Product R&D, Technology, and Systems Development**—Activities, costs, and assets relating to product R&D, process R&D, process design improvement, equipment design, computer software development, telecommunications systems, computer-assisted design and engineering, database capabilities, and development of computerized support systems.

- **Human Resources Management**—Activities, costs, and assets associated with the recruitment, hiring, training, development, and compensation of all types of personnel; labor relations activities; and development of knowledge-based skills and core competencies.

- **General Administration**—Activities, costs, and assets relating to general management, accounting and finance, legal and regulatory affairs, safety and security, management information systems, forming strategic alliances and collaborating with strategic partners, and other "overhead" functions.

Source: Based on the discussion in Michael E. Porter, *Competitive Advantage* (New York: Free Press, 1985), pp. 37–43.

---

who bear risks and provide capital. Tracking the profit margin along with the value-creating activities is critical because unless an enterprise succeeds in delivering customer value profitably (with a sufficient return on invested capital), it can't survive for long. Attention to a company's profit formula in

---

CONCEPTS & CONNECTIONS 4.1

THE VALUE CHAIN FOR KP MACLANE, A PRODUCER OF POLO SHIRTS

Value Chain Activities and Costs in Producing and Selling a Women's Polo Shirt

1. Cotton-blend fabric from France	$ 6.80
2. Fabric for placket and vent	$ 0.99
3. 4 buttons, including 1 extra	$ 0.12
4. Thread	$ 0.09
5. Labels	$ 1.10
6. Hang tag	$ 0.40
7. Waste fabric	$ 0.85
8. Labor	$ 11.05
9. Packing materials	$ 0.17
10. Shipping materials to factory; shirt to store	$ 5.00
11. Hand-embroidered linen bag	$ 3.00
12. Total company costs	$ 29.57
13. Wholesale markup over company costs (company operating profit)	$ 35.43
14. Wholesale price	$ 65.00
15. Retailer's markup	$ 90.00
16. Retail price	$155.00

Source: Christina Binkley, "What Goes into a $155 Price Tag," *The Wall Street Journal,* U.S. Home Edition, On Style, February 2, 2012, http://online.wsj.com/article_email/SB10001424052970204652904577195252388913754-IMyQjAxMTAyMDAwMzEwNDMyWj.html?mod=wsj_share_email.

---

addition to its customer value proposition is the essence of a sound business model, as described in Chapter 1. Concepts & Connections 4.1 shows representative costs for various activities performed by KP MacLane, a maker of upscale polo shirts.

Benchmarking: A Tool for Assessing Whether a Company's Value Chain Activities Are Competitive

Benchmarking entails comparing how different companies perform various value chain activities—how materials are purchased, how inventories are managed, how products are assembled, how customer orders are filled and shipped, and how maintenance is performed—and then making cross-company comparisons of the costs and effectiveness of these activities.[12] The objectives of benchmarking are to identify the best practices in performing an activity and to emulate those best practices when they are possessed by others.

> **CORE CONCEPT**
>
> **Benchmarking** is a potent tool for learning which companies are best at performing particular activities and then using their techniques (or "best practices") to improve the cost and effectiveness of a company's own internal activities.

Xerox led the way in the use of benchmarking to become more cost-competitive by deciding not to restrict its benchmarking efforts to its office equipment rivals, but by comparing itself to *any company* regarded as "world class" in performing activities relevant to Xerox's business. Other companies quickly picked up on Xerox's approach. Toyota managers got their idea for just-in-time inventory deliveries by studying how U.S. supermarkets replenished their shelves. Southwest Airlines reduced the turnaround time of its aircraft at each scheduled stop by studying pit crews on the auto-racing circuit. More than 80 percent of Fortune 500 companies reportedly use benchmarking for comparing themselves against rivals on cost and other competitively important measures.

The tough part of benchmarking is not whether to do it, but rather how to gain access to information about other companies' practices and costs. Sometimes benchmarking can be accomplished by collecting information from published reports, trade groups, and industry research firms and by talking to knowledgeable industry analysts, customers, and suppliers. Sometimes field trips to the facilities of competing or noncompeting companies can be arranged to observe how things are done, compare practices and processes, and perhaps exchange data on productivity and other cost components. However, such companies, even if they agree to host facilities tours and answer questions, are unlikely to share competitively sensitive cost information. Furthermore, comparing two companies' costs may not involve comparing apples to apples if the two companies employ different cost accounting principles to calculate the costs of particular activities.

However, a fairly reliable source of benchmarking information has emerged. The explosive interest of companies in benchmarking costs and identifying best practices has prompted consulting organizations (e.g., Accenture, A. T. Kearney, Benchnet—The Benchmarking Exchange, Towers Watson, and Best Practices, LLC) and several councils and associations (e.g., the APQC, the Qualserve Benchmarking Clearinghouse, and the Strategic Planning Institute's Council on Benchmarking) to gather benchmarking data, distribute information about best practices, and provide comparative cost data without identifying the names of particular companies. Having an independent group gather the information and report it in a manner that disguises the names of individual companies avoids the disclosure of competitively sensitive data and lessens the potential for unethical behavior on the part of company personnel in gathering their own data about competitors.

The Value Chain System for an Entire Industry

A company's value chain is embedded in a larger system of activities that includes the value chains of its suppliers and the value chains of whatever distribution channel allies it utilizes in getting its product or service to end users. The value chains of forward channel partners are relevant because (1) the costs and margins of a company's distributors and retail dealers are part of the price the consumer ultimately pays, and (2) the activities that distribution allies perform affect the company's customer value proposition. For these reasons, companies normally work closely with their suppliers and forward channel allies to per-

> A company's customer value proposition and cost competitiveness depend not only on internally performed activities (its own company value chain), but also on the value chain activities of its suppliers and forward channel allies.

form value chain activities in mutually beneficial ways. For instance, motor vehicle manufacturers work closely with their forward channel allies (local automobile dealers) to ensure that owners are satisfied with dealers' repair and maintenance services.[13] Also, many automotive parts suppliers have built plants near the auto assembly plants they supply to facilitate just-in-time deliveries, reduce warehousing and shipping costs, and promote close collaboration on parts design and production scheduling. Irrigation equipment companies, suppliers of grape-harvesting and winemaking equipment, and firms making barrels, wine bottles, caps, corks, and labels all have facilities in the California wine country to be close to the nearly 700 winemakers they supply.[14] The lesson here is that a company's value chain activities are often closely linked to the value chains of its suppliers and the forward allies.

As a consequence, *accurately assessing the competitiveness of a company's cost structure and customer value proposition requires that company managers understand an industry's entire value chain system for delivering a product or service to customers, not just the company's own value chain.* A typical industry value chain that incorporates the value-creating activities, costs, and margins of suppliers and forward channel allies (if any) is shown in Figure 4.2. However, industry value chains vary significantly by industry. For example, the primary value chain activities in the bottled water industry (spring operation or water purification, processing of basic ingredients used in flavored or vitamin-enhanced water, bottling, wholesale distribution, advertising, and retail merchandising) differ from those for the computer software industry (programming, disk loading, marketing, distribution). Producers of bathroom and kitchen faucets depend heavily on the activities of wholesale distributors and building supply retailers in winning sales to home builders and do-it-yourselfers, but producers of papermaking machines internalize their distribution activities by selling directly to the operators of paper plants.

Strategic Options for Remedying a Cost or Value Disadvantage

The results of value chain analysis and benchmarking may disclose cost or value disadvantages relative to key rivals. These competitive disadvantages are likely to lower a company's relative profit margin or weaken its customer value proposition. In such instances, actions to improve a company's value chain are called for to boost profitability or to allow for the addition of new

---

FIGURE 4.2 **Representative Value Chain for an Entire Industry**

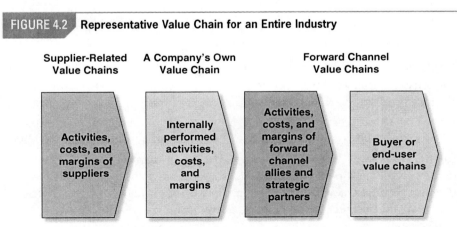

Source: Based in part on the single-industry value chain displayed in Michael E. Porter, *Competitive Advantage* (New York: Free Press, 1985), p. 35.

features that drive customer value. There are three main areas in a company's overall value chain where important differences between firms in costs and value can occur: a company's own internal activities, the suppliers' part of the industry value chain, and the forward channel portion of the industry chain.

Improving Internally Performed Value Chain Activities

Managers can pursue any of several strategic approaches to reduce the costs of internally performed value chain activities and improve a company's cost competitiveness.

1. *Implement the use of best practices* throughout the company, particularly for high-cost activities.

2. *Try to eliminate some cost-producing activities* by revamping the value chain. Many retailers have found that donating returned items to charitable organizations and taking the appropriate tax deduction results in a smaller loss than incurring the costs of the value chain activities involved in reverse logistics.

3. *Relocate high-cost activities* (such as manufacturing) to geographic areas such as China, Latin America, or Eastern Europe where they can be performed more cheaply.

4. *Outsource certain internally performed activities* to vendors or contractors if they can perform them more cheaply than can be done in-house.

5. *Invest in productivity-enhancing, cost-saving technological improvements* (robotics, flexible manufacturing techniques, state-of-the-art electronic networking).

6. *Find ways to detour around the activities or items where costs are high—* computer chip makers regularly design around the patents held by others to avoid paying royalties; automakers have substituted lower-cost plastic for metal at many exterior body locations.

7. *Redesign the product* and/or some of its components to facilitate speedier and more economical manufacture or assembly.

8. *Try to make up the internal cost disadvantage* by reducing costs in the supplier or forward channel portions of the industry value chain—usually a last resort.

Rectifying a weakness in a company's customer value proposition can be accomplished by applying one or more of the following approaches:

1. Implement the use of best practices throughout the company, particularly for activities that are important for creating customer value—product design, product quality, or customer service.

2. Adopt best practices for marketing, brand management, and customer relationship management to improve brand image and customer loyalty.

3. Reallocate resources to activities having a significant impact on value delivered to customers—larger R&D budgets, new state-of-the-art production facilities, new distribution centers, modernized service centers, or enhanced budgets for marketing campaigns.

Additional approaches to managing value chain activities that drive costs, uniqueness, and value are discussed in Chapter 5.

Improving Supplier-Related Value Chain Activities   Supplier-related cost disadvantages can be attacked by pressuring suppliers for lower prices, switching to lower-priced substitute inputs, and collaborating closely with suppliers to identify mutual cost-saving opportunities.[15] For example, just-in-time deliveries from suppliers can lower a company's inventory and internal logistics costs, eliminate capital expenditures for additional warehouse space, and improve cash flow and financial ratios by reducing accounts payable. In a few instances, companies may find that it is cheaper to integrate backward into the business of high-cost suppliers and make the item in-house instead of buying it from outsiders.

Similarly, a company can enhance its customer value proposition through its supplier relationships. Some approaches include selecting and retaining suppliers that meet higher-quality standards, providing quality-based incentives to suppliers, and integrating suppliers into the design process. When fewer defects exist in components provided by suppliers this not only improves product quality and reliability, but it can also lower costs because there is less disruption to production processes and lower warranty expenses.

Improving Value Chain Activities of Forward Channel Allies   There are three main ways to combat a cost disadvantage in the forward portion of the industry value chain: (1) Pressure dealer-distributors and other forward channel allies to reduce their costs and markups; (2) work closely with forward channel allies to identify win-win opportunities to reduce costs—for example, a chocolate manufacturer learned that by shipping its bulk chocolate in liquid form in tank cars instead of 10-pound molded bars, it could not only save its candy bar manufacturing customers the costs associated with unpacking and melting but also eliminate its own costs of molding bars and packing them; and (3) change to a more economical distribution strategy or perhaps integrate forward into company-owned retail outlets. Dell Computer's direct sales model eliminated all activities, costs, and margins of distributors, dealers, and retailers by allowing buyers to purchase customized PCs directly from Dell.

A company can improve its customer value proposition through the activities of forward channel partners by the use of (1) cooperative advertising and promotions with forward channel allies; (2) training programs for dealers, distributors, or retailers to improve the purchasing experience or customer service; and (3) creating and enforcing operating standards for resellers or franchisees to ensure consistent store operations. Harley-Davidson, for example, enhances the shopping experience and perceptions of buyers by selling through dealers that represent Harley-Davidson motorcycles exclusively and operate under strict operating guidelines developed by Harley-Davidson.

How Value Chain Activities Relate to Resources and Capabilities

A close relationship exists between the value-creating activities that a company performs and its resources and capabilities. When companies engage in a value-creating activity, they do so by drawing on specific company resources and capabilities that underlie and enable the activity. For example, brand-building activities that enhance a company's customer value proposition can depend on human resources, such as experienced brand managers, as well as organizational capabilities related to developing and executing effective marketing campaigns. Distribution activities that lower costs may derive from organizational capabilities in inventory management and resources such as cutting-edge inventory tracking systems.

Because of the linkage between activities and enabling resources and capabilities, value chain analysis complements resource and capability analysis as another tool for assessing a company's competitive advantage. Resources and capabilities that are *both valuable and rare* provide a company with the *necessary preconditions* for competitive advantage. When these assets are deployed in the form of a value-creating activity, *that potential is realized.* Resource analysis is a valuable tool for assessing the competitive advantage potential of resources and capabilities. But the actual competitive benefit provided by resources and capabilities can only be assessed objectively after they are deployed in the form of activities.

Question 4: What Is the Company's Competitive Strength Relative to Key Rivals?

LO4 Learn how to evaluate a company's competitive strength relative to key rivals.

An additional component of evaluating a company's situation is developing a comprehensive assessment of the company's overall competitive strength. Making this determination requires answers to two questions:

1. How does the company rank relative to competitors on each of the important factors that determine market success?

2. All things considered, does the company have a net competitive advantage or disadvantage versus major competitors?

Step 1 in doing a competitive strength assessment is to list the industry's key success factors and other telling measures of competitive strength or weakness (6 to 10 measures usually suffice). Step 2 is to assign a weight to each measure of competitive strength based on its perceived importance in shaping competitive success. (The sum of the weights for each measure must add up to 1.0.) Step 3 is to calculate weighted strength ratings by scoring each competitor on each strength measure (using a 1 to 10 rating scale where 1 is very weak and 10 is very strong) and multiplying the assigned rating by the assigned weight. Step 4 is to sum the weighted strength ratings on each factor to get an overall measure of competitive strength for each company being rated. Step 5 is to use the overall strength ratings to draw conclusions about the size and extent of the company's net competitive advantage or disadvantage and to take specific note of areas of strength and weakness. Table 4.3 on page 86 provides an example of a competitive strength assessment, using the hypothetical ABC Company against four rivals. ABC's total score of 5.95 signals a net competitive advantage over Rival 3 (with a score of 2.10) and Rival 4 (with a score of 3.70), but indicates a net competitive disadvantage against Rival 1 (with a score of 7.70) and Rival 2 (with an overall score of 6.85).

Interpreting the Competitive Strength Assessments

Competitive strength assessments provide useful conclusions about a company's competitive situation. The ratings show how a company compares against rivals, factor by factor or capability by capability, thus revealing where it is strongest and weakest. Moreover, the overall competitive strength scores indicate whether the company is at a net competitive advantage or disadvantage against each rival.

> A company's competitive strength scores pinpoint its strengths and weaknesses against rivals and point to offensive and defensive strategies capable of producing first-rate results.

In addition, the strength ratings provide guidelines for designing wise offensive and defensive strategies. For example, consider the ratings and weighted scores in Table 4.3. If ABC Co. wants to go on the offensive to win additional sales and market share, such an offensive probably needs to be aimed directly at winning customers away from Rivals 3 and 4 (which have lower overall strength scores) rather than Rivals 1 and 2 (which have higher overall strength scores). ABC's advantages over Rival 4 tend to be in areas that are moderately important to competitive success in the industry, but ABC outclasses Rival 3 on the two most heavily weighted strength factors—relative cost position and customer service capabilities. Therefore, Rival 3 should be viewed as the primary target of ABC's offensive strategies, with Rival 4 being a secondary target.

A competitively astute company should utilize the strength scores in deciding what strategic moves to make. When a company has important competitive strengths in areas where one or more rivals are weak, it makes sense to consider offensive moves to exploit rivals' competitive weaknesses. When a company has competitive weaknesses in important areas where one or more rivals are strong, it makes sense to consider defensive moves to curtail its vulnerability.

Question 5: What Strategic Issues and Problems Must Be Addressed by Management?

The final and most important analytical step is to zero in on exactly what strategic issues company managers need to address. This step involves drawing on the results of both industry and competitive analysis and the evaluations of the company's internal situation. The task here is to get a clear fix on exactly what industry and competitive challenges confront the company, which of the company's internal weaknesses need fixing, and what specific problems merit front-burner attention by company managers. *Pinpointing the precise things that management needs to worry about sets the agenda for deciding what actions to take next to improve the company's performance and business outlook.*

LO5 Understand how a comprehensive evaluation of a company's external and internal situations can assist managers in making critical decisions about their next strategic moves.

If the items on management's "worry list" are relatively minor, which suggests the company's strategy is mostly on track and reasonably well matched to the company's overall situation, company managers seldom need to go much beyond fine-tuning the present strategy. If, however, the issues and problems confronting the company are serious and indicate the present strategy is not well suited for the road ahead, the task of crafting a better strategy has got to go to the top of management's action agenda.

> Compiling a "worry list" of problems and issues creates an agenda for managerial strategy making.

TABLE 4.3

Illustration of a Competitive Strength Assessment

Key Success Factor/Strength Measure	Importance Weight	ABC CO. Strength Rating	ABC CO. Score	RIVAL 1 Strength Rating	RIVAL 1 Score	RIVAL 2 Strength Rating	RIVAL 2 Score	RIVAL 3 Strength Rating	RIVAL 3 Score	RIVAL 4 Strength Rating	RIVAL 4 Score
Quality/product performance	0.10	8	0.80	5	0.50	10	1.00	1	0.10	6	0.60
Reputation/image	0.10	8	0.80	7	0.70	10	1.00	1	0.10	6	0.60
Manufacturing capability	0.10	2	0.20	10	1.00	4	0.40	5	0.50	1	0.10
Technological skills	0.05	10	0.50	1	0.05	7	0.35	3	0.15	8	0.40
Dealer network/distribution capability	0.05	9	0.45	4	0.20	10	0.50	5	0.25	1	0.05
New-product innovation capability	0.05	9	0.45	4	0.20	10	0.50	5	0.25	1	0.05
Financial resources	0.10	5	0.50	10	1.00	7	0.70	3	0.30	1	0.10
Relative cost position	0.30	5	1.50	10	3.00	3	0.95	1	0.30	4	1.20
Customer service capabilities	0.15	5	0.75	7	1.05	10	1.50	1	0.15	4	0.60
Sum of importance weights	1.00										
Weighted overall strength rating			**5.95**		**7.70**		**6.85**		**2.10**		**3.70**

(Rating scale: 1 = very weak; 10 = very strong)

KEY POINTS

In analyzing a company's own particular competitive circumstances and its competitive position vis-à-vis key rivals, consider five key questions:

1. *How well is the present strategy working?* This involves evaluating the strategy in terms of the company's financial performance and competitive strength and market standing. The stronger a company's current overall performance, the less likely the need for radical strategy changes. The weaker a company's performance and/or the faster the changes in its external situation (which can be gleaned from industry and competitive analysis), the more its current strategy must be questioned.

2. *Do the company's resources and capabilities have sufficient competitive power to give it a sustainable advantage over competitors?* The answer to this question comes from conducting the four tests of a resource's competitive power—the VRIN tests. If a company has resources and capabilities that are competitively *valuable* and *rare*, the firm will have the potential for a competitive advantage over market rivals. If its resources and capabilities are also hard to copy (*inimitable*) with no good substitutes (*nonsubstitutable*), then the firm may be able to sustain this advantage even in the face of active efforts by rivals to overcome it.

   SWOT analysis can be used to assess if a company's resources and capabilities are sufficient to seize market opportunities and overcome external threats to its future well-being. The two most important parts of SWOT analysis are (1) drawing conclusions about what story the compilation of strengths, weaknesses, opportunities, and threats tells about the company's overall situation, and (2) acting on the conclusions to better match the company's strategy to its internal strengths and market opportunities, to correct the important internal weaknesses, and to defend against external threats. A company's strengths and competitive assets are strategically relevant because they are the most logical and appealing building blocks for strategy; internal weaknesses are important because they may represent vulnerabilities that need correction. External opportunities and threats come into play because a good strategy necessarily aims at capturing a company's most attractive opportunities and at defending against threats to its well-being.

3. *Are the company's cost structure and customer value proposition competitive?* One telling sign of whether a company's situation is strong or precarious is whether its costs are competitive with those of industry rivals. Another sign is how it compares with rivals in terms of its customer value proposition. Value chain analysis and benchmarking are essential tools in determining whether the company is performing particular functions and activities well, whether its costs are in line with competitors, whether it is able to offer an attractive value proposition to customers, and whether particular internal activities and business processes need improvement. Value chain analysis complements resource and capability analysis because of the tight linkage between activities and enabling resources and capabilities.

4. *Is the company competitively stronger or weaker than key rivals?* The key appraisals here involve how the company matches up against key rivals on industry key success factors and other chief determinants of competitive success and whether and why the company has a competitive advantage or disadvantage. Quantitative competitive strength assessments, using the method presented in Table 4.3, indicate where a company is competitively strong and weak and provide insight into the company's ability to defend or enhance its market position. As a rule a company's

competitive strategy should be built around its competitive strengths and should aim at shoring up areas where it is competitively vulnerable. When a company has important competitive strengths in areas where one or more rivals are weak, it makes sense to consider offensive moves to exploit rivals' competitive weaknesses. When a company has important competitive weaknesses in areas where one or more rivals are strong, it makes sense to consider defensive moves to curtail its vulnerability.

5. *What strategic issues and problems merit front-burner managerial attention?* This analytical step zeros in on the strategic issues and problems that stand in the way of the company's success. It involves using the results of both industry and competitive analysis and company situation analysis to identify a "worry list" of issues to be resolved for the company to be financially and competitively successful in the years ahead. Actually deciding upon a strategy and what specific actions to take comes after the list of strategic issues and problems that merit front-burner management attention has been developed.

Good company situation analysis, like good industry and competitive analysis, is a valuable precondition for good strategy making.

 ## ASSURANCE OF LEARNING EXERCISES

LO1

1. Using the financial ratios provided in the Appendix and the financial statement information for Macy's, Inc., below, calculate the following ratios for Macy's for both 2011 and 2012.

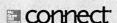

   a. Gross profit margin.
   b. Operating profit margin.
   c. Net profit margin.
   d. Times interest earned coverage.
   e. Return on shareholders' equity.
   f. Return on assets.
   g. Debt-to-equity ratio.
   h. Days of inventory.
   i. Inventory turnover ratio.
   j. Average collection period.

   Based on these ratios, did Macy's financial performance improve, weaken, or remain about the same from 2011 to 2012?

Consolidated Statements of Income for Macy's, Inc., 2011–2012 (in millions, except per share data)

	2012	2011
Net sales	$ 27,686	$ 26,405
Cost of sales	(16,538)	(15,738)
Gross margin	11,148	10,667
Selling, general, and administrative expenses	(8,482)	(8,281)
Impairments, store closing costs and gain on sale of leases	(5)	25
Operating income	2,661	2,411
		(continued)

Consolidated Statements of Income for Macy's, Inc., 2011–2012 (in millions, except per share data)

	2012	2011
Interest expense	(425)	(447)
Premium on early retirement of debt	(137)	—
Interest income	3	4
Income before income taxes	2,102	1,968
Federal, state, and local income tax expense	(767)	(712)
Net income	$ 1,335	$ 1,256
Basic earnings per share	$ 3.29	$ 2.96
Diluted earnings per share	$ 3.24	$ 2.92

Consolidated Balance Sheets for Macy's, Inc., 2011–2012 (in millions, except per share data)

ASSETS	FEBRUARY 2, 2012	JANUARY 28, 2011
Current Assets:		
Cash and cash equivalents	$ 1,836	$ 2,827
Receivables	371	368
Merchandise inventories	5,308	5,117
Prepaid expenses and other current assets	361	465
Total Current Assets	7,876	8,777
Property and Equipment – net	8,196	8,420
Goodwill	3,743	3,743
Other Intangible Assets – net	561	598
Other Assets	615	557
Total Assets	$ 20,991	$ 22,095
LIABILITIES AND SHAREHOLDERS' EQUITY		
Current Liabilities:		
Short-term debt	$ 124	$ 1,103
Merchandise accounts payable	1,579	1,593
Accounts payable and accrued liabilities	2,610	2,788
Income taxes	355	371
Deferred income taxes	407	408
Total Current Liabilities	5,075	6,263
Long-Term Debt	6,806	6,655
Deferred Income Taxes	1,238	1,141
Other Liabilities	1,821	2,103
Shareholders' Equity:		
Common stock (387.7 and 414.2 shares outstanding)	4	5
Additional paid-in capital	3,872	5,408
Accumulated equity	5,108	4,015
Treasury stock	(2,002)	(2,434)
Accumulated other comprehensive loss	(931)	(1,061)
Total Shareholders' Equity	6,051	5,933
Total Liabilities and Shareholders' Equity	$ 20,991	$ 22,095

Source: Macy's, Inc., 2012 10-K.

LO2 2. Panera Bread operates more than 1,600 bakery-cafés in 44 states and Canada. How many of the four tests of the competitive power of a resource does the store network pass? Explain your answer.

LO3 3. Review the information in Concepts & Connections 4.1 concerning the value chain average costs of producing and selling an upscale polo shirt and compare this with the representative value chain depicted in Figure 4.1. Then answer the following questions:

   a. Which of the company's primary value chain activities account for the largest percentage of its operating expenses?

   b. What support activities described in Figure 4.1 would be necessary at KP MacLane?

   c. What value chain activities might be important in securing or maintaining a competitive advantage for a producer of upscale, branded shirts like KP MacLane?

LO4 4. Using the methodology illustrated in Table 4.3 and your knowledge as an automobile owner, prepare a competitive strength assessment for General Motors and its rivals Ford, Chrysler, Toyota, and Honda. Each of the five automobile manufacturers should be evaluated on the key success factors/strength measures of cost competitiveness, product-line breadth, product quality and reliability, financial resources and profitability, and customer service. What does your competitive strength assessment disclose about the overall competitiveness of each automobile manufacturer? What factors account most for Toyota's competitive success? Does Toyota have competitive weaknesses that were disclosed by your analysis? Explain.

▶ EXERCISES FOR SIMULATION PARTICIPANTS

LO1 1. Using the formulas in the Appendix and the data in your company's latest financial statements, calculate the following measures of financial performance for your company:

   a. Operating profit margin

   b. Return on total assets

   c. Current ratio

   d. Working capital

   e. Long-term debt-to-capital ratio

   f. Price-earnings ratio

LO1 2. Based on your company's latest financial statements and all of the other available data regarding your company's performance that appear in the Industry Report, list the three measures of financial performance on which your company did "best" and the three measures on which your company's financial performance was "worst."

LO1 3. What hard evidence can you cite that indicates your company's strategy is working fairly well (or perhaps not working so well, if your company's performance is lagging that of rival companies)?

LO2 4. What internal strengths and weaknesses does your company have? What external market opportunities for growth and increased profitability exist for your company? What external threats to your company's future well-being and profitability do you and your co-managers see? What does the preceding SWOT analysis indicate about your company's present situation and future prospects—where on the scale from "exceptionally strong" to "alarmingly weak" does the attractiveness of your company's situation rank?

5. Does your company have any core competencies? If so, what are they?   LO2

6. What are the key elements of your company's value chain? Refer to Figure 4.1 in developing your answer.   LO3

7. Using the methodology illustrated in Table 4.3, do a weighted competitive strength assessment for your company and two other companies that you and your co-managers consider to be very close competitors.   LO4

 ENDNOTES

1. Birger Wernerfelt, "A Resource-Based View of the Firm," *Strategic Management Journal* 5, no. 5 (September–October 1984); Jay Barney, "Firm Resources and Sustained Competitive Advantage," *Journal of Management* 17, no. 1 (1991); Margaret A. Peteraf, "The Cornerstones of Competitive Advantage: A Resource-Based View," *Strategic Management Journal* 14, no. 3 (March 1993).

2. Birger Wernerfelt, "A Resource-Based View of the Firm," *Strategic Management Journal* 5, no. 5 (September–October 1984), pp. 171–80; Jay Barney, "Firm Resources and Sustained Competitive Advantage," *Journal of Management* 17, no. 1 (1991); and Margaret A. Peteraf, "The Cornerstones of Competitive Advantage: A Resource-Based View," *Strategic Management Journal* 14, no. 3 (March 1993).

3. R. Amit and P. Schoemaker, "Strategic Assets and Organizational Rent," *Strategic Management Journal* 14, no. 1 (1993).

4. David J. Collis and Cynthia A. Montgomery, "Competing on Resources: Strategy in the 1990s," *Harvard Business Review* 73, no. 4 (July–August 1995).

5. George Stalk, Philip Evans, and Lawrence E. Schulman, "Competing on Capabilities: The New Rules of Corporate Strategy," *Harvard Business Review* 70, no. 2 (March–April 1992).

6. David J. Teece, Gary Pisano, and Amy Shuen, "Dynamic Capabilities

and Strategic Management," *Strategic Management Journal* 18, no. 7 (1997); and Constance E. Helfat and Margaret A. Peteraf, "The Dynamic Resource-Based View: Capability Lifecycles," *Strategic Management Journal* 24, no. 10 (2003).

7. C. Montgomery, "Of Diamonds and Rust: A New Look at Resources" in *Resource-Based and Evolutionary Theories of the Firm,* ed. C. Montgomery (Boston: Kluwer Academic Publishers, 1995), pp. 251–68.

8. D. Teece, G. Pisano, and A. Shuen, "Dynamic Capabilities and Strategic Management," *Strategic Management Journal* 18, no. 7 (1997); K. Eisenhardt and J. Martin, "Dynamic Capabilities: What Are They?" *Strategic Management Journal* 21, nos. 10–11 (2000); M. Zollo and S. Winter, "Deliberate Learning and the Evolution of Dynamic Capabilities," *Organization Science* 13 (2002); and C. Helfat et al., *Dynamic Capabilities: Understanding Strategic Change in Organizations* (Malden, MA: Blackwell, 2007).

9. W. Powell, K. Koput, and L. Smith-Doerr, "Interorganizational Collaboration and the Locus of Innovation," *Administrative Science Quarterly* 41, no. 1 (1996).

10. M. Peteraf, "The Cornerstones of Competitive Advantage: A Resource-Based View," *Strategic Management Journal,* March 1993, pp. 179–91.

11. Michael E. Porter, *Competitive Advantage* (New York: Free Press, 1985).

12. Gregory H. Watson, *Strategic Benchmarking: How to Rate Your Company's Performance Against the World's Best* (New York: John Wiley & Sons, 1993); Robert C. Camp, *Benchmarking: The Search for Industry Best Practices That Lead to Superior Performance* (Milwaukee: ASQC Quality Press, 1989); Christopher E. Bogan and Michael J. English, *Benchmarking for Best Practices: Winning through Innovative Adaptation* (New York: McGraw-Hill, 1994); and Dawn Iacobucci and Christie Nordhielm, "Creative Benchmarking," *Harvard Business Review* 78, no. 6 (November–December 2000).

13. M. Hegert and D. Morris, "Accounting Data for Value Chain Analysis," *Strategic Management Journal* 10 (1989); Robin Cooper and Robert S. Kaplan, "Measure Costs Right: Make the Right Decisions," *Harvard Business Review* 66, no. 5 (September–October 1988); and John K. Shank and Vijay Govindarajan, *Strategic Cost Management* (New York: Free Press, 1993).

14. Michael E. Porter, "Clusters and the New Economics of Competition," *Harvard Business Review* 76, no. 6 (November–December 1998).

15. Reuben E. Stone, "Leading a Supply Chain Turnaround," *Harvard Business Review* 82, no. 10 (October 2004).

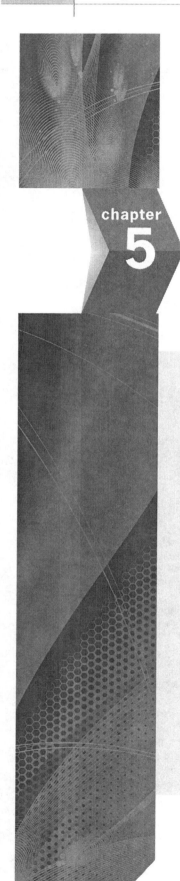

The Five Generic Competitive Strategies

LEARNING OBJECTIVES

LO1 Understand what distinguishes each of the five generic strategies and why some of these strategies work better in certain kinds of industry and competitive conditions than in others.

LO2 Learn the major avenues for achieving a competitive advantage based on lower costs.

LO3 Gain command of the major avenues for developing a competitive advantage based on differentiating a company's product or service offering from the offerings of rivals.

LO4 Recognize the required conditions for delivering superior value to customers through the use of a hybrid of low-cost provider and differentiation strategies.

There are several basic approaches to competing successfully and gaining a competitive advantage, but they all involve giving buyers what they perceive as superior value compared to the offerings of rival sellers. A superior value proposition can be based on offering a good product at a lower price, a superior product that is worth paying more for, or a best-value offering that represents an attractive combination of price, features, quality, service, and other appealing attributes.

This chapter describes the five *generic competitive strategy options* for building competitive advantage and delivering superior value to customers. Which of the five to employ is a company's first and foremost choice in crafting an overall strategy and beginning its quest for competitive advantage.

The Five Generic Competitive Strategies

A company's **competitive strategy** *deals exclusively with the specifics of management's game plan for competing successfully*—its specific efforts to please customers, strengthen its market position, counter the maneuvers of rivals, respond to shifting market conditions, and achieve a particular competitive advantage. The chances are remote that any two companies—even companies in the same industry—will employ competitive strategies that are exactly alike. However, when one strips away the details to get at the real substance, the two biggest factors that distinguish one competitive strategy from another boil down to (1) whether a company's market target is broad or narrow, and (2) whether the company is pursuing a competitive advantage linked to lower costs or differentiation. These two factors give rise to the five competitive strategy options shown in Figure 5.1 and listed below.[1]

LO1 Understand what distinguishes each of the five generic strategies and why some of these strategies work better in certain kinds of industry and competitive conditions than in others.

1. *A low-cost provider strategy*—striving to achieve lower overall costs than rivals and appealing to a broad spectrum of customers, usually by underpricing rivals.

2. *A broad differentiation strategy*—seeking to differentiate the company's product or service from rivals' in ways that will appeal to a broad spectrum of buyers.

> **CORE CONCEPT**
>
> A **competitive strategy** concerns the specifics of management's game plan for competing successfully and securing a competitive advantage over rivals in the marketplace.

3. *A focused low-cost strategy*—concentrating on a narrow buyer segment (or market niche) and outcompeting rivals by having lower costs than rivals and thus being able to serve niche members at a lower price.

4. *A focused differentiation strategy*—concentrating on a narrow buyer segment (or market niche) and outcompeting rivals by offering niche members customized attributes that meet their tastes and requirements better than rivals' products.

5. *A best-cost provider strategy*—giving customers more value for the money by satisfying buyers' expectations on key quality/features/performance/service attributes while beating their price expectations. This option is a *hybrid* strategy that blends elements of low-cost provider and differentiation strategies; the aim is to have the lowest (best) costs and prices among sellers offering products with comparable differentiating attributes.

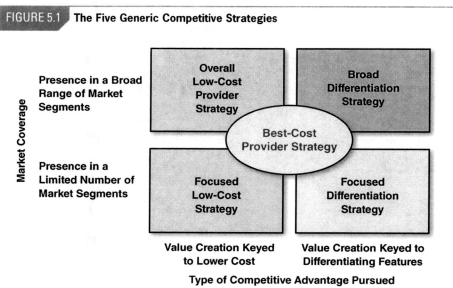

FIGURE 5.1   **The Five Generic Competitive Strategies**

Source: This is an author-expanded version of a three-strategy classification discussed in Michael E. Porter, *Competitive Strategy* (New York: Free Press, 1980), pp. 35–40.

The remainder of this chapter explores the ins and outs of the five generic competitive strategies and how they differ.

Low-Cost Provider Strategies

Striving to be the industry's overall low-cost provider is a powerful competitive approach in markets with many price-sensitive buyers. A company achieves low-cost leadership when it becomes the industry's lowest-cost provider rather than just being one of perhaps several competitors with low costs. Successful low-cost providers boast meaningfully lower costs than rivals, but not necessarily the absolutely lowest possible cost. In striving for a cost advantage over rivals, managers must include features and services that buyers consider essential. A product offering that is too frills-free can be viewed by consumers as offering little value, regardless of its pricing.

> **CORE CONCEPT**
>
> A **low-cost leader**'s basis for competitive advantage is lower overall costs than competitors. Success in achieving a low-cost edge over rivals comes from eliminating and/or curbing "nonessential" activities and/or outmanaging rivals in performing essential activities.

A company has two options for translating a low-cost advantage over rivals into attractive profit performance. Option 1 is to use the lower-cost edge to underprice competitors and attract price-sensitive buyers in great enough numbers to increase total profits. Option 2 is to maintain the present price, be content with the present market share, and use the lower-cost edge to earn a higher profit margin on each unit sold, thereby raising the firm's total profits and overall return on investment.

The Two Major Avenues for Achieving Low-Cost Leadership

To achieve a low-cost edge over rivals, a firm's cumulative costs across its overall value chain must be lower than competitors' cumulative costs. There are two major avenues for accomplishing this:[2]

1. Performing essential value chain activities more cost-effectively than rivals.

2. Revamping the firm's overall value chain to eliminate or bypass some cost-producing activities.

Cost-Efficient Management of Value Chain Activities   For a company to do a more cost-efficient job of managing its value chain than rivals, managers must launch a concerted, ongoing effort to ferret out cost-saving opportunities in every part of the value chain. No activity can escape cost-saving scrutiny, and all company personnel must be expected to use their talents and ingenuity to come up with innovative and effective ways to keep costs down. Particular attention needs to be paid to **cost drivers**, which are factors that have an especially strong effect on the costs of a company's value chain activities. The number of products in a company's product line, its capacity utilization, the type of components used in the assembly of its products, and the extent of its employee benefits package are all factors affecting the company's overall cost position. Figure 5.2 shows the most important cost drivers. Cost-saving approaches that demonstrate effective management of the cost drivers in a company's value chain include:

> **CORE CONCEPT**
>
> A **cost driver** is a factor having a strong effect on the cost of a company's value chain activities and cost structure.

- *Striving to capture all available economies of scale.* Economies of scale stem from an ability to lower unit costs by increasing the scale of operation. For example, occasions may arise when a large plant is more economical to operate than a small or medium-sized plant or when a large distribution center is more cost efficient than a small one.

- *Taking full advantage of experience and learning curve effects.* The cost of performing an activity can decline over time as the learning and experience of company personnel build.

- *Trying to operate facilities at full capacity.* Whether a company is able to operate at or near full capacity has a big impact on unit costs when its value chain contains activities associated with substantial fixed costs. Higher rates of capacity utilization allow depreciation and other fixed costs to be spread over a larger unit volume, thereby lowering fixed costs per unit.

- *Substituting lower-cost inputs whenever there's little or no sacrifice in product quality or product performance.* If the costs of certain raw materials and parts are "too high," a company can switch to using lower-cost alternatives when they exist.

LO2 Learn the major avenues for achieving a competitive advantage based on lower costs.

FIGURE 5.2 Important Cost Drivers in a Company's Value Chain

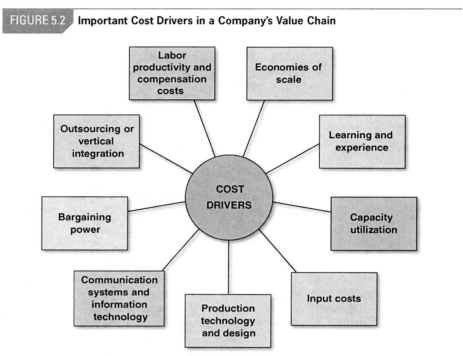

Sources: Adapted by the authors from M. Porter, *The Competitive Advantage: Creating and Sustaining Superior Performance* (New York: Free Press, 1985).

- *Employing advanced production technology and process design to improve overall efficiency.* Often production costs can be cut by utilizing design for manufacture (DFM) procedures and computer-assisted design (CAD) techniques that enable more integrated and efficient production methods, investing in highly automated robotic production technology, and shifting to production processes that enable manufacturing multiple versions of a product as cost efficiently as mass producing a single version. A number of companies are ardent users of total quality management systems, business process reengineering, Six Sigma methodology, and other business process management techniques that aim at boosting efficiency and reducing costs.

- *Using communication systems and information technology to achieve operating efficiencies.* For example, sharing data and production schedules with suppliers, coupled with the use of enterprise resource planning (ERP) and manufacturing execution system (MES) software, can reduce parts inventories, trim production times, and lower labor requirements.

- *Using the company's bargaining power vis-à-vis suppliers to gain concessions.* A company may have sufficient bargaining clout with suppliers to win price discounts on large-volume purchases or realize other cost as on p. 97 savings.

- *Being alert to the cost advantages of outsourcing and vertical integration.* Outsourcing the performance of certain value chain activities can be more economical than performing them in-house if outside specialists, by virtue of their expertise and volume, can perform the activities at lower cost.

- *Pursuing ways to boost labor productivity and lower overall compensation costs.* A company can economize on labor costs by using incentive compensation systems that promote high productivity, installing labor-saving equipment, shifting production from geographic areas where pay scales are high to geographic areas where pay scales are low, and avoiding the use of union labor where possible (because costly work rules can stifle productivity and because of union demands for above-market pay scales and costly fringe benefits).

Revamping the Value Chain   Dramatic cost advantages can often emerge from reengineering the company's value chain in ways that eliminate costly work steps and bypass certain cost-producing value chain activities. Such value chain revamping can include:

- *Selling directly to consumers and cutting out the activities and costs of distributors and dealers.* To circumvent the need for distributors–dealers, a company can (1) create its own direct sales force (which adds the costs of maintaining and supporting a sales force but may be cheaper than utilizing independent distributors and dealers to access buyers), and/or (2) conduct sales operations at the company's website (costs for website operations and shipping may be a substantially cheaper way to make sales to customers than going through distributor–dealer channels). Costs in the wholesale/retail portions of the value chain frequently represent 35 to 50 percent of the price final consumers pay, so establishing a direct sales force or selling online may offer big cost savings.

- *Streamlining operations by eliminating low-value-added or unnecessary work steps and activities.* Southwest Airlines has achieved considerable cost savings by reconfiguring the traditional value chain of commercial airlines to eliminate low-value-added activities and work steps. Southwest does not offer assigned seating, baggage transfer to connecting airlines, or first-class seating and service, thereby eliminating all the cost-producing activities associated with these features. Also, the company's carefully designed point-to-point route system minimizes connections, delays, and total trip time for passengers, allowing about 75 percent of Southwest passengers to fly nonstop to their destinations and at the same time helping reduce Southwest's costs for flight operations.

- *Improving supply chain efficiency to reduce materials handling and shipping costs.* Collaborating with suppliers to streamline the ordering and purchasing process, to reduce inventory carrying costs via just-in-time inventory practices, to economize on shipping and materials handling, and to ferret out other cost-saving opportunities is a much-used approach to cost reduction. A company with a distinctive competence in cost-efficient supply chain management, such as BASF (the world's leading chemical company), can sometimes achieve a sizable cost advantage over less adept rivals.

Concepts & Connections 5.1 describes Walmart's broad approach to managing its value chain in the retail grocery portion of its business to achieve a dramatic cost advantage over rival supermarket chains and become the world's biggest grocery retailer.

CONCEPTS & CONNECTIONS 5.1

HOW WALMART MANAGED ITS VALUE CHAIN TO ACHIEVE A LOW-COST ADVANTAGE OVER RIVAL SUPERMARKET CHAINS

Walmart has achieved a very substantial cost and pricing advantage over rival supermarket chains by both revamping portions of the grocery retailing value chain and outmanaging its rivals in efficiently performing various value chain activities. Its cost advantage stems from a series of initiatives and practices:

- Instituting extensive information sharing with vendors via online systems that relay sales at its checkout counters directly to suppliers of the items, thereby providing suppliers with real-time information on customer demand and preferences (creating an estimated 6 percent cost advantage).

- Pursuing global procurement of some items and centralizing most purchasing activities so as to leverage the company's buying power (creating an estimated 2.5 percent cost advantage).

- Investing in state-of-the-art automation at its distribution centers, efficiently operating a truck fleet that makes daily deliveries to Walmart's stores, and putting assorted other cost-saving practices into place at its headquarters, distribution centers, and stores (resulting in an estimated 4 percent cost advantage).

- Striving to optimize the product mix and achieve greater sales turnover (resulting in about a 2 percent cost advantage).

- Installing security systems and store operating procedures that lower shrinkage rates (producing a cost advantage of about 0.5 percent).

- Negotiating preferred real estate rental and leasing rates with real estate developers and owners of its store sites (yielding a cost advantage of 2 percent).

- Managing and compensating its workforce in a manner that produces lower labor costs (yielding an estimated 5 percent cost advantage).

Altogether, these value chain initiatives give Walmart an approximately 22 percent cost advantage over Kroger, Safeway, and other leading supermarket chains. With such a sizable cost advantage, Walmart has been able to underprice its rivals and become the world's leading supermarket retailer.

Sources: www.walmart.com; and Marco Iansiti and Roy Levien, "Strategy as Ecology," *Harvard Business Review* 82, no. 3 (March 2004), p. 70.

When a Low-Cost Provider Strategy Works Best

A competitive strategy predicated on low-cost leadership is particularly powerful when:

1. *Price competition among rival sellers is especially vigorous.* Low-cost providers are in the best position to compete offensively on the basis of price and to survive price wars.

2. *The products of rival sellers are essentially identical and are readily available from several sellers.* Commodity-like products and/or ample supplies set the stage for lively price competition; in such markets, it is the less efficient, higher-cost companies that are most vulnerable.

3. *There are few ways to achieve product differentiation that have value to buyers.* When the product or service differences between brands do not matter much to buyers, buyers nearly always shop the market for the best price.

4. *Buyers incur low costs in switching their purchases from one seller to another.* Low switching costs give buyers the flexibility to shift purchases to lower-priced sellers having equally good products. A low-cost leader is

well positioned to use low price to induce its customers not to switch to rival brands.

5. *The majority of industry sales are made to a few, large-volume buyers.* Low-cost providers are in the best position among sellers in bargaining with high-volume buyers because they are able to beat rivals' pricing to land a high-volume sale while maintaining an acceptable profit margin.

6. *Industry newcomers use introductory low prices to attract buyers and build a customer base.* The low-cost leader can use price cuts of its own to make it harder for a new rival to win customers.

As a rule, the more price-sensitive buyers are, the more appealing a low-cost strategy becomes. A low-cost company's ability to set the industry's price floor and still earn a profit erects protective barriers around its market position.

Pitfalls to Avoid in Pursuing a Low-Cost Provider Strategy

Perhaps the biggest pitfall of a low-cost provider strategy is getting carried away with *overly aggressive price cutting* and ending up with lower, rather than higher, profitability. A low-cost/low-price advantage results in superior profitability only if (1) prices are cut by less than the size of the cost advantage or (2) the added volume is large enough to bring in a bigger total profit despite lower margins per unit sold. Thus, a company with a 5 percent cost advantage cannot cut prices 20 percent, end up with a volume gain of only 10 percent, and still expect to earn higher profits!

A second big pitfall is *relying on an approach to reduce costs that can be easily copied by rivals.* The value of a cost advantage depends on its sustainability. Sustainability, in turn, hinges on whether the company achieves its cost advantage in ways difficult for rivals to replicate or match. If rivals find it relatively easy or inexpensive to imitate the leader's low-cost methods, then the leader's advantage will be too short-lived to yield a valuable edge in the marketplace.

A third pitfall is becoming *too fixated on cost reduction.* Low costs cannot be pursued so zealously that a firm's offering ends up being too features-poor to gain the interest of buyers. Furthermore, a company driving hard to push its costs down has to guard against misreading or ignoring increased buyer preferences for added features or declining buyer price sensitivity. Even if these mistakes are avoided, a low-cost competitive approach still carries risk. Cost-saving technological breakthroughs or process improvements by rival firms can nullify a low-cost leader's hard-won position.

Broad Differentiation Strategies

Differentiation strategies are attractive whenever buyers' needs and preferences are too diverse to be fully satisfied by a standardized product or service. A company attempting to succeed through differentiation must study buyers' needs and behavior carefully to learn what buyers think has value and what they are willing to

> **CORE CONCEPT**
> The essence of a **broad differentiation strategy** is to offer unique product or service attributes that a wide range of buyers find appealing and worth paying for.

pay for. Then the company must include these desirable features to clearly set itself apart from rivals lacking such product or service attributes.

Successful differentiation allows a firm to:

- Command a premium price, and/or
- Increase unit sales (because additional buyers are won over by the differentiating features), and/or
- Gain buyer loyalty to its brand (because some buyers are strongly attracted to the differentiating features and bond with the company and its products).

Differentiation enhances profitability whenever the extra price the product commands outweighs the added costs of achieving the differentiation. Company differentiation strategies fail when buyers don't value the brand's uniqueness and/or when a company's approach to differentiation is easily copied or matched by its rivals.

Approaches to Differentiation

LO3 Gain command of the major avenues for developing a competitive advantage based on differentiating a company's product or service offering from the offerings of rivals.

Companies can pursue differentiation from many angles: a unique taste (Red Bull, Listerine), multiple features (Microsoft Office, Apple iPad), wide selection and one-stop shopping (Home Depot, Amazon.com), superior service (Ritz-Carlton, Nordstrom), spare parts availability (Caterpillar guarantees 48-hour spare parts delivery to any customer anywhere in the world or else the part is furnished free), engineering design and performance (Mercedes-Benz, BMW), luxury and prestige (Rolex, Gucci, Chanel), product reliability (Whirlpool and Bosch in large home appliances), quality manufacturing (Michelin in tires, Toyota and Honda in automobiles), technological leadership (3M Corporation in bonding and coating products), a full range of services (Charles Schwab in stock brokerage), and a complete line of products (Campbell soups, Frito-Lay snack foods).

The most appealing approaches to differentiation are those that are hard or expensive for rivals to duplicate. Resourceful competitors can, in time, clone almost any product or feature or attribute. If Coca-Cola introduces a vitamin-enhanced bottled water, so can Pepsi; if Firestone offers customers attractive financing terms, so can Goodyear. As a rule, differentiation yields a longer-lasting and more profitable competitive edge when it is based on product innovation, technical superiority, product quality and reliability, comprehensive customer service, and unique competitive capabilities. Such differentiating attributes tend to be tough for rivals to copy or offset profitably, and buyers widely perceive them as having value.

> Easy-to-copy differentiating features cannot produce sustainable competitive advantage; differentiation based on hard-to-copy competencies and capabilities tends to be more sustainable.

Managing the Value Chain in Ways That Enhance Differentiation

Success in employing a differentiation strategy results from management's ability to offer superior customer value through the addition of product/service attributes and features that differentiate a company's offering from the offerings of rivals. Differentiation opportunities can exist in activities all along an industry's value chain and particularly in activities and factors that meaningfully impact customer value. Such activities are referred to as **uniqueness drivers**—analogous to cost drivers—but have a high impact on differentiation rather than a company's overall cost position. Figure 5.3 lists important uniqueness drivers found in a company's value chain. Ways that managers can enhance differentiation through the systematic management of uniqueness drivers include the following:

- *Seeking out high-quality inputs.* Input quality can ultimately spill over to affect the performance or quality of the company's end product. Starbucks, for example, gets high ratings on its coffees partly because it has very strict specifications on the coffee beans purchased from suppliers.

> **CORE CONCEPT**
> A **uniqueness driver** is a value chain activity or factor that can have a strong effect on customer value and creating differentiation.

- *Striving for innovation and technological advances.* Successful innovation is the route to more frequent first-on-the-market victories and is a powerful differentiator. If the innovation proves hard to replicate, through patent protection or other means, it can provide a company with a first-mover advantage that is sustainable.

- *Creating superior product features, design, and performance.* The physical and functional features of a product have a big influence on differentiation. Styling and appearance are big differentiating factors in the apparel and

FIGURE 5.3   **Important Uniqueness Drivers in a Company's Value Chain**

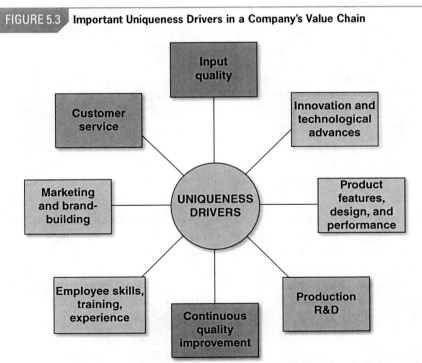

Source: Adapted from M. Porter, *The Competitive Advantage: Creating and Sustaining Superior Performance* (New York: Free Press, 1985).

motor vehicle industries. Size and weight matter in binoculars and smart-phones. Most companies employing broad differentiation strategies make a point of incorporating innovative and novel features in their product/service offering, especially those that improve performance.

- *Investing in production-related R&D activities.* Engaging in production R&D may permit custom-order manufacture at an efficient cost, provide wider product variety and selection, or improve product quality. Many manufacturers have developed flexible manufacturing systems that allow different models and product versions to be made on the same assembly line. Being able to provide buyers with made-to-order products can be a potent differentiating capability.

- *Pursuing continuous quality improvement.* Quality control processes reduce product defects, prevent premature product failure, extend product life, make it economical to offer longer warranty coverage, improve economy of use, result in more end-user convenience, enhance product appearance, or improve customer service.

- *Emphasizing human resource management activities that improve the skills, expertise, and knowledge of company personnel.* A company with high-caliber intellectual capital often has the capacity to generate the kinds of ideas that drive product innovation, technological advances, better product design and product performance, improved production techniques, and higher product quality.

- *Increasing emphasis on marketing and brand-building activities.* The manner in which a company conducts its marketing and brand management activities has a significant influence on customer perceptions of the value of a company's product offering and the price customers will pay for it. A highly skilled and competent sales force, effectively communicated product information, eye-catching ads, in-store displays, and special promotional campaigns can all cast a favorable light on the differentiating attributes of a company's product/service offering and contribute to greater brand-name awareness and brand-name power.

- *Improving customer service or adding additional services.* Better customer service, in areas such as delivery, returns, and repair, can be as important in creating differentiation as superior product features.

Revamping the Value Chain System to Increase Differentiation Just as pursuing a cost advantage can involve the entire value chain system, the same is true for a differentiation advantage. As was discussed in Chapter 4, activities performed upstream by suppliers or downstream by distributors and retailers can have a meaningful effect on customers' perceptions of a company's offerings and its value proposition. Approaches to enhancing differentiation through changes in the value chain system include:

- *Coordinating with channel allies to enhance customer value.* Coordinating with downstream partners such as distributors, dealers, brokers, and retailers can contribute to differentiation in a variety of ways. Many manufacturers work directly with retailers on in-store displays and signage, joint advertising campaigns, and providing sales clerks with product knowledge and tips on sales techniques—all to enhance customer buying experiences. Companies can work with distributors and shippers to ensure fewer "out-of-stock" annoyances, quicker delivery to customers, more-accurate order filling, lower shipping costs, and a variety of shipping choices to customers.

- *Coordinating with suppliers to better address customer needs.* Collaborating with suppliers can also be a powerful route to a more effective differentiation strategy. This is particularly true for companies that engage only in assembly operations, such as Dell in PCs and Ducati in motorcycles. Close coordination with suppliers can also enhance differentiation by speeding up new-product development cycles or speeding delivery to end customers. Strong relationships with suppliers can also mean that the company's supply requirements are prioritized when industry supply is insufficient to meet overall demand.

Delivering Superior Value via a Differentiation Strategy

While it is easy enough to grasp that a successful differentiation strategy must offer value in ways unmatched by rivals, a big issue in crafting a differentiation strategy is deciding what is valuable to customers. Typically, value can be delivered to customers in three basic ways.

1. *Include product attributes and user features that lower the buyer's costs.* Commercial buyers value products that can reduce their cost of doing business. For example, making a company's product more economical for a buyer to use can be done by reducing the buyer's raw materials waste (providing cut-to-size components), reducing a buyer's inventory requirements (providing just-in-time deliveries), increasing product reliability to lower a buyer's repair and maintenance costs, and providing free technical support. Similarly, consumers find value in differentiating features that will reduce their expenses. Rising costs for gasoline prices have spurred the efforts of motor vehicle manufacturers worldwide to introduce models with better fuel economy.

2. *Incorporate tangible features that improve product performance.* Commercial buyers and consumers alike value higher levels of performance in many types of products. Product reliability, output, durability, convenience, and ease of use are aspects of product performance that differentiate products offered to buyers. Mobile phone manufacturers are currently in a race to improve the performance of their products through the introduction of next-generation phones with added functionality and greater ease of use.

3. *Incorporate intangible features that enhance buyer satisfaction in noneconomic ways.* Toyota's Prius appeals to environmentally conscious motorists who wish to help reduce global carbon dioxide emissions. Bentley, Ralph Lauren, Louis Vuitton, Tiffany, Cartier, and Rolex have differentiation-based competitive advantages linked to buyer desires for status, image, prestige, upscale fashion, superior craftsmanship, and the finer things in life.

> Differentiation can be based on *tangible* or *intangible* features and attributes.

Perceived Value and the Importance of Signaling Value

The price premium commanded by a differentiation strategy reflects *the value actually delivered* to the buyer and *the value perceived* by the buyer. The value of certain differentiating features is rather easy for buyers to detect, but in some instances buyers may have trouble assessing what their experience with the product will be. Successful differentiators go to great lengths to make buyers knowledgeable about a product's value and incorporate signals of value such as attractive packaging; extensive ad campaigns; the quality of brochures and sales presentations; the seller's list of customers; the length of time the firm has been in business; and the professionalism, appearance, and personality of the seller's employees. Such signals of value may be as important as actual value (1) when the nature of differentiation is subjective or hard to quantify, (2) when buyers are making a first-time purchase, (3) when repurchase is infrequent, and (4) when buyers are unsophisticated.

When a Differentiation Strategy Works Best

Differentiation strategies tend to work best in market circumstances where:

1. *Buyer needs and uses of the product are diverse.* Diverse buyer preferences allow industry rivals to set themselves apart with product attributes that appeal to particular buyers. For instance, the diversity of consumer preferences for menu selection, ambience, pricing, and customer service gives restaurants exceptionally wide latitude in creating differentiated concepts. Other industries offering opportunities for differentiation based upon diverse buyer needs and uses include magazine publishing, automobile manufacturing, footwear, kitchen appliances, and computers.

2. *There are many ways to differentiate the product or service that have value to buyers.* Industries that allow competitors to add features to product attributes are well suited to differentiation strategies. For example, hotel chains can differentiate on such features as location, size of room, range of guest services, in-hotel dining, and the quality and luxuriousness of bedding and furnishings. Similarly, cosmetics producers are able to differentiate based upon prestige and image, formulations that fight the signs of aging, UV light protection, exclusivity of retail locations, the inclusion of antioxidants and natural ingredients, or prohibitions against animal testing.

3. *Few rival firms are following a similar differentiation approach.* The best differentiation approaches involve trying to appeal to buyers on the basis of attributes that rivals are not emphasizing. A differentiator encounters less head-to-head rivalry when it goes its own separate way to create uniqueness and does not try to outdifferentiate rivals on the very same attributes. When many rivals are all claiming "ours tastes better than theirs" or "ours gets your clothes cleaner than theirs," competitors tend to end up chasing the same buyers with very similar product offerings.

4. *Technological change is fast-paced and competition revolves around rapidly evolving product features.* Rapid product innovation and frequent introductions of next-version products heighten buyer interest and provide space for companies to pursue distinct differentiating paths. In video game

hardware and video games, golf equipment, PCs, mobile phones, and automobile navigation systems, competitors are locked into an ongoing battle to set themselves apart by introducing the best next-generation products; companies that fail to come up with new and improved products and distinctive performance features quickly lose out in the marketplace.

Pitfalls to Avoid in Pursuing a Differentiation Strategy

Differentiation strategies can fail for any of several reasons. *A differentiation strategy keyed to product or service attributes that are easily and quickly copied is always suspect.* Rapid imitation means that no rival achieves meaningful differentiation, because whatever new feature one firm introduces that strikes the fancy of buyers is almost immediately added by rivals. This is why a firm must search out sources of uniqueness that are time-consuming or burdensome for rivals to match if it hopes to use differentiation to win a sustainable competitive edge over rivals.

Differentiation strategies can also falter when buyers see little value in the unique attributes of a company's product. Thus, even if a company sets the attributes of its brand apart from its rivals' brands, its strategy can fail because of trying to differentiate on the basis of something that does not deliver adequate value to buyers. Any time many potential buyers look at a company's differentiated product offering and conclude "so what," the company's differentiation strategy is in deep trouble; buyers will likely decide the product is not worth the extra price and sales will be disappointingly low.

Overspending on efforts to differentiate is a strategy flaw that can erode profitability. Company efforts to achieve differentiation nearly always raise costs. The trick to profitable differentiation is either to keep the costs of achieving differentiation below the price premium the differentiating attributes can command in the marketplace or to offset thinner profit margins by selling enough additional units to increase total profits. If a company goes overboard in pursuing costly differentiation, it could be saddled with unacceptably thin profit margins or even losses. The need to contain differentiation costs is why many companies add little touches of differentiation that add to buyer satisfaction but are inexpensive to institute.

Other common pitfalls and mistakes in crafting a differentiation strategy include:

- *Overdifferentiating so that product quality or service levels exceed buyers' needs.* Buyers are unlikely to pay extra for features and attributes that will go unused. For example, consumers are unlikely to purchase programmable large appliances such as washers, dryers, and ovens if they are satisfied with manually controlled appliances.

- *Trying to charge too high a price premium.* Even if buyers view certain extras or deluxe features as "nice to have," they may still conclude that the added benefit or luxury is not worth the price differential over that of lesser differentiated products.

- *Being timid and not striving to open up meaningful gaps in quality or service or performance features vis-à-vis the products of rivals.* Tiny differences between rivals' product offerings may not be visible or important to buyers.

A low-cost provider strategy can always defeat a differentiation strategy when buyers are satisfied with a basic product and don't think "extra" attributes are worth a higher price.

Focused (or Market Niche) Strategies

What sets focused strategies apart from low-cost leadership or broad differentiation strategies is a concentration on a narrow piece of the total market. The targeted segment, or niche, can be defined by geographic uniqueness or by special product attributes that appeal only to niche members. The advantages of focusing a company's entire competitive effort on a single market niche are considerable, especially for smaller and medium-sized companies that may lack the breadth and depth of resources to tackle going after a national customer base with a "something for everyone" lineup of models, styles, and product selection. Community Coffee, the largest family-owned specialty coffee retailer in the United States, has a geographic focus on the state of Louisiana and communities across the Gulf of Mexico. Community holds only a 1.1 percent share of the national coffee market, but has recorded sales in excess of $100 million and has won a 50 percent share of the coffee business in the 11-state region where its coffee is distributed. Examples of firms that concentrate on a well-defined market niche keyed to a particular product or buyer segment include Discovery Channel and Comedy Central (in cable TV), Google (in Internet search engines), Porsche (in sports cars), and CGA, Inc. (a specialist in providing insurance to cover the cost of lucrative hole-in-one prizes at golf tournaments). Microbreweries, local bakeries, bed-and-breakfast inns, and local owner-managed retail boutiques are all good examples of enterprises that have scaled their operations to serve narrow or local customer segments.

A Focused Low-Cost Strategy

A focused strategy based on low cost aims at securing a competitive advantage by serving buyers in the target market niche at a lower cost and a lower price than rival competitors. This strategy has considerable attraction when a firm can lower costs significantly by limiting its customer base to a well-defined buyer segment. The avenues to achieving a cost advantage over rivals also serving the target market niche are the same as for low-cost leadership—outmanage rivals in keeping the costs to a bare minimum and searching for innovative ways to bypass or reduce nonessential activities. The only real difference between a low-cost provider strategy and a focused low-cost strategy is the size of the buyer group to which a company is appealing.

Focused low-cost strategies are fairly common. Producers of private-label goods are able to achieve low costs in product development, marketing, distribution, and advertising by concentrating on making generic items similar to name-brand merchandise and selling directly to retail chains wanting a low-priced store brand. The Perrigo Company has become a leading manufacturer of over-the-counter health care products with 2012 sales of more than

CONCEPTS & CONNECTIONS 5.2

ARAVIND EYE CARE SYSTEM'S FOCUSED LOW-COST STRATEGY

Cataracts, the largest cause of preventable blindness, can be treated with a quick surgical procedure that restores sight; however, poverty and limited access to care prevent millions worldwide from obtaining surgery. The Aravind Eye Care System has found a way to address this problem, with a focused low-cost strategy that has made cataract surgery not only affordable for more people in India, but also free for the very poorest. On the basis of this strategy, Aravind has achieved world renown and become the largest provider of eye care in the world.

High volume and high efficiency are at the cornerstone of Aravind's strategy. The Aravind network of five eye hospitals in India has become one of the most productive systems in the world, conducting about 300,000 surgeries a year in addition to seeing more than 2.6 million outpatients each year. Using the unique model of screenings at camps all over the country, Aravind reaches a broad cross-section of the market for surgical treatment. Additionally, Aravind attains very high staff productivity with each surgeon performing more than 2,500 surgeries annually, compared to 125 for a comparable American surgeon.

This level of productivity (with no loss in quality of care) was achieved through the development of a standardized system of surgical treatment, capitalizing on the fact that cataract removal is a fairly routine process. Aravind streamlined as much of the process as possible, reducing discretionary elements to a minimum, and tracking outcomes to ensure continuous process improvement. At Aravind's hospitals, no time is wasted between surgeries as different teams of support staff prepare patients for surgery and bring them to the operating theater; surgeons simply turn from one table to another to perform surgery on the next prepared patient. Aravind also drove costs down through the creation of its own manufacturing division, Aurolab, to produce intraocular lenses, suture needles, pharmaceuticals, and surgical blades in India.

Aravind's low costs allow it to keep prices for cataract surgery very low—about $10 per patient, compared to an average cost of $1,500 for surgery in the United States. Nevertheless, the system provides surgical outcomes and quality comparable to clinics in the United States. As a result of its unique fee system and effective management, Aravind is also able to provide free eye care to 60 percent of its patients from the revenue generated from paying patients.

Sources: Developed with Avni V. Patel. G. Natchiar, A. L. Robin, R. Thulasiraj, et al., "Attacking the Backlog of India's Curable Blind; The Aravind Eye Hospital Model," *Archives of Ophthalmology* 112, no. 7 (July 1994), pp. 987–93; D. F. Chang, "Tackling the Greatest Challenge in Cataract Surgery," *British Journal of Ophthalmology* 89, no. 9 (September 2005), pp. 1073–77; and McKinsey & Co., "Driving Down the Cost of High-Quality Care," *Health International*, December 2011.

$3.2 billion by focusing on producing private-label brands for retailers such as Walmart, CVS, Walgreens, Rite Aid, and Safeway. Even though Perrigo doesn't make branded products, a focused low-cost strategy is appropriate for the makers of branded products as well. Concepts & Connections 5.2 describes how Aravind's focus on lowering the costs of cataract removal allowed the company to address the needs of the "bottom of the pyramid" in India's population where blindness due to cataracts is an endemic problem.

A Focused Differentiation Strategy

Focused differentiation strategies are keyed to offering carefully designed products or services to appeal to the unique preferences and needs of a narrow, well-defined group of buyers (as opposed to a broad differentiation strategy aimed at many buyer groups and market segments). Companies such as Four Seasons Hotels and Resorts, Chanel, Gucci, and Louis Vuitton employ successful differentiation-based focused strategies targeted at affluent buyers wanting products and services with world-class attributes. Indeed, most markets contain a buyer segment willing to pay a price premium for the very finest items available, thus opening the strategic window for some competitors to pursue differentiation-based focused strategies aimed at the very top of the market pyramid.

Another successful focused differentiator is "fashion food retailer" Trader Joe's, a 369-store, 33-state chain that is a combination gourmet deli and food warehouse. Customers shop Trader Joe's as much for entertainment as for conventional grocery items; the store stocks out-of-the-ordinary culinary treats such as raspberry salsa, salmon burgers, and jasmine fried rice, as well as the standard goods normally found in supermarkets. What sets Trader Joe's apart is not just its unique combination of food novelties and competitively priced grocery items but also its capability to turn an otherwise mundane grocery excursion into a whimsical treasure hunt that is just plain fun. Concepts & Connections 5.3 describes the focused differentiation strategy of Popchips in the snack food industry.

When a Focused Low-Cost or Focused Differentiation Strategy Is Viable

A focused strategy aimed at securing a competitive edge based on either low cost or differentiation becomes increasingly attractive as more of the following conditions are met:

- The target market niche is big enough to be profitable and offers good growth potential.
- Industry leaders have chosen not to compete in the niche—focusers can avoid battling head-to-head against the industry's biggest and strongest competitors.
- It is costly or difficult for multisegment competitors to meet the specialized needs of niche buyers and at the same time satisfy the expectations of mainstream customers.
- The industry has many different niches and segments, thereby allowing a focuser to pick a niche suited to its resource strengths and capabilities.
- Few, if any, rivals are attempting to specialize in the same target segment.

The Risks of a Focused Low-Cost or Focused Differentiation Strategy

Focusing carries several risks. The *first major risk* is the chance that competitors will find effective ways to match the focused firm's capabilities in serving the target niche. In the lodging business, large chains such as Marriott and Hilton have launched multibrand strategies that allow them to compete effectively in several lodging segments simultaneously. Marriott has flagship hotels with a full complement of services and amenities that allow it to attract travelers and vacationers going to major resorts; it has J.W. Marriott and Ritz-Carlton hotels that provide deluxe comfort and service to business and leisure travelers; it

CONCEPTS & CONNECTIONS 5.3

POPCHIPS'S FOCUSED DIFFERENTIATION STRATEGY

Potato chips are big business: Americans spend $7 billion annually on their consumption. But the industry is a hard one to break into; it's a mature, slow-growth industry dominated by a few large competitors. Frito-Lay, maker of Lays and Ruffles, has a commanding 60 percent market share. These characteristics are enough to dissuade most potential entrants, but not Popchips, a small potato chip start-up. Despite difficult odds, Popchips has made impressive inroads into the industry with the help of a *focused differentiation strategy.* Popchips was founded in 2007 by Keith Belling, a serial entrepreneur, and Pat Turpin, a former Costco snack executive. Their idea was simple: Take advantage of high-income purchasers' growing desire for tasty, low-fat snacks. Using an innovative cooking method, they found a way to halve the fat content in potato chips while preserving the flavor.

Popchips has a differentiated product. But its real point of differentiation is in its brand and distribution strategy. Most potato chips have mass distribution and a broad buyer base. Belling and Turpin decided from the outset to narrow their distribution and their targeted buyers. They hoped that focusing on a market niche would allow their product to stand out from the bags of Lays and cans of Pringles in aisles all over America. Popchips's target: upper-income, health-conscious urban and suburban consumers.

To that end, the firm signed distribution deals with Whole Foods, Target, and, reflecting Turpin's roots, Costco. Popchips

marketing emphasizes social marketing and word-of-mouth recommendations. The company sends samples to key taste-makers who tweet, blog, or recommend the product in traditional media. Ashton Kutcher, MTV's former *Punk'd* host, was so impressed with the chips that he volunteered to promote them. Like *Punk'd,* Popchips advertising is irreverent, with taglines like "love. without the handles."

Popchips's differentiation strategy is succeeding. Between 2009 and 2011, the company's sales accounted for nearly all potato chip sales growth at natural supermarket stores, such as Whole Foods. Popchips now has nearly 15 percent market share in this niche distribution channel. The company's 2010 sales were $45.7 million, more than double the 2009 figure. That's particularly impressive given that the industry growth rate has been a paltry 4 percent. In 2011, Forbes put Popchips on its list of America's most promising companies.

Developed with Dennis L. Huggins.

Sources: Molly *Maier,* "Chips, Pretzels and Corn Snacks - US - January 2012," Mintel, January 2012, www.oxygen.mintel.com (accessed February 1, 2012); Lindsay Blakely and Caitlin Elsaesser, "One Snacker at a Time: How Popchips Grew without Losing Its Character," *CBS News,* January 2011, www.cbsnews.com (accessed February 1, 2012; Laura Petrecca, "Popchips CEO Keith Belling Is 'Poptimist' on Healthy Snacks," *USA Today,* March 2010, www.usatoday.com (accessed February 13, 2012); http://www.forbes.com/sites/brettnelson/2011/11/30/americas-most-promising-companies-the-top-20/, accessed February 28, 2012; Popchips website.

---

has Courtyard by Marriott and SpringHill Suites brands for business travelers looking for moderately priced lodging; it has Marriott Residence Inns and TownePlace Suites designed as a "home away from home" for travelers staying five or more nights; and it has more than 670 Fairfield Inn locations that cater to travelers looking for quality lodging at an "affordable" price. Multibrand strategies are attractive to large companies such as Marriott precisely because they enable a company to enter a market niche and siphon business away from companies that employ a focus strategy.

A *second risk* of employing a focus strategy is the potential for the preferences and needs of niche members to shift over time toward the product attributes desired by the majority of buyers. An erosion of the differences across buyer segments lowers entry barriers into a focuser's market niche and provides an open invitation for rivals in adjacent segments to begin competing for the focuser's customers. A *third risk* is that the segment may become so attractive it is soon inundated with competitors, intensifying rivalry and splintering segment profits.

Best-Cost Provider Strategies

LO4 Recognize the required conditions for delivering superior value to customers through the use of a hybrid of low-cost provider and differentiation strategies.

As Figure 5.1 indicates, **best-cost provider strategies** are a *hybrid* of low-cost provider and differentiation strategies that aim at satisfying buyer expectations on key quality/features/performance/service attributes and beating customer expectations on price. Companies pursuing best-cost strategies aim squarely at the sometimes great mass of value-conscious buyers looking for a good-to-very-good product or service at an economical price. The essence of a best-cost provider strategy is giving customers *more value for the money* by satisfying buyer desires for appealing features/performance/quality/service and charging a lower price for these attributes compared to rivals with similar-caliber product offerings.[3]

To profitably employ a best-cost provider strategy, a company *must have the capability to incorporate attractive or upscale attributes at a lower cost than rivals.* This capability is contingent on (1) a superior value chain configuration that eliminates or minimizes activities that do not add value, (2) unmatched efficiency in managing essential value chain activities, and (3) core competencies that allow differentiating attributes to be incorporated at a low cost. When a company can incorporate appealing features, good-to-excellent product performance or quality, or more satisfying customer service into its product offering *at a lower cost than rivals,* then it enjoys "best-cost" status—it is the low-cost provider of a product or service with *upscale attributes.* A best-cost provider can use its low-cost advantage to underprice rivals whose products or services have similar upscale attributes and still earn attractive profits.

> **CORE CONCEPT**
>
> **Best-cost provider strategies** are a *hybrid* of low-cost provider and differentiation strategies that aim at satisfying buyer expectations on key quality/features/performance/service attributes and beating customer expectations on price.

Concepts & Connections 5.4 describes how Toyota has applied the principles of a best-cost provider strategy in producing and marketing its Lexus brand.

When a Best-Cost Provider Strategy Works Best

A best-cost provider strategy works best in markets where product differentiation is the norm and attractively large numbers of value-conscious buyers can be induced to purchase midrange products rather than the basic products of low-cost producers or the expensive products of top-of-the-line differentiators. A best-cost provider usually needs to position itself near the middle of the market with either a medium-quality product at a below-average price or a high-quality product at an average or slightly higher-than-average price. Best-cost provider strategies also work well in recessionary times when great masses of buyers become value-conscious and are attracted to economically priced products and services with especially appealing attributes.

The Danger of an Unsound Best-Cost Provider Strategy

A company's biggest vulnerability in employing a best-cost provider strategy is not having the requisite core competencies and efficiencies in managing value chain activities to support the addition of differentiating features without significantly increasing costs. A company with a modest degree of

CONCEPTS & CONNECTIONS 5.4

TOYOTA'S BEST-COST PRODUCER STRATEGY FOR ITS LEXUS LINE

Toyota Motor Company is widely regarded as a low-cost producer among the world's motor vehicle manufacturers. Despite its emphasis on product quality, Toyota has achieved low-cost leadership because it has developed considerable skills in efficient supply chain management and low-cost assembly capabilities, and because its models are positioned in the low-to-medium end of the price spectrum, where high production volumes are conducive to low unit costs. But when Toyota decided to introduce its new Lexus models to compete in the luxury-car market, it employed a classic best-cost provider strategy. Toyota took the following four steps in crafting and implementing its Lexus strategy:

- Designing an array of high-performance characteristics and upscale features into the Lexus models so as to make them comparable in performance and luxury to other high-end models and attractive to Mercedes-Benz, BMW, Audi, Jaguar, Cadillac, and Lincoln buyers.

- Transferring its capabilities in making high-quality Toyota models at low cost to making premium-quality Lexus models at costs below other luxury-car makers. Toyota's supply chain capabilities and low-cost assembly know-how allowed it to incorporate high-tech performance features

and upscale quality into Lexus models at substantially less cost than comparable Mercedes and BMW models.

- Using its relatively lower manufacturing costs to underprice comparable Mercedes and BMW models. Toyota believed that with its cost advantage it could price attractively equipped Lexus cars low enough to draw price-conscious buyers away from Mercedes and BMW. Toyota's pricing policy also allowed it to induce Toyota, Honda, Ford, or GM owners desiring more luxury to switch to a Lexus. Lexus's pricing advantage over Mercedes and BMW was sometimes quite significant. For example, in 2013 the Lexus RX 350, a midsize SUV, carried a sticker price in the $39,000–$54,000 range (depending on how it was equipped), whereas variously equipped Mercedes ML 350 SUVs had price tags in the $47,000–$96,000 range, and a BMW X5 SUV could range anywhere from $47,000 to $89,000, depending on the optional equipment chosen.

- Establishing a new network of Lexus dealers, separate from Toyota dealers, dedicated to providing a level of personalized, attentive customer service unmatched in the industry.

differentiation and no real cost advantage will most likely find itself squeezed between the firms using low-cost strategies and those using differentiation strategies. Low-cost providers may be able to siphon customers away with the appeal of a lower price (despite having marginally less appealing product attributes). High-end differentiators may be able to steal customers away with the appeal of appreciably better product attributes (even though their products carry a somewhat higher price tag). Thus, a successful best-cost provider must offer buyers *significantly* better product attributes to justify a price above what low-cost leaders are charging. Likewise, it has to achieve significantly lower costs in providing upscale features so that it can outcompete high-end differentiators on the basis of a *significantly* lower price.

Successful Competitive Strategies Are Resource Based

For a company's competitive strategy to succeed in delivering good performance and the intended competitive edge over rivals, it has to be well matched to a company's internal situation and underpinned by an appropriate set of

> A company's competitive strategy should be well matched to its internal situation and predicated on leveraging its collection of competitively valuable resources and competencies.

resources, know-how, and competitive capabilities. To succeed in employing a low-cost provider strategy, a company has to have the resources and capabilities to keep its costs below those of its competitors; this means having the expertise to cost-effectively manage value chain activities better than rivals and/or the innovative capability to bypass certain value chain activities being performed by rivals. To succeed in strongly differentiating its product in ways that are appealing to buyers, a company must have the resources and capabilities (such as better technology, strong skills in product innovation, expertise in customer service) to incorporate unique attributes into its product offering that a broad range of buyers will find appealing and worth paying for. Strategies focusing on a narrow segment of the market require the capability to do an outstanding job of satisfying the needs and expectations of niche buyers. Success in employing a strategy keyed to a best-value offering requires the resources and capabilities to incorporate upscale product or service attributes at a lower cost than rivals.

 KEY POINTS

1. Early in the process of crafting a strategy, company managers have to decide which of the five basic competitive strategies to employ—overall low-cost, broad differentiation, focused low-cost, focused differentiation, or best-cost provider.

2. In employing a low-cost provider strategy, a company must do a better job than rivals of cost-effectively managing internal activities and/or it must find innovative ways to eliminate or bypass cost-producing activities. Particular attention should be paid to cost drivers, which are factors having a strong effect on the cost of a company's value chain activities and cost structure. Low-cost provider strategies work particularly well when price competition is strong and the products of rival sellers are very weakly differentiated. Other conditions favoring a low-cost provider strategy are when supplies are readily available from eager sellers, when there are not many ways to differentiate that have value to buyers, when the majority of industry sales are made to a few large buyers, when buyer switching costs are low, and when industry newcomers are likely to use a low introductory price to build market share.

3. Broad differentiation strategies seek to produce a competitive edge by incorporating attributes and features that set a company's product/service offering apart from rivals in ways that buyers consider valuable and worth paying for. Such features and attributes are best integrated through the systematic management of uniqueness—value chain activities or factors that can have a strong effect on customer value and creating differentiation. Successful differentiation allows a firm to (1) command a premium price for its product, (2) increase unit sales (because additional buyers are won over by the differentiating features), and/or (3) gain buyer loyalty to its brand (because some buyers are strongly attracted to the differentiating features and bond with the company and its products).

Differentiation strategies work best in markets with diverse buyer preferences where there are big windows of opportunity to strongly differentiate a company's product offering from those of rival brands, in situations where few other rivals are pursuing a similar differentiation approach, and in circumstances where technological change is fast-paced and competition centers on rapidly evolving product features. A differentiation strategy is doomed when competitors are able to quickly copy most or all of the appealing product attributes a company comes up with, when a company's differentiation efforts meet with a ho-hum or so-what market reception, or when a company erodes profitability by overspending on efforts to differentiate its product offering.

4. A focus strategy delivers competitive advantage either by achieving lower costs than rivals in serving buyers comprising the target market niche or by offering niche buyers an appealingly differentiated product or service that meets their needs better than rival brands. A focused strategy becomes increasingly attractive when the target market niche is big enough to be profitable and offers good growth potential, when it is costly or difficult for multisegment competitors to put capabilities in place to meet the specialized needs of the target market niche and at the same time satisfy the expectations of their mainstream customers, when there are one or more niches that present a good match with a focuser's resource strengths and capabilities, and when few other rivals are attempting to specialize in the same target segment.

5. Best-cost provider strategies stake out a middle ground between pursuing a low-cost advantage and a differentiation-based advantage and between appealing to the broad market as a whole and a narrow market niche. The aim is to create competitive advantage by giving buyers more value for the money—satisfying buyer expectations on key quality/features/performance/service attributes while beating customer expectations on price. To profitably employ a best-cost provider strategy, a company *must have the capability to incorporate attractive or upscale attributes at a lower cost than rivals*. This capability is contingent on (1) a superior value chain configuration, (2) unmatched efficiency in managing essential value chain activities, and (3) resource strengths and core competencies that allow differentiating attributes to be incorporated at a low cost. A best-cost provider strategy works best in markets where opportunities to differentiate exist and where many buyers are sensitive to price and value.

6. Deciding which generic strategy to employ is perhaps the most important strategic commitment a company makes—it tends to drive the rest of the strategic actions a company decides to undertake and it sets the whole tone for the pursuit of a competitive advantage over rivals.

ASSURANCE OF LEARNING EXERCISES

1. Best Buy is the largest consumer electronics retailer in the United States with 2012 sales of almost $50 billion. The company competes aggressively on price with rivals such as Costco Wholesale, Sam's Club, Walmart, and Target, but is also known by consumers for its first-rate customer service. Best Buy customers have commented that the retailer's sales staff is exceptionally knowledgeable about products and can direct them to the exact location of difficult-to-find items. Best Buy customers also appreciate that demonstration models of PC monitors, digital

LO1, LO2,
LO3, LO4

media players, and other electronics are fully powered and ready for in-store use. Best Buy's Geek Squad tech support and installation services are additional customer service features valued by many customers.

How would you characterize Best Buy's competitive strategy? Should it be classified as a low-cost provider strategy? a differentiation strategy? a best-cost strategy? Explain your answer.

LO2

connect

2. Concepts & Connections 5.1 discusses Walmart's low-cost advantage in the supermarket industry. Based on information provided in the illustration, explain how Walmart has built its low-cost advantage in the supermarket industry and why a low-cost provider strategy is well suited to the industry.

LO1, LO2, LO3, LO4

3. Stihl is the world's leading manufacturer and marketer of chain saws with annual sales exceeding $2 billion. With innovations dating to its 1929 invention of the gasoline-powered chain saw, the company holds more than 1,000 patents related to chain saws and outdoor power tools. The company's chain saws, leaf blowers, and hedge trimmers sell at price points well above competing brands and are sold only by its network of some 8,000 independent dealers.

How would you characterize Stihl's competitive strategy? Should it be classified as a low-cost provider strategy? a differentiation strategy? a best-cost strategy? Also, has the company chosen to focus on a narrow piece of the market or does it appear to pursue a broad market approach? Explain your answer.

LO3

connect

4. Explore BMW's website at www.bmwgroup.com and see if you can identify at least three ways in which the company seeks to differentiate itself from rival automakers. Is there reason to believe that BMW's differentiation strategy has been successful in producing a competitive advantage? Why or why not?

EXERCISES FOR SIMULATION PARTICIPANTS

LO1, LO2, LO3, LO4

1. Which one of the five generic competitive strategies best characterizes your company's strategic approach to competing successfully?

2. Which rival companies appear to be employing a low-cost provider strategy?

3. Which rival companies appear to be employing a broad differentiation strategy?

4. Which rival companies appear to be employing a best-cost provider strategy?

5. Which rival companies appear to be employing some type of focus strategy?

6. What is your company's action plan to achieve a sustainable competitive advantage over rival companies? List at least three (preferably more than three) specific kinds of decision entries on specific decision screens that your company has made or intends to make to win this kind of competitive edge over rivals.

ENDNOTES

1. Michael E. Porter, *Competitive Strategy: Techniques for Analyzing Industries and Competitors* (New York: Free Press, 1980), chap. 2; and Michael E. Porter, "What Is Strategy?"

Harvard Business Review 74, no. 6 (November–December 1996).

2. Michael E. Porter, *Competitive Advantage* (New York: Free Press, 1985).

3. Peter J. Williamson and Ming Zeng, "Value-for-Money Strategies for Recessionary Times," *Harvard Business Review* 87, no. 3 (March 2009).

chapter

7

Strategies for Competing in International Markets

LEARNING OBJECTIVES

LO1 Develop an understanding of the primary reasons companies choose to compete in international markets.

LO2 Learn why and how differing market conditions across countries influence a company's strategy choices in international markets.

LO3 Gain familiarity with the five general modes of entry into foreign markets.

LO4 Learn the three main options for tailoring a company's international strategy to cross-country differences in market conditions and buyer preferences.

LO5 Understand how multinational companies are able to use international operations to improve overall competitiveness.

LO6 Gain an understanding of the unique characteristics of competing in developing-country markets.

Any company that aspires to industry leadership in the twenty-first century must think in terms of global, not domestic, market leadership. The world economy is globalizing at an accelerating pace as countries previously closed to foreign companies open their markets, as countries with previously planned economies embrace market or mixed economies, as information technology shrinks the importance of geographic distance, and as ambitious, growth-minded companies race to build stronger competitive positions in the markets of more and more countries. The forces of globalization are changing the competitive landscape in many industries, offering companies attractive new opportunities but at the same time introducing new competitive threats. Companies in industries where these forces are greatest are under considerable pressure to develop strategies for competing successfully in international markets.

This chapter focuses on strategy options for expanding beyond domestic boundaries and competing in the markets of either a few or many countries. We will discuss the factors that shape the choice of strategy in international markets and the specific market circumstances that support the adoption of multidomestic, transnational, and global strategies. The chapter also includes sections on strategy options for entering foreign markets; how international operations may be used to improve overall competitiveness; and the special circumstances of competing in such emerging markets as China, India, Brazil, Russia, and Eastern Europe.

Why Companies Expand into International Markets

LO1 Develop an understanding of the primary reasons companies choose to compete in international markets.

A company may opt to expand outside its domestic market for any of five major reasons:

1. *To gain access to new customers.* Expanding into foreign markets offers potential for increased revenues, profits, and long-term growth and becomes an especially attractive option when a company's home markets are mature. Honda has done this with its classic 50-cc motorcycle, the Honda Cub, which is still selling well in developing markets, more than 50 years after it was introduced in Japan.

2. *To achieve lower costs and enhance the firm's competitiveness.* Many companies are driven to sell in more than one country because domestic sales volume alone is not large enough to fully capture manufacturing economies of scale or learning curve effects. The relatively small size of country markets in Europe explains why companies such as Michelin, BMW, and Nestlé long ago began selling their products all across Europe and then moved into markets in North America and Latin America.

3. *To further exploit its core competencies.* A company may be able to leverage its competencies and capabilities into a position of competitive advantage in foreign markets as well as domestic markets. Walmart is capitalizing on its considerable expertise in discount retailing to expand into the United Kingdom, Japan, China, and Latin America. Walmart executives are particularly excited about the company's growth opportunities in China.

4. *To gain access to resources and capabilities located in foreign markets.* An increasingly important motive for entering foreign markets is to acquire resources and capabilities that cannot be accessed as readily in a company's home market. Companies often enter into cross-border alliances, make acquisitions abroad, or establish operations in foreign countries to access local resources such as distribution networks, low-cost labor, natural resources, or specialized technical knowledge.[1]

5. *To spread its business risk across a wider market base.* A company spreads business risk by operating in a number of foreign countries rather than depending entirely on operations in its domestic market. Thus, if the economies of North American countries turn down for a period of time, a company with operations across much of the world may be sustained by buoyant sales in Latin America, Asia, or Europe.

Factors That Shape Strategy Choices in International Markets

Four important factors shape a company's strategic approach to competing in foreign markets: (1) the degree to which there are important cross-country differences in demographic, cultural, and market conditions; (2) whether opportunities exist to gain a location-based advantage based on wage rates, worker productivity, inflation rates, energy costs, tax rates, and other factors that impact cost structure; (3) the risks of adverse shifts in currency exchange rates; and (4) the extent to which governmental policies affect the local business climate.

LO2 Learn why and how differing market conditions across countries influence a company's strategy choices in international markets.

Cross-Country Differences in Demographic, Cultural, and Market Conditions

Buyer tastes for a particular product or service sometimes differ substantially from country to country. For example, Italian coffee drinkers prefer espressos, but in North America the preference is for milder-roasted coffees. In parts of Asia, refrigerators are a status symbol and may be placed in the living room, leading to preferences for stylish designs and colors; bright blue and red are popular colors in India. People in Hong Kong and Japan prefer compact appliances, but in Taiwan large appliances are more popular. Consequently, companies operating in a global marketplace must wrestle with *whether and how much to customize their offerings in each different country market to match the tastes and preferences of local buyers or whether to pursue a strategy of offering a mostly standardized product worldwide.* While making products that are closely matched to local tastes makes them more appealing to local buyers, customizing a company's products country by country may raise production and distribution costs. Greater standardization of a global company's product offering, on the other hand, can lead to scale economies and learning curve effects, thus contributing to the achievement of a low-cost advantage. *The tension between the market pressures to localize a company's product offerings country by country and the competitive pressures to lower costs is one of the big strategic issues that participants in foreign markets have to resolve.*

Understandably, differing population sizes, income levels, and other demographic factors give rise to considerable differences in market size and growth rates from country to country. In emerging markets such as India, China, Brazil, and Malaysia, market growth potential is far higher for such products as PCs, mobile phones, steel, credit cards, and electric energy than in the more mature economies of Britain, Canada, and Japan. The potential for market growth in automobiles is explosive in China, where 2010 sales of new vehicles amounted to 18 million, surpassing U.S. sales of 11.6 million and making China the world's largest market for the second year in a row.[2] Owing to widely differing population demographics and income levels, there is a far bigger market for luxury automobiles in the United States and Germany than in Argentina, India, Mexico, and Thailand. Cultural influences can also affect consumer demand for a product. For instance, in China, many parents are reluctant to purchase PCs even when they can afford them because of concerns that their children will be distracted from their schoolwork by surfing the web, playing PC-based video games, and downloading and listening to pop music.

Market growth can be limited by the lack of infrastructure or established distribution and retail networks in emerging markets. India has well-developed national channels for distribution of goods to the nation's 3 million retailers, whereas in China distribution is primarily local. Also, the competitive rivalry in some country marketplaces is only moderate, while others are characterized by strong or fierce competition. The managerial challenge at companies with international or global operations is how best to tailor a company's strategy to take all these cross-country differences into account.

Opportunities for Location-Based Cost Advantages

Differences from country to country in wage rates, worker productivity, energy costs, environmental regulations, tax rates, inflation rates, and the like are often so big that *a company's operating costs and profitability are significantly impacted by where its production, distribution, and customer service activities are located.* Wage rates, in particular, vary enormously from country to country. For example, in 2011, hourly compensation for manufacturing workers averaged about $1.36 in China, $2.01 in the Philippines, $6.48 in Mexico, $9.17 in Hungary, $9.34 in Taiwan, $11.65 in Brazil, $12.91 in Portugal, $18.91 in South Korea, $35.53 in the United States, $35.71 in Japan, $36.56 in Canada, $47.38 in Germany, and $64.15 in Norway.[3] Not surprisingly, China has emerged as the manufacturing capital of the world—virtually all of the world's major manufacturing companies now have facilities in China. A manufacturer can also gain cost advantages by locating its manufacturing and assembly plants in countries with less costly government regulations, low taxes, low energy costs, and cheaper access to essential natural resources.

The Risks of Adverse Exchange Rate Shifts

When companies produce and market their products and services in many different countries, they are subject to the impacts of sometimes favorable and sometimes unfavorable changes in currency exchange rates. The rates of exchange between different currencies can vary by as much as 20 to

40 percent annually, with the changes occurring sometimes gradually and sometimes swiftly. Sizable shifts in exchange rates, which tend to be hard to predict because of the variety of factors involved and the uncertainties surrounding when and by how much these factors will change, *shuffle the global cards of which countries represent the low-cost manufacturing location* and *which rivals have the upper hand in the marketplace.*

To illustrate the competitive risks associated with fluctuating exchange rates, consider the case of a U.S. company that has located manufacturing facilities in Brazil (where the currency is reals—pronounced *ray-alls*) and that exports most of its Brazilian-made goods to markets in the European Union (where the currency is euros). To keep the numbers simple, assume the exchange rate is 4 Brazilian reals for 1 euro and that the product being made in Brazil has a manufacturing cost of 4 Brazilian reals (or 1 euro). Now suppose that for some reason the exchange rate shifts from 4 reals per euro to 5 reals per euro (meaning the real has declined in value and the euro is stronger). Making the product in Brazil is now more cost-competitive because a Brazilian good costing 4 reals to produce has fallen to only 0.8 euro at the new exchange rate (4 reals divided by 5 reals per euro = 0.8 euro). On the other hand, should the value of the Brazilian real grow stronger in relation to the euro—resulting in an exchange rate of 3 reals to 1 euro—the same Brazilian-made good formerly costing 4 reals to produce now has a cost of 1.33 euros (4 reals divided by 3 reals per euro = 1.33). This increase in the value of the real has eroded the cost advantage of the Brazilian manufacturing facility for goods shipped to Europe and affects the ability of the U.S. company to underprice European producers of similar goods. Thus, *the lesson of fluctuating exchange rates is that companies that export goods to foreign countries always gain in competitiveness when the currency of the country in which the goods are manufactured is weak. Exporters are disadvantaged when the currency of the country where goods are being manufactured grows stronger.*

The Impact of Government Policies on the Business Climate in Host Countries

National governments enact all kinds of measures affecting business conditions and the operation of foreign companies in their markets. It matters whether these measures create a favorable or unfavorable business climate. Governments of countries eager to spur economic growth, create more jobs, and raise living standards for their citizens usually make a special effort to create a business climate that outsiders will view favorably. They may provide such incentives as reduced taxes, low-cost loans, and site-development assistance to companies agreeing to construct or expand production and distribution facilities in the host country.

On the other hand, governments sometimes enact policies that, from a business perspective, make locating facilities within a country's borders less attractive. For example, the nature of a company's operations may make it particularly costly to achieve compliance with environmental regulations in certain countries. Some governments, wishing to discourage foreign imports, may enact deliberately burdensome customs procedures and requirements or impose tariffs or quotas on imported goods. Host-country governments may also specify that products contain a certain percentage of locally produced parts and components, require prior approval of capital spending projects, limit withdrawal of funds from the country, and require local ownership stakes in foreign-company operations in the host country. Such governmental actions make a country's business climate unattractive, and in some cases may be sufficiently onerous as to discourage a company from locating facilities in that country or sell its products there.

A country's business climate is also a function of the political and economic risks associated with operating within its borders. **Political risks** have to do with the instability of weak governments or the potential for future elections to produce government leaders hostile to foreign-owned businesses. **Economic risks** have to do with the threat of piracy and lack of protection for the company's intellectual property and the stability of a country's economy—whether inflation rates might skyrocket or whether uncontrolled deficit spending on the part of government could lead to a breakdown of the country's monetary system and prolonged economic distress.

> **CORE CONCEPT**
>
> **Political risks** stem from instability or weakness in national governments and hostility to foreign business; **economic risks** stem from the stability of a country's monetary system, economic and regulatory policies, and the lack of property rights protections.

Strategy Options for Entering Foreign Markets

LO3 Gain familiarity with the five general modes of entry into foreign markets.

A company choosing to expand outside its domestic market may elect one of the following five general modes of entry into a foreign market:

1. *Maintain a national (one-country) production base and export goods to foreign markets.*

2. *License foreign firms to produce and distribute the company's products abroad.*

3. *Employ a franchising strategy.*

4. *Establish a subsidiary in a foreign market via acquisition or internal development.*

5. *Rely on strategic alliances or joint ventures with foreign partners to enter new country markets.*

The following sections discuss the five general options in more detail.

Export Strategies

Using domestic plants as a production base for exporting goods to foreign markets is an excellent initial strategy for pursuing international sales. It is a conservative way to test the international waters. The amount of capital needed to begin exporting is often quite minimal, and existing production capacity may be sufficient to make goods for export. With an export-based entry strategy, a manufacturer can limit its involvement in foreign markets by contracting with foreign wholesalers experienced in importing to handle the entire distribution and marketing function in their countries or regions of the world. If it is more advantageous to maintain control over these functions, however, a manufacturer can establish its own distribution and sales organizations in some or all of the target foreign markets. Either way, a home-based production and export strategy helps the firm minimize its direct investments in foreign countries.

An export strategy is vulnerable when (1) manufacturing costs in the home country are substantially higher than in foreign countries where rivals have plants, (2) the costs of shipping the product to distant foreign markets are relatively high, or (3) adverse shifts occur in currency exchange rates. Unless an exporter can both keep its production and shipping costs competitive with rivals and successfully hedge against unfavorable changes in currency exchange rates, its success will be limited.

Licensing Strategies

Licensing as an entry strategy makes sense when a firm with valuable technical know-how or a unique patented product has neither the internal organizational capability nor the resources to enter foreign markets. Licensing also has the advantage of avoiding the risks of committing resources to country markets that are unfamiliar, politically volatile, economically unstable, or otherwise risky. By licensing the technology or the production rights to foreign-based firms, the firm does not have to bear the costs and risks of entering foreign markets on its own, yet it is able to generate income from royalties. The big disadvantage of licensing is the risk of providing valuable technological know-how to foreign companies and thereby losing some degree of control over its use. Also, monitoring licensees and safeguarding the company's proprietary know-how can prove quite difficult in some circumstances. But if the royalty potential is considerable and the companies to whom the licenses are being granted are both trustworthy and reputable, then licensing can be a very attractive option. Many software and pharmaceutical companies use licensing strategies.

Franchising Strategies

While licensing works well for manufacturers and owners of proprietary technology, franchising is often better suited to the global expansion efforts of service and retailing enterprises. McDonald's, Yum! Brands (the parent of A&W, Pizza Hut, KFC, Long John Silver's, and Taco Bell), the UPS Store, 7-Eleven, and Hilton Hotels have all used franchising to build a presence in international markets. Franchising has much the same advantages as licensing. The franchisee bears most of the costs and risks of establishing foreign locations, so a franchisor has to expend only the resources to recruit, train, support, and monitor franchisees. The big problem a franchisor faces is maintaining quality control. In many cases, foreign franchisees do not always exhibit strong commitment to consistency and standardization, especially when the local culture does not stress the same kinds of quality concerns. Another problem that can arise is whether to allow foreign franchisees to modify the franchisor's product offering to better satisfy the tastes and expectations of local buyers. Should McDonald's allow its franchised units in Japan to modify Big Macs slightly to suit Japanese tastes? Should the franchised KFC units in China be permitted to substitute spices that appeal to Chinese consumers? Or should the same menu offerings be rigorously and unvaryingly required of all franchisees worldwide?

Foreign Subsidiary Strategies

While exporting, licensing, and franchising rely upon the resources and capabilities of allies in international markets to deliver goods or services to buyers, companies pursuing international expansion may elect to take responsibility for the performance of all essential value chain activities in foreign markets. Companies that prefer direct control over all aspects of operating in a foreign market can establish a wholly owned subsidiary, either by acquiring a foreign company or by establishing operations from the ground up via internal development.

Acquisition is the quicker of the two options, and it may be the least risky and cost-efficient means of hurdling such entry barriers as gaining access to local distribution channels, building supplier relationships, and establishing working relationships with key government officials and other constituencies. Buying an ongoing operation allows the acquirer to move directly to the task of transferring resources and personnel to the newly acquired business, integrating and redirecting the activities of the acquired business into its own operation, putting its own strategy into place, and accelerating efforts to build a strong market position.[4]

The big issue an acquisition-minded firm must consider is whether to pay a premium price for a successful local company or to buy a struggling competitor at a bargain price. If the buying firm has little knowledge of the local market but ample capital, it is often better off purchasing a capable, strongly positioned firm—unless the acquisition price is prohibitive. However, when the acquirer sees promising ways to transform a weak firm into a strong one and has the resources and managerial know-how to do it, a struggling company can be the better long-term investment.

Entering a new foreign country via internal development and building a foreign subsidiary from scratch makes sense when a company already operates in a number of countries, has experience in getting new subsidiaries up and running and overseeing their operations, and has a sufficiently large pool of resources and competencies to rapidly equip a new subsidiary with the personnel and capabilities it needs to compete successfully and profitably. Four other conditions make an internal start-up strategy appealing:

- When creating an internal start-up is cheaper than making an acquisition.
- When adding new production capacity will not adversely impact the supply–demand balance in the local market.
- When a start-up subsidiary has the ability to gain good distribution access (perhaps because of the company's recognized brand name).
- When a start-up subsidiary will have the size, cost structure, and resources to compete head-to-head against local rivals.

Alliance and Joint Venture Strategies

Strategic alliances, joint ventures, and other cooperative agreements with foreign companies are a favorite and potentially fruitful means for entering a foreign market or strengthening a firm's competitiveness in world markets.[5] Historically, export-minded firms in industrialized nations sought alliances with firms in less-developed countries to import and market their products locally—such arrangements were often necessary to win approval for entry from the host country's government. Both Japanese and American companies are actively forming alliances with European companies to strengthen their ability to compete in the 28-nation European Union (and the three countries that are candidates to become EU members) and to capitalize on the opening of Eastern European markets. Many U.S. and European companies are allying with Asian companies in their efforts to enter markets in China, India, Malaysia, Thailand, and other Asian countries. Many foreign companies, of course, are particularly interested in strategic partnerships that will strengthen their ability to gain a foothold in the U.S. market.

However, cooperative arrangements between domestic and foreign companies have strategic appeal for reasons besides gaining better access to attractive country markets.[6] A second big appeal of cross-border alliances is to capture economies of scale in production and/or marketing. By joining forces in producing components, assembling models, and marketing their products, companies can realize cost savings not achievable with their own small volumes. A third motivation for entering into a cross-border alliance is to fill gaps in technical expertise and/or knowledge of local markets (buying habits and product preferences of consumers, local customs, and so on). A fourth motivation for cross-border alliances is to share distribution facilities and dealer networks, and to mutually strengthen each partner's access to buyers.

A fifth benefit is that cross-border allies can direct their competitive energies more toward mutual rivals and less toward one another; teaming up may help them close the gap on leading companies. A sixth driver of cross-border alliances comes into play when companies wanting to enter a new foreign market conclude that alliances with local companies are an effective way to establish working relationships with key officials in the host-country government.[7] And, finally, alliances can be a particularly useful way for companies across the world to gain agreement on important technical standards—they have been used to arrive at standards for assorted PC devices, Internet-related technologies, high-definition televisions, and mobile phones.

What makes cross-border alliances an attractive strategic means of gaining the aforementioned types of benefits (as compared to acquiring or merging with foreign-based companies) is that entering into alliances and strategic partnerships allows a company to preserve its independence and avoid using perhaps scarce financial resources to fund acquisitions. Furthermore, an alliance offers the flexibility to readily disengage once its purpose has been served or if the benefits prove elusive, whereas an acquisition is a more permanent sort of arrangement.[8] Concepts & Connections 7.1 discusses how California-based Solazyme, a maker of biofuels and other green products, has used cross-border strategic alliances to fuel its growth.

CONCEPTS & CONNECTIONS 7.1

SOLAZYME'S CROSS-BORDER ALLIANCES WITH UNILEVER, SEPHORA, QANTAS, AND ROQUETTE

Solazyme, a California-based company that produces oils from algae for nutritional, cosmetic, and biofuel products, was named "America's Fastest-Growing Manufacturing Company" by *Inc.* magazine in 2011. The company has fueled its rapid growth through a variety of cross-border strategic alliances with much larger partners. These partnerships have not only facilitated Solazyme's entry into new markets, but they have also created value through resource sharing and risk spreading.

Its partnership with Unilever, a British–Dutch consumer goods company, has focused on collaborative R&D. Projects under way are aimed at meeting the growing demand for completely renewable, natural, and sustainable personal care products through the use of algal oils. By further developing Solazyme's technology platform, the partnership will enable the production of Solazyme's oils and other biomaterials efficiently and at large scale.

Solazyme has entered into a variety of marketing and distribution agreements with French cosmetics company Sephora (now part of LVMH). In March 2011, Solazyme launched its luxury skin care brand, Algenist, with Sephora's help. Sephora has also agreed to distribute Solazyme's anti-aging skin care line, making it available in Sephora stores and at Sephora.com.

In 2011, Solazyme also signed a contract with Australian airline Qantas to supply, test, and refine Solazyme's jet fuel

product, SolaJet. Solazyme stands to gain valuable input on how to design and distribute its product while receiving media attention and the marketing advantage of a well-known customer. On the other hand, Qantas hopes to better understand how it will achieve its sustainability goals while building its reputation as a sustainability leader in the airline industry.

Because its algae require sugar to produce oil, Solazyme has an interest in securing a stable supply of this feedstock. For this purpose, Solazyme created a 50/50 joint venture with French starch processor Roquette to develop, produce, and market food products globally. By working with Roquette to source feedstock and manufacture final food products, Solazyme lowered its exposure to sugar price fluctuations while taking advantage of Roquette's manufacturing infrastructure and expertise. In return, Roquette gained access to Solazyme's innovative technological resources.

Developed with John L. Gardner.

Sources: Company website; http://gigaom.com/cleantech/solazyme-draws-richard-branson-unilever-to-algae/; www.businessgreen.com/bg/news/2026103/qantas-inks-solazyme-algae-biofuel-deal; www.reuters.com/article/2012/02/22/us-smallbiz-solazyme-feb-idUSTRE81L1ZO20120222; www.foodnavigator-usa.com/Business/Solazyme-Roquette-JV-prepares-for-January-2012-launch-of-unique-algal-flour, accessed March 4, 2012.

The Risks of Strategic Alliances with Foreign Partners   Alliances and joint ventures with foreign partners have their pitfalls, however. Cross-border allies typically have to overcome language and cultural barriers and figure out how to deal with diverse (or perhaps conflicting) operating practices. The communication, trust-building, and coordination costs are high in terms of management time.[9] It is not unusual for partners to discover they have conflicting objectives and strategies, deep differences of opinion about how to proceed, or important differences in corporate values and ethical standards. Tensions build, working relationships cool, and the hoped-for benefits never materialize. The recipe for successful alliances requires many meetings of many people working in good faith over a period of time to iron out what is to be shared, what is to remain proprietary, and how the cooperative arrangements will work.[10]

Even if the alliance becomes a win-win proposition for both parties, there is the danger of becoming overly dependent on foreign partners for essential expertise and competitive capabilities. If a company is aiming for global market leadership and needs to develop capabilities of its own, then at some juncture cross-border merger or acquisition may have to be substituted for cross-border alliances and joint ventures. One of the lessons about cross-border alliances is that they are more effective in helping a company establish a beachhead of new opportunity in world markets than they are in enabling a company to achieve and sustain global market leadership.

International Strategy: The Three Principal Options

Broadly speaking, a company's **international strategy** is simply its strategy for competing in two or more countries simultaneously. Typically, a company will start to compete internationally by entering just one or perhaps a select few foreign markets, selling its products or services in countries where there is a ready market for them. But as it expands further internationally, it will have to confront head-on the conflicting pressures of local responsiveness versus efficiency gains from standardizing its product offering globally. As discussed earlier in the chapter, deciding upon the degree to vary its competitive approach to fit the specific market conditions and buyer preferences in each host country is perhaps the foremost strategic issue that must be addressed when operating in two or more foreign markets.[11] Figure 7.1 shows a company's three strategic approaches for competing internationally and resolving this issue.

> **CORE CONCEPT**
>
> A company's **international strategy** is its strategy for competing in two or more countries simultaneously.

LO4 Learn the three main options for tailoring a company's international strategy to cross-country differences in market conditions and buyer preferences.

Multidomestic Strategy—A Think Local, Act Local Approach to Strategy Making

A **multidomestic strategy** or **think local, act local** approach to strategy making is essential when there are significant country-to-country differences in customer preferences and buying habits, when there are significant cross-country differences in distribution channels and marketing methods, when host governments enact regulations requiring that products sold locally meet strict manufacturing specifications or performance standards, and when the trade restrictions of host governments are so diverse and complicated that they preclude a uniform, coordinated worldwide market approach. With localized strategies, a company often has different product versions for different countries and sometimes sells the products under different brand names. Government requirements for gasoline additives that help reduce carbon monoxide, smog, and other emissions are almost never the same from country to country. BP utilizes localized strategies in its gasoline and service station

> **CORE CONCEPT**
>
> A **multidomestic strategy** calls for varying a company's product offering and competitive approach from country to country in an effort to be responsive to significant cross-country differences in customer preferences, buyer purchasing habits, distribution channels, or marketing methods. **Think local, act local** strategy-making approaches are also essential when host-government regulations or trade policies preclude a uniform, coordinated worldwide market approach.

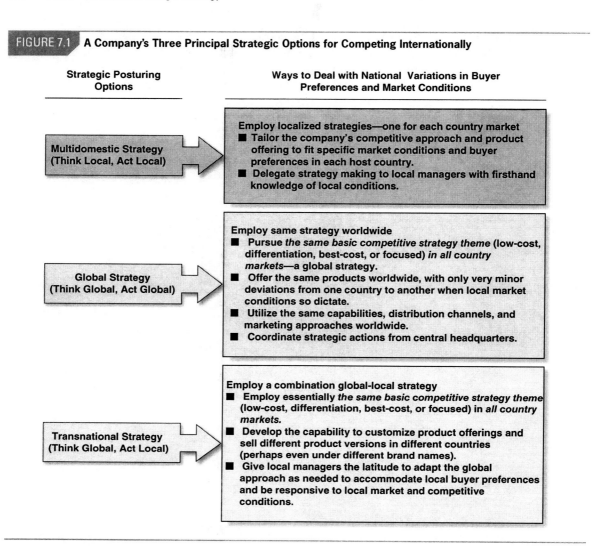

FIGURE 7.1   **A Company's Three Principal Strategic Options for Competing Internationally**

business segment because of these cross-country formulation differences and because of customer familiarity with local brand names. For example, the company markets gasoline in the United States under its BP and Arco brands, but markets gasoline in Germany, Belgium, Poland, Hungary, and the Czech Republic under the Aral brand. Companies in the food products industry often vary the ingredients in their products and sell the localized versions under local brand names to cater to country-specific tastes and eating preferences. The strength of employing a set of localized or multidomestic strategies is that the company's actions and business approaches are deliberately crafted to appeal to the tastes and expectations of buyers in each country and to stake out the most attractive market positions vis-à-vis local competitors.[12]

However, think local, act local strategies have two big drawbacks: (1) They hinder transfer of a company's competencies and resources across country boundaries because the strategies in different host countries can be grounded in varying competencies and capabilities; and (2) they do not promote building a single, unified competitive advantage, especially one based on low cost. Companies employing highly localized or multidomestic strategies face big hurdles in achieving low-cost leadership *unless* they find ways to customize their products and *still* be in a position to capture scale economies and learning curve effects. Toyota's unique mass customization production capability has been key to its ability to effectively adapt product offerings to local buyer tastes, while maintaining low-cost leadership.

Global Strategy—A Think Global, Act Global Approach to Strategy Making

While multidomestic strategies are best suited for industries where a fairly high degree of local responsiveness is important, global strategies are best suited for globally standardized industries. A **global strategy** is one in which the company's approach is predominantly the same in all countries—it sells the same products under the same brand names everywhere, utilizes much the same distribution channels in all countries, and competes on the basis of the same capabilities and marketing approaches worldwide. Although the company's strategy or product offering may be adapted in very minor ways to accommodate specific situations in a few host countries, the company's fundamental competitive approach (low-cost, differentiation, or focused) remains very much intact worldwide and local managers stick close to the global strategy. A **think global, act global** strategic theme prompts company managers to integrate and coordinate the company's strategic moves worldwide and to expand into most if not all nations where there is significant buyer demand. It puts considerable strategic emphasis on building a *global* brand name and aggressively pursuing opportunities to transfer ideas, new products, and capabilities from one country to another.

> **CORE CONCEPT**
>
> **Global strategies** employ the same basic competitive approach in all countries where a company operates and are best suited to industries that are globally standardized in terms of customer preferences, buyer purchasing habits, distribution channels, or marketing methods. This is the **think global, act global** strategic theme.

Ford's global design strategy is a move toward a think global, act global strategy by the company and involves the development and production of standardized models with country-specific modifications limited primarily to what is required to meet local country emission and safety standards. The 2010 Ford Fiesta and 2011 Ford Focus were the company's first global design models to be marketed in Europe, North America, Asia, and Australia. Whenever country-to-country differences are small enough to be accommodated within the framework of a global strategy, a global strategy is preferable to localized strategies because a company can more readily unify its operations and focus on establishing a brand image and reputation that is uniform from country to country. Moreover, with a global strategy a company is better able to focus its full resources on securing a sustainable low-cost or differentiation-based competitive advantage over both domestic rivals and global rivals.

Transnational Strategy—A Think Global, Act Local Approach to Strategy Making

A **transnational strategy** is a **think global, act local** approach to developing strategy that accommodates cross-country variations in buyer tastes, local customs, and market conditions while also striving for the benefits of standardization. This middle-ground approach entails utilizing the same basic competitive theme (low-cost, differentiation, or focused) in each country but allows local managers the latitude to (1) incorporate whatever country-specific variations in product attributes are needed to best satisfy local buyers and (2) make whatever adjustments in production, distribution, and marketing are needed to respond to local market conditions and compete successfully against local rivals. Both McDonald's and KFC have discovered ways to customize their menu offerings in various countries without compromising costs, product quality, and operating effectiveness. Otis Elevator found that a transnational strategy delivers better results than a global strategy when competing in countries such as China where local needs are highly differentiated. In 2000, it switched from its customary single-brand approach to a multibrand strategy aimed at serving different segments of the market. By 2009, it had doubled its market share in China and increased its revenues sixfold.[13]

> **CORE CONCEPT**
>
> A **transnational strategy** is a **think global, act local** approach to strategy making that involves employing essentially the same strategic theme (low-cost, differentiation, focused, best-cost) in all country markets, while allowing some country-to-country customization to fit local market conditions.

As a rule, most companies that operate multinationally endeavor to employ as global a strategy as customer needs and market conditions permit. Electronic Arts has two major design studios—one in Vancouver, British Columbia, and one in Los Angeles—and smaller design studios in San Francisco, Orlando, London, and Tokyo. This dispersion of design studios helps EA to design games that are specific to different cultures—for example, the London studio took the lead in designing the popular FIFA Soccer game to suit European tastes and to replicate the stadiums, signage, and team rosters; the U.S. studio took the lead in designing games involving NFL football, NBA basketball, and NASCAR racing.

Using International Operations to Improve Overall Competitiveness

LO5 Understand how multinational companies are able to use international operations to improve overall competitiveness.

A firm can gain competitive advantage by expanding outside its domestic market in two important ways. One, it can use location to lower costs or help achieve greater product differentiation. And two, it can use cross-border coordination in ways that a domestic-only competitor cannot.

Using Location to Build Competitive Advantage

To use location to build competitive advantage, a company must consider two issues: (1) whether to concentrate each internal process in a few countries or to disperse performance of each process to many nations, and (2) in which countries to locate particular activities.

When to Concentrate Internal Processes in a Few Locations

Companies tend to concentrate their activities in a limited number of locations in the following circumstances:

- *When the costs of manufacturing or other activities are significantly lower in some geographic locations than in others.* For example, much of the world's athletic footwear is manufactured in Asia (China and Korea) because of low labor costs; much of the production of circuit boards for PCs is located in Taiwan because of both low costs and the high-caliber technical skills of the Taiwanese labor force.

- *When there are significant scale economies.* The presence of significant economies of scale in components production or final assembly means a company can gain major cost savings from operating a few super-efficient plants as opposed to a host of small plants scattered across the world. Makers of digital cameras and LED TVs located in Japan, South Korea, and Taiwan have used their scale economies to establish a low-cost advantage.

- *When there is a steep learning curve associated with performing an activity.* In some industries, learning curve effects in parts manufacture or assembly are so great that a company establishes one or two large plants from which it serves the world market. The key to riding down the learning curve is to concentrate production in a few locations to increase the accumulated volume at a plant (and thus the experience of the plant's workforce) as rapidly as possible.

- *When certain locations have superior resources, allow better coordination of related activities, or offer other valuable advantages.* A research unit or a sophisticated production facility may be situated in a particular nation because of its pool of technically trained personnel. Samsung became a leader in memory chip technology by establishing a major R&D facility in Silicon Valley and transferring the know-how it gained back to headquarters and its plants in South Korea.

> Companies that compete multinationally can pursue competitive advantage in world markets by locating their value chain activities in whichever nations prove most advantageous.

When to Disperse Internal Processes Across Many Locations

There are several instances when dispersing a process is more advantageous than concentrating it in a single location. Buyer-related activities, such as distribution to dealers, sales and advertising, and after-sale service, usually must take place close to buyers. This makes it necessary to physically locate the capability to perform such activities in every country market where a global firm has major customers. For example, large public accounting firms have numerous international offices to service the foreign operations of their multinational corporate clients. Dispersing activities to many locations is also competitively important when high transportation costs, diseconomies of large size, and trade barriers make it too expensive to operate from a central location. In addition, it is strategically advantageous to disperse activities to hedge against the risks of fluctuating exchange rates and adverse political developments.

Using Cross-Border Coordination to Build Competitive Advantage

Multinational and global competitors are able to coordinate activities across different countries to build competitive advantage.[14] If a firm learns how to assemble its product more efficiently at, say, its Brazilian plant, the accumulated expertise and knowledge can be shared with assembly plants in other world locations. Also, knowledge gained in marketing a company's product in Great Britain, for instance, can readily be exchanged with company personnel in New Zealand or Australia. Other examples of cross-border coordination include shifting production from a plant in one country to a plant in another to take advantage of exchange rate fluctuations and to respond to changing wage rates, energy costs, or changes in tariffs and quotas.

Efficiencies can also be achieved by shifting workloads from where they are unusually heavy to locations where personnel are underutilized. Whirlpool's efforts to link its product R&D and manufacturing operations in North America, Latin America, Europe, and Asia allowed it to accelerate the discovery of innovative appliance features, coordinate the introduction of these features in the appliance products marketed in different countries, and create a cost-efficient worldwide supply chain. Whirlpool's conscious efforts to integrate and coordinate its various operations around the world have helped it become a low-cost producer and also speed product innovations to market, thereby giving Whirlpool an edge over rivals worldwide.

Strategies for Competing in the Markets of Developing Countries

LO6 Gain an understanding of the unique characteristics of competing in developing-country markets.

Companies racing for global leadership have to consider competing in developing-economy markets such as China, India, Brazil, Indonesia, Thailand, Poland, Russia, and Mexico—countries where the business risks are considerable but where the opportunities for growth are huge, especially as their economies develop and living standards climb toward levels in the industrialized world.[15] For example, in 2010 China was the world's second-largest economy (behind the United States) based upon purchasing power, and its population of 1.3 billion people made it the world's largest market for many commodities and types of consumer goods. China's growth in demand for consumer goods put it on track to become the world's largest market for luxury goods by 2014.[16] Thus, no company pursuing global market leadership can afford to ignore the strategic importance of establishing competitive market positions in China, India, other parts of the Asian-Pacific region, Latin America, and Eastern Europe. Concepts & Connections 7.2 describes Yum! Brands' strategy to boost its sales and market share in China.

Tailoring products to fit conditions in an emerging country market such as China, however, often involves more than making minor product changes and becoming more familiar with local cultures. McDonald's has had to offer vegetable burgers in parts of Asia and to rethink its prices, which are often high by local standards and affordable only by the well-to-do. Kellogg has struggled to introduce its cereals successfully because consumers in many

CONCEPTS & CONNECTIONS 7.2

YUM! BRANDS' STRATEGY FOR BECOMING THE LEADING FOOD SERVICE BRAND IN CHINA

In 2013, Yum! Brands operated more than 38,000 restaurants in more than 117 countries. Its best-known brands were KFC, Taco Bell, Pizza Hut, A&W, and Long John Silver's. In 2012, its fastest growth in revenues came from its 5,700-plus restaurants in China, which recorded operating profits of $963 million during the year. KFC was the largest quick-service chain in China, with 4,260 units in 2012, while Pizza Hut was the largest casual-dining chain, with 987 units. Yum! Brands planned to open at least 700 new restaurant locations annually in China, including new Little Sheep units and East Dawning units, which had menus offering traditional Chinese food. All Yum! Brands menu items for China were developed in its R&D facility in Shanghai.

In addition to adapting its menu to local tastes and adding new units at a rapid pace, Yum! Brands adapted the restaurant ambience and decor to appeal to local consumer preferences and behavior. The company changed its KFC store formats to provide educational displays that supported parents' priorities for their children and to make KFC a fun place for children to visit. The typical KFC outlet in China averaged two birthday parties per day.

In 2012, Yum! Brands operated 58 KFC, Taco Bell, Pizza Hut, A&W, and Long John Silver's restaurants for every 1 million Americans. The company's more than 5,700 units in China represented only two restaurants per 1 million Chinese. Yum! Brands management believed that its strategy keyed to continued expansion in the number of units in China, and additional menu refinements would allow its operating profits from restaurants located in China to account for nearly 50 percent of systemwide operating profits by 2017.

Sources: Yum! Brands 2012 10K; information posted at www.yum.com.

less-developed countries do not eat cereal for breakfast—changing habits is difficult and expensive. Single-serving packages of detergents, shampoos, pickles, cough syrup, and cooking oils are very popular in India because they allow buyers to conserve cash by purchasing only what they need immediately. Thus, many companies find that trying to employ a strategy akin to that used in the markets of developed countries is hazardous.[17] Experimenting with some, perhaps many, local twists is usually necessary to find a strategy combination that works.

Strategy Options for Competing in Developing-Country Markets

Several strategy options for tailoring a company's strategy to fit the sometimes unusual or challenging circumstances presented in developing-country markets are the following:

- *Prepare to compete on the basis of low price.* Consumers in emerging markets are often highly focused on price, which can give low-cost local competitors the edge unless a company can find ways to attract buyers with bargain prices as well as better products. For example, when Unilever entered the market for laundry detergents in India, it developed a low-cost detergent (named Wheel) that was not harsh to the skin, constructed new super-efficient production facilities, distributed the product to local merchants by handcarts, and crafted an economical marketing campaign that included painted signs on buildings and demonstrations near stores—the new brand quickly captured $100 million in sales and was the top detergent brand in India in 2011 based on dollar sales. Unilever later replicated the strategy with low-price shampoos and deodorants in India and in South America with a detergent brand named Ala.

- *Modify aspects of the company's business model or strategy to accommodate local circumstances (but not so much that the company loses the advantage of global scale and global branding).* For instance when Dell entered China, it discovered that individuals and businesses were not accustomed to placing orders via the Internet. To adapt, Dell modified its direct sales model to rely more heavily on phone and fax orders and decided to be patient in getting Chinese customers to place Internet orders. Further, because numerous Chinese government departments and state-owned enterprises insisted that hardware vendors make their bids through distributors and systems integrators (as opposed to dealing directly with Dell salespeople as did large enterprises in other countries), Dell opted to use third parties in marketing its products to this buyer segment (although it did sell through its own sales force where it could). But Dell was careful not to abandon those parts of its business model that gave it a competitive edge over rivals.

- *Try to change the local market to better match the way the company does business elsewhere.* A multinational company often has enough market clout to drive major changes in the way a local country market operates. When Japan's Suzuki entered India in 1981, it triggered a quality revolution among Indian auto parts manufacturers. Local parts and components suppliers teamed up with Suzuki's vendors in Japan and worked with Japanese experts to produce higher-quality products. Over the next two decades, Indian companies became very proficient in making top-notch parts and components for vehicles, won more prizes for quality than companies in any country other than Japan, and broke into the global market as suppliers to many automakers in Asia and other parts of the world. Mahindra and Mahindra, one of India's premier automobile manufacturers, has been recognized by a number of organizations for its product quality. Among its most noteworthy awards was its number-one ranking by J.D. Power Asia Pacific for new-vehicle overall quality.

- *Stay away from those emerging markets where it is impractical or uneconomical to modify the company's business model to accommodate local circumstances.* Home Depot expanded into Mexico in 2001 and China in 2006, but has avoided entry into other emerging countries because its value proposition of good quality, low prices, and attentive customer service relies on (1) good highways and logistical systems to minimize store inventory costs, (2) employee stock ownership to help motivate store personnel to provide good customer service, and (3) high labor costs for housing construction and home repairs to encourage homeowners to engage in do-it-yourself projects. Relying on these factors in the U.S. and Canadian markets has worked spectacularly for Home Depot, but Home Depot has found that it cannot count on these factors in nearby Latin America.

Company experiences in entering developing markets such as China, India, Russia, and Brazil indicate that profitability seldom comes quickly or easily. Building a market for the company's products can often turn into a long-term process that involves reeducation of consumers, sizable investments in advertising and promotion to alter tastes and buying habits, and upgrades of the local infrastructure (the supplier base, transportation systems, distribution channels, labor markets, and capital markets). In such cases, a company must be patient, work within the system to improve the infrastructure, and lay the foundation for generating sizable revenues and profits once conditions are ripe for market takeoff.

> Profitability in emerging markets rarely comes quickly or easily—new entrants have to adapt their business models and strategies to local conditions and be patient in earning a profit.

KEY POINTS

1. Competing in international markets allows multinational companies to (1) gain access to new customers, (2) achieve lower costs and enhance the firm's competitiveness by more easily capturing scale economies or learning curve effects, (3) leverage core competencies refined domestically in additional country markets, (4) gain access to resources and capabilities located in foreign markets, and (5) spread business risk across a wider market base.

2. Companies electing to expand into international markets must consider cross-country differences in buyer tastes, market sizes, and growth potential; location-based cost drivers; adverse exchange rates; and host-government policies when evaluating strategy options.

3. Options for entering foreign markets include maintaining a national (one-country) production base and exporting goods to foreign markets, licensing foreign firms to use the company's technology or produce and distribute the company's products, employing a franchising strategy, establishing a foreign subsidiary, and using strategic alliances or other collaborative partnerships.

4. In posturing to compete in foreign markets, a company has three basic options: (1) a multidomestic or think local, act local approach to crafting a strategy, (2) a global or think global, act global approach to crafting a strategy, and (3) a transnational strategy or combination think global, act local approach. A "think local, act local" or multicountry strategy is appropriate for industries or companies that must vary their product offerings and competitive approaches from country to country to accommodate differing buyer preferences and market conditions. A "think global, act global" approach (or global strategy) works best in markets that support employing the same basic competitive approach (low-cost, differentiation, focused) in all country markets and marketing essentially the same products under the same brand names in all countries where the company operates. A "think global, act local" approach can be used when it is feasible for a company to employ essentially the same basic competitive strategy in all markets, but still customize its product offering and some aspect of its operations to fit local market circumstances.

5. There are two general ways in which a firm can gain competitive advantage (or offset domestic disadvantages) in global markets. One way involves locating various value chain activities among nations in a manner that lowers costs or achieves greater product differentiation. A second way draws on a multinational or global competitor's ability to deepen or broaden its resources and capabilities and to coordinate its dispersed activities in ways that a domestic-only competitor cannot.

6. Companies racing for global leadership have to consider competing in emerging markets such as China, India, Brazil, Indonesia, and Mexico—countries where the business risks are considerable but the opportunities for growth are huge. To succeed in these markets, companies often have to (1) compete on the basis of low price, (2) be prepared to modify aspects of the company's business model or strategy to accommodate local circumstances (but not so much that the company loses the advantage of global scale and global branding), and/or (3) try to change the local market to better match the way the company does business elsewhere. Profitability is unlikely to come quickly or easily in emerging markets, typically because of the investments needed to alter buying habits and tastes and/or the need for infrastructure upgrades. And there may be times when a company should simply stay away from certain emerging markets until conditions for entry are better suited to its business model and strategy.

▶ ASSURANCE OF LEARNING EXERCISES

LO1, LO3   1. Chile's largest producer of wine, Concha y Toro, chooses to compete in Europe, North America, the Caribbean, and Asia using an export strategy. Go to the investor relations section of the company's website (www.conchaytoro.com/the-company/investor-relations/) to review the company's press releases, annual reports, and presentations. Why does it seem that the company has avoided developing vineyards and wineries in wine growing regions outside of South America? For what reasons does Concha y Toro likely have to pursue exporting rather than stick to a domestic-only sales and distribution strategy?

LO1, LO3   2. Collaborative agreements with foreign companies in the form of strategic alliances or joint ventures are widely used as a means of entering foreign markets. They are also used as a means of acquiring resources and capabilities by learning from foreign partners. And they are used to put together powerful combinations of complementary resources and capabilities by accessing the complementary resources and capabilities of a foreign partner. Concepts & Connections 7.1 provides examples of four cross-border strategic alliances in which Solazyme has participated. What were each of these partnerships (with Unilever, Sephora, Qantas, and Roquette) designed to achieve, and why would they make sense for a company such as Solazyme? (Analyze each partnership separately based on the information provided in the capsule.)

connect

LO2, LO4   3. Assume you are in charge of developing the strategy for a multinational company selling products in some 50 countries around the world. One of the issues you face is whether to employ a multidomestic, a transnational, or a global strategy.

connect

   a. If your company's product is mobile phones, do you think it would make better strategic sense to employ a multidomestic strategy, a transnational strategy, or a global strategy? Why?

b. If your company's product is dry soup mixes and canned soups, would a multidomestic strategy seem to be more advisable than a transnational or global strategy? Why or why not?

c. If your company's product is large home appliances such as washing machines, ranges, ovens, and refrigerators, would it seem to make more sense to pursue a multidomestic strategy or a transnational strategy or a global strategy? Why?

4. Using your university library's subscription to Lexis-Nexis, EBSCO, or a similar database, identify and discuss three key strategies that Volkswagen is using to compete in China.   LO5, LO6

 EXERCISES FOR SIMULATION PARTICIPANTS

The questions below are for simulation participants whose companies operate in an international market arena. If your company competes only in a single country, then skip the questions in this section.

1. To what extent, if any, have you and your co-managers adapted your company's strategy to take shifting exchange rates into account? In other words, have you undertaken any actions to try to minimize the impact of adverse shifts in exchange rates?   LO2

2. To what extent, if any, have you and your co-managers adapted your company's strategy to consider geographic differences in import tariffs or import duties?   LO2

3. Which one of the following best describes the strategic approach your company is taking to try to compete successfully on an international basis?   LO4

- Multidomestic or think local, act local approach.
- Global or think global, act global approach.
- Transnational or think global, act local approach.

Explain your answer and indicate two or three chief elements of your company's strategy for competing in two or more different geographic regions.

 ENDNOTES

1. A. C. Inkpen and A. Dinur, "Knowledge Management Processes and International Joint Ventures," *Organization Science* 9, no. 4 (July–August 1998); P. Dussauge, B. Garrette, and W. Mitchell, "Learning from Competing Partners: Outcomes and Durations of Scale and Link Alliances in Europe, North America and Asia," *Strategic Management Journal* 21, no. 2 (February 2000); C. Dhanaraj, M. A. Lyles, H. K. Steensma, et al., "Managing Tacit and Explicit Knowledge Transfer in IJVS: The Role of Relational Embeddedness and the Impact on Performance," *Journal of International Business Studies* 35, no. 5 (September 2004); K. W. Glaister and P. J. Buckley, "Strategic Motives for International Alliance Formation," *Journal of Management Studies* 33, no. 3 (May 1996); J. Anand and B. Kogut, "Technological Capabilities of Countries, Firm Rivalry and Foreign Direct Investment," *Journal of International Business Studies* 28, no. 3 (1997); J. Anand and A. Delios, "Absolute and Relative Resources as Determinants of International Acquisitions," *Strategic Management Journal* 23, no. 2 (February 2002); A. Seth, K. Song, and A. Pettit, "Value Creation and Destruction in Cross-Border Acquisitions: An Empirical Analysis of Foreign Acquisitions of U.S. Firms," *Strategic Management Journal* 23, no. 10 (October 2002); J. Anand, L. Capron, and W. Mitchell, "Using Acquisitions to Access Multinational Diversity: Thinking Beyond the Domestic Versus Cross-Border M&A Comparison," *Industrial & Corporate Change* 14, no. 2 (April 2005).

2. "China Car Sales 'Overtook the US' in 2009," *BBC News*, January 11, 2010, http://news.bbc.co.uk/2/hi/8451887.stm.

3. News release by U.S. Department of Labor, Bureau of Labor Statistics, "International Comparisons of Hourly Compensation Costs in Manufacturing, 2011," December 19, 2012.

4. E. Pablo, "Determinants of Cross-Border M&As in Latin America," *Journal of Business Research* 62, no. 9 (2009); R. Olie, "Shades of Culture and Institutions in International Mergers," *Organization Studies* 15, no. 3 (1994); and K. E. Meyer, M. Wright, and S. Pruthi, "Institutions, Resources, and Entry Strategies in Emerging Economies," *Strategic Management Journal* 30, no. 5 (2009).

5. Joel Bleeke and David Ernst, "The Way to Win in Cross-Border Alliances," *Harvard Business Review* 69, no. 6 (November–December 1991); and Gary Hamel, Yves L. Doz, and C. K. Prahalad, "Collaborate with Your Competitors—and Win," *Harvard Business Review* 67, no. 1 (January–February 1989).

6. Yves L. Doz and Gary Hamel, *Alliance Advantage* (Boston: Harvard Business School Press, 1998); Bleeke and Ernst, "The Way to Win in Cross-Border Alliances"; Hamel, Doz, and Prahalad, "Collaborate with Your Competitors—and Win"; and Michael Porter, *The Competitive Advantage of Nations* (New York: Free Press, 1990).

7. H. Kurt Christensen, "Corporate Strategy: Managing a Set of Businesses," in *The Portable MBA in Strategy*, ed. Liam Fahey and Robert M. Randall (New York: John Wiley & Sons, 2001).

8. Jeffrey H. Dyer, Prashant Kale, and Harbir Singh, "When to Ally and When to Acquire," *Harvard Business Review* 82, no. 7/8 (July–August 2004).

9. Rosabeth Moss Kanter, "Collaborative Advantage: The Art of the Alliance," *Harvard Business Review* 72, no. 4 (July–August 1994).

10. Jeremy Main, "Making Global Alliances Work," *Fortune*, December 19, 1990, p. 125.

11. Pankaj Ghemawat, "Managing Differences: The Central Challenge of Global Strategy," *Harvard Business Review* 85, no. 3 (March 2007).

12. C. A. Bartlett and S. Ghoshal, *Managing Across Borders: The Transnational Solution*, 2nd ed. (Boston: Harvard Business School Press, 1998).

13. Lynn S. Paine, "The China Rules," *Harvard Business Review* 88, no. 6 (June 2010) pp. 103-8.

14. C. K. Prahalad and Yves L. Doz, *The Multinational Mission* (New York: Free Press, 1987), pp. 58–60.

15. David J. Arnold and John A. Quelch, "New Strategies in Emerging Markets," *Sloan Management Review* 40, no. 1 (Fall 1998); and C. K. Prahalad, *The Fortune at the Bottom of the Pyramid: Eradicating Poverty through Profits* (Upper Saddle River, NJ: Wharton, 2005).

16. Brenda Cherry, "What China Eats (and Drinks and . . .)," *Fortune*, October 4, 2004, pp. 152–53; "A Ravenous Dragon," *The Economist* 386, no. 8571 (March 15, 2008), online edition; and "China: Just the Facts," *Journal of Commerce*, June 2, 2008, p. 24.

17. Tarun Khanna, Krishna G. Palepu, and Jayant Sinha, "Strategies That Fit Emerging Markets," *Harvard Business Review* 83, no. 6 (June 2005); and Arindam K. Bhattacharya and David C. Michael, "How Local Companies Keep Multinationals at Bay," *Harvard Business Review* 86, no. 3 (March 2008).

Corporate Strategy: Diversification and the Multibusiness Company

chapter

8

LEARNING OBJECTIVES

LO1   Understand when and how diversifying into multiple businesses can enhance shareholder value.

LO2   Gain an understanding of how related diversification strategies can produce cross-business strategic fit capable of delivering competitive advantage.

LO3   Become aware of the merits and risks of corporate strategies keyed to unrelated diversification.

LO4   Gain command of the analytical tools for evaluating a company's diversification strategy.

LO5   Understand a diversified company's four main corporate strategy options for solidifying its diversification strategy and improving company performance.

This chapter moves up one level in the strategy-making hierarchy, from strategy making in a single-business enterprise to strategy making in a diversified enterprise. Because a diversified company is a collection of individual businesses, the strategy-making task is more complicated. In a one-business company, managers have to come up with a plan for competing successfully in only a single industry environment—the result is what Chapter 2 labeled as *business strategy* (or *business-level strategy*). But in a diversified company, the strategy-making challenge involves assessing multiple industry environments and developing a *set* of business strategies, one for each industry arena in which the diversified company operates. And top executives at a diversified company must still go one step further and devise a companywide or *corporate strategy* for improving the attractiveness and performance of the company's overall business lineup and for making a rational whole out of its diversified collection of individual businesses.

In most diversified companies, corporate-level executives delegate considerable strategy-making authority to the heads of each business, usually giving them the latitude to craft a business strategy suited to their particular industry and competitive circumstances and holding them accountable for producing good results. But the task of crafting a diversified company's overall corporate strategy falls squarely in the lap of top-level executives and involves four distinct facets:

1. *Picking new industries to enter and deciding on the means of entry.* The decision to pursue business diversification requires that management decide what new industries offer the best growth prospects and whether to enter by starting a new business from the ground up, acquiring a company already in the target industry, or forming a joint venture or strategic alliance with another company.

2. *Pursuing opportunities to leverage cross-business value chain relationships into competitive advantage.* Companies that diversify into businesses with strategic fit across the value chains of their business units have a much better chance of gaining a $1 + 1 = 3$ effect than multibusiness companies lacking strategic fit.

3. *Establishing investment priorities and steering corporate resources into the most attractive business units.* A diversified company's business units are usually not equally attractive, and it is incumbent on corporate management to channel resources into areas where earnings potentials are higher.

4. *Initiating actions to boost the combined performance of the corporation's collection of businesses.* Corporate strategists must craft moves to improve the overall performance of the corporation's business lineup and sustain increases in shareholder value. Strategic options for diversified corporations include *(a)* sticking closely with the existing business lineup and pursuing opportunities presented by these businesses, *(b)* broadening the scope of diversification by entering additional industries, *(c)* retrenching to a narrower scope of diversification by divesting poorly performing businesses, and *(d)* broadly restructuring the business lineup with multiple divestitures and/or acquisitions.

The first portion of this chapter describes the various means a company can use to diversify and explores the pros and cons of related versus unrelated diversification strategies. The second part of the chapter looks at how to evaluate the attractiveness of a diversified company's business lineup, decide whether it has a good diversification strategy, and identify ways to improve its future performance.

When Business Diversification Becomes a Consideration

As long as a single-business company can achieve profitable growth opportunities in its present industry, there is no urgency to pursue diversification. However, a company's opportunities for growth can become limited if the industry becomes competitively unattractive. Consider, for example, what the growing use of debit cards and online bill payment have done to the check printing business and what mobile phone companies and marketers of Voice over Internet Protocol (VoIP) have done to the revenues of long-distance providers such as AT&T, British Telecommunications, and NTT in Japan. Thus, *diversifying into new industries always merits strong consideration whenever a single-business company encounters diminishing market opportunities and stagnating sales in its principal business.*[1]

LO1 Understand when and how diversifying into multiple businesses can enhance shareholder value.

Building Shareholder Value: The Ultimate Justification for Business Diversification

Diversification must do more for a company than simply spread its business risk across various industries. In principle, diversification cannot be considered a success unless it results in *added shareholder value*—value that shareholders cannot capture on their own by spreading their investments across the stocks of companies in different industries.

Business diversification stands little chance of building shareholder value without passing the following three tests:[2]

1. *The industry attractiveness test.* The industry to be entered through diversification must offer an opportunity for profits and return on investment that is equal to or better than that of the company's present business(es).

2. *The cost-of-entry test.* The cost to enter the target industry must not be so high as to erode the potential for good profitability. A Catch-22 can prevail here, however. The more attractive an industry's prospects are for growth and good long-term profitability, the more expensive it can be to enter. It's easy for acquisitions of companies in highly attractive industries to fail the cost-of-entry test.

3. *The better-off test.* Diversifying into a new business must offer potential for the company's existing businesses and the new business to perform better together under a single corporate umbrella than they would perform operating as independent, stand-alone businesses. For example, let's say company A diversifies by purchasing company B in another industry.

If A and B's consolidated profits in the years to come prove no greater than what each could have earned on its own, then A's diversification won't provide its shareholders with added value. Company A's shareholders could have achieved the same $1 + 1 = 2$ result by merely purchasing stock in company B. Shareholder value is not created by diversification unless it produces a $1 + 1 = 3$ effect.

> Creating added value for shareholders via diversification requires building a multibusiness company where the whole is greater than the sum of its parts.

Diversification moves that satisfy all three tests have the greatest potential to grow shareholder value over the long term. Diversification moves that can pass only one or two tests are suspect.

Approaches to Diversifying the Business Lineup

The means of entering new industries and lines of business can take any of three forms: acquisition, internal development, or joint ventures with other companies.

Diversification by Acquisition of an Existing Business

Acquisition is a popular means of diversifying into another industry. Not only is it quicker than trying to launch a new operation, but it also offers an effective way to hurdle such entry barriers as acquiring technological know-how, establishing supplier relationships, achieving scale economies, building brand awareness, and securing adequate distribution. Buying an ongoing operation allows the acquirer to move directly to the task of building a strong market position in the target industry, rather than getting bogged down in the fine points of launching a start-up.

The big dilemma an acquisition-minded firm faces is whether to pay a premium price for a successful company or to buy a struggling company at a bargain price.[3] If the buying firm has little knowledge of the industry but has ample capital, it is often better off purchasing a capable, strongly positioned firm—unless the price of such an acquisition is prohibitive and flunks the cost-of-entry test. However, when the acquirer sees promising ways to transform a weak firm into a strong one, a struggling company can be the better long-term investment.

Entering a New Line of Business through Internal Development

Achieving diversification through *internal development* involves starting a new business subsidiary from scratch. Generally, forming a start-up subsidiary to enter a new business has appeal only when (1) the parent company already has in-house most or all of the skills and resources needed to compete effectively; (2) there is ample time to launch the business; (3) internal entry has lower costs than entry via acquisition; (4) the targeted industry is populated with many relatively small firms such that the new start-up does not have to compete against large, powerful rivals; (5) adding new production capacity will not adversely impact the supply–demand balance in the industry; and

(6) incumbent firms are likely to be slow or ineffective in responding to a new entrant's efforts to crack the market.

Using Joint Ventures to Achieve Diversification

A joint venture to enter a new business can be useful in at least two types of situations.[4] First, a joint venture is a good vehicle for pursuing an opportunity that is too complex, uneconomical, or risky for one company to pursue alone. Second, joint ventures make sense when the opportunities in a new industry require a broader range of competencies and know-how than an expansion-minded company can marshal. Many of the opportunities in biotechnology call for the coordinated development of complementary innovations and tackling an intricate web of technical, political, and regulatory factors simultaneously. In such cases, pooling the resources and competencies of two or more companies is a wiser and less risky way to proceed.

However, as discussed in Chapters 6 and 7, partnering with another company—in the form of either a joint venture or a collaborative alliance—has significant drawbacks due to the potential for conflicting objectives, disagreements over how to best operate the venture, culture clashes, and so on. Joint ventures are generally the least durable of the entry options, usually lasting only until the partners decide to go their own ways.

Choosing the Diversification Path: Related versus Unrelated Businesses

> **CORE CONCEPT**
>
> **Related businesses** possess competitively valuable cross-business value chain and resource matchups; **unrelated businesses** have dissimilar value chains and resources requirements, with no competitively important cross-business value chain relationships.

Once a company decides to diversify, its first big corporate strategy decision is whether to diversify into **related businesses, unrelated businesses**, or some mix of both (see Figure 8.1). *Businesses are said to be related when their value chains possess competitively valuable cross-business relationships.* These value chain matchups present opportunities for the businesses to perform better under the same corporate umbrella than they could by operating as stand-alone entities. *Businesses are said to be unrelated when the activities comprising their respective value chains and resource requirements are so dissimilar that no competitively valuable cross-business relationships are present.*

LO2 Gain an understanding of how related diversification strategies can produce cross-business strategic fit capable of delivering competitive advantage.

The next two sections explore the ins and outs of related and unrelated diversification.

Diversifying into Related Businesses

A related diversification strategy involves building the company around businesses whose value chains possess competitively valuable strategic fit, as shown in Figure 8.2. **Strategic fit** exists whenever one or more activities comprising the

> **CORE CONCEPT**
>
> **Strategic fit** exists when value chains of different businesses present opportunities for cross-business skills transfer, cost sharing, or brand sharing.

FIGURE 8.1   **Strategic Themes of Multibusiness Corporation**

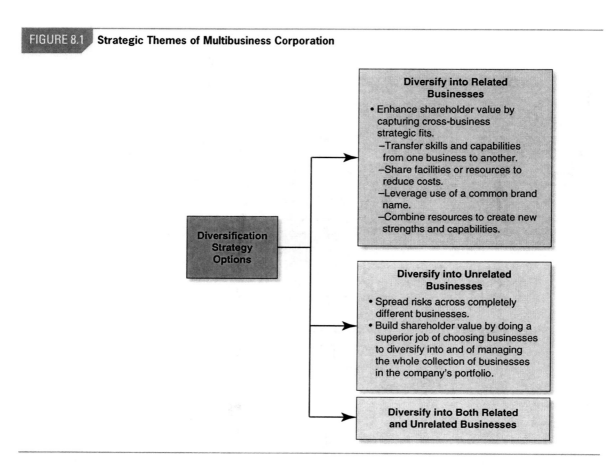

value chains of different businesses are sufficiently similar to present opportunities for:[5]

- *Transferring competitively valuable resources, expertise, technological know-how, or other capabilities from one business to another.* Google's technological know-how and innovation capabilities refined in its Internet search business have aided considerably in the development of its Android mobile operating system and Chrome operating system for computers. After acquiring Marvel Comics in 2009, Walt Disney Company shared Marvel's iconic characters such as Spider-Man, Iron Man, and the Black Widow with many of the other Disney businesses, including its theme parks, retail stores, motion picture division, and video game business.

- *Cost sharing between separate businesses where value chain activities can be combined.* For instance, it is often feasible to manufacture the products of different businesses in a single plant or have a single sales force for the products of different businesses if they are marketed to the same types of customers.

- *Brand sharing between business units that have common customers or that draw upon common core competencies.* For example, Yamaha's name in motorcycles gave it instant credibility and recognition in entering the personal watercraft business, allowing it to achieve a significant market share

---

FIGURE 8.2   **Related Diversification Is Built upon Competitively Valuable Strategic Fit in Value Chain Activities**

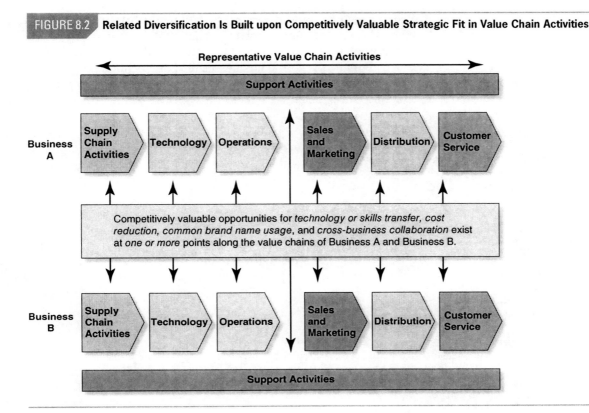

---

without spending large sums on advertising to establish a brand identity for the WaveRunner. Likewise, Apple's reputation for producing easy-to-operate computers was a competitive asset that facilitated the company's diversification into digital music players and smartphones.

Cross-business strategic fit can exist anywhere along the value chain—in R&D and technology activities, in supply chain activities, in manufacturing, in sales and marketing, or in distribution activities. Likewise, different businesses can often use the same administrative and customer service infrastructure. For instance, a cable operator that diversifies as a broadband provider can use the same customer data network, the same customer call centers and local offices, the same billing and customer accounting systems, and the same customer service infrastructure to support all its products and services.[6]

Strategic Fit and Economies of Scope

Strategic fit in the value chain activities of a diversified corporation's different businesses opens up opportunities for economies of scope— a concept distinct from *economies of scale*. Economies of *scale* are cost savings that accrue directly from a larger operation; for example, unit costs may be lower in a large plant than in a small

> **CORE CONCEPT**
>
> **Economies of scope** are cost reductions stemming from strategic fit along the value chains of related businesses (thereby, a larger scope of operations), whereas *economies of scale* accrue from a larger operation.

plant. **Economies of scope,** however, stem directly from cost-saving strategic fit along the value chains of related businesses. Such economies are open only to a multibusiness enterprise and are the result of a related diversification strategy that allows sibling businesses to share technology, perform R&D together, use common manufacturing or distribution facilities, share a common sales force or distributor/dealer network, and/or share the same administrative infrastructure. *The greater the cross-business economies associated with cost-saving strategic fit, the greater the potential for a related diversification strategy to yield a competitive advantage based on lower costs than rivals.*

The Ability of Related Diversification to Deliver Competitive Advantage and Gains in Shareholder Value

Economies of scope and the other strategic-fit benefits provide a dependable basis for earning higher profits and returns than what a diversified company's businesses could earn as stand-alone enterprises. Converting the competitive advantage potential into greater profitability is what fuels $1 + 1 = 3$ gains in shareholder value—the necessary outcome for satisfying the *better-off test.* There are three things to bear in mind here: (1) Capturing cross-business strategic fit via related diversification builds shareholder value in ways that shareholders cannot replicate by simply owning a diversified portfolio of stocks; (2) the capture of cross-business strategic-fit benefits is possible only through related diversification; and (3) the benefits of cross-business strategic fit are not automatically realized—*the benefits materialize only after management has successfully pursued internal actions to capture them.*[7]

Diversifying into Unrelated Businesses

LO3 Become aware of the merits and risks of corporate strategies keyed to unrelated diversification.

An unrelated diversification strategy discounts the importance of pursuing cross-business strategic fit and, instead, focuses squarely on entering and operating businesses in industries that allow the company as a whole to increase its earnings. Companies that pursue a strategy of unrelated diversification generally exhibit a willingness to diversify into *any* industry where senior managers see opportunity to realize improved financial results. Such companies are frequently labeled *conglomerates* because their business interests range broadly across diverse industries.

Companies that pursue unrelated diversification nearly always enter new businesses by acquiring an established company rather than by internal development. The premise of acquisition-minded corporations is that growth by acquisition can deliver enhanced shareholder value through upward-trending corporate revenues and earnings and a stock price that *on average* rises enough year after year to amply reward and please shareholders. Three types of acquisition candidates are usually of particular interest: (1) businesses that have bright growth prospects but are short on investment capital, (2) undervalued companies that can be acquired at a bargain price, and (3) struggling companies whose operations can be turned around with the aid of the parent company's financial resources and managerial know-how.

Building Shareholder Value through Unrelated Diversification

Given the absence of cross-business strategic fit with which to capture added competitive advantage, the task of building shareholder value via unrelated diversification ultimately hinges on the ability of the parent company to improve its businesses via other means. To succeed with a corporate strategy keyed to unrelated diversification, corporate executives must:

- Do a superior job of identifying and acquiring new businesses that can produce consistently good earnings and returns on investment.

- Do an excellent job of negotiating favorable acquisition prices.

- Do such a good job *overseeing* and *parenting* the firm's businesses that they perform at a higher level than they would otherwise be able to do through their own efforts alone. The parenting activities of corporate executives can take the form of providing expert problem-solving skills, creative strategy suggestions, and first-rate advice and guidance on how to improve competitiveness and financial performance to the heads of the various business subsidiaries.[8]

The Pitfalls of Unrelated Diversification

Unrelated diversification strategies have two important negatives that undercut the pluses: very demanding managerial requirements and limited competitive advantage potential.

Demanding Managerial Requirements   Successfully managing a set of fundamentally different businesses operating in fundamentally different industry and competitive environments is an exceptionally difficult proposition for corporate-level managers. The greater the number of businesses a company is in and the more diverse they are, the more difficult it is for corporate managers to:

1. Stay abreast of what's happening in each industry and each subsidiary.

2. Pick business-unit heads having the requisite combination of managerial skills and know-how to drive gains in performance.

3. Tell the difference between those strategic proposals of business-unit managers that are prudent and those that are risky or unlikely to succeed.

4. Know what to do if a business unit stumbles and its results suddenly head downhill.[9]

As a rule, the more unrelated businesses that a company has diversified into, the more corporate executives are forced to "manage by the numbers"—that is, keep a close track on the financial and operating results of each subsidiary and assume that the heads of the various subsidiaries have most everything under control so long as the latest key financial and operating measures look good. Managing by the numbers works if the heads of the various business units are quite capable and consistently meet their numbers. But problems arise when things start

> Unrelated diversification requires that corporate executives rely on the skills and expertise of business-level managers to build competitive advantage and boost the performance of individual businesses.

to go awry and corporate management has to get deeply involved in turning around a business it does not know much about.

Limited Competitive Advantage Potential The second big negative associated with unrelated diversification is that such a strategy *offers limited potential for competitive advantage beyond what each individual business can generate on its own.* Unlike a related diversification strategy, there is no cross-business strategic fit to draw on for reducing costs; transferring capabilities, skills, and technology; or leveraging use of a powerful brand name and thereby adding to the competitive advantage possessed by individual businesses. *Without the competitive advantage potential of strategic fit, consolidated performance of an unrelated group of businesses is unlikely to be better than the sum of what the individual business units could achieve independently in most instances.*

Misguided Reasons for Pursuing Unrelated Diversification

Competently overseeing a set of widely diverse businesses can turn out to be much harder than it sounds. In practice, comparatively few companies have proved that they have top management capabilities that are up to the task. Far more corporate executives have failed than been successful at delivering consistently good financial results with an unrelated diversification strategy.[10] Odds are that the result of unrelated diversification will be 1 + 1 = 2 or less. In addition, management sometimes undertakes a strategy of unrelated diversification for the wrong reasons.

- *Risk reduction.* Managers sometimes pursue unrelated diversification to reduce risk by spreading the company's investments over a set of diverse industries. But this cannot create long-term shareholder value alone since the company's shareholders can more efficiently reduce their exposure to risk by investing in a diversified portfolio of stocks and bonds.

- *Growth.* While unrelated diversification may enable a company to achieve rapid or continuous growth in revenues, only profitable growth can bring about increases in shareholder value and justify a strategy of unrelated diversification.

- *Earnings stabilization.* In a broadly diversified company, there's a chance that market downtrends in some of the company's businesses will be partially offset by cyclical upswings in its other businesses, thus producing somewhat less earnings volatility. In actual practice, however, there's no convincing evidence that the consolidated profits of firms with unrelated diversification strategies are more stable than the profits of firms with related diversification strategies.

- *Managerial motives.* Unrelated diversification can provide benefits to managers such as higher compensation, which tends to increase with firm size and degree of diversification. Diversification for this reason alone is far more likely to reduce shareholder value than to increase it.

Diversifying into Both Related and Unrelated Businesses

There's nothing to preclude a company from diversifying into both related and unrelated businesses. Indeed, the business makeup of diversified companies varies considerably. Some diversified companies are really *dominant-business enterprises*—one major "core" business accounts for 50 to 80 percent of total revenues and a collection of small related or unrelated businesses accounts for the remainder. Some diversified companies are *narrowly diversified* around a few (two to five) related or unrelated businesses. Others are *broadly diversified* around a wide-ranging collection of related businesses, unrelated businesses, or a mixture of both. And a number of multibusiness enterprises have diversified into *several unrelated groups of related businesses*. There's ample room for companies to customize their diversification strategies to incorporate elements of both related and unrelated diversification.

Evaluating the Strategy of a Diversified Company

Strategic analysis of diversified companies builds on the methodology used for single-business companies discussed in Chapters 3 and 4 but utilizes tools that streamline the overall process. The procedure for evaluating the pluses and minuses of a diversified company's strategy and deciding what actions to take to improve the company's performance involves six steps:

LO4   Gain command of the analytical tools for evaluating a company's diversification strategy.

1. Assessing the attractiveness of the industries the company has diversified into.
2. Assessing the competitive strength of the company's business units.
3. Evaluating the extent of cross-business strategic fit along the value chains of the company's various business units.
4. Checking whether the firm's resources fit the requirements of its present business lineup.
5. Ranking the performance prospects of the businesses from best to worst and determining a priority for allocating resources.
6. Crafting new strategic moves to improve overall corporate performance.

The core concepts and analytical techniques underlying each of these steps are discussed further in this section of the chapter.

Step 1: Evaluating Industry Attractiveness

A principal consideration in evaluating the caliber of a diversified company's strategy is the attractiveness of the industries in which it has business operations. The more attractive the industries (both individually and as a group) a diversified company is in, the better its prospects for good long-term performance. A simple and reliable analytical tool for gauging industry attractiveness involves calculating quantitative industry attractiveness scores based upon the following measures:

- *Market size and projected growth rate.* Big industries are more attractive than small industries, and fast-growing industries tend to be more attractive than slow-growing industries, other things being equal.

- *The intensity of competition.* Industries where competitive pressures are relatively weak are more attractive than industries with strong competitive pressures.
- *Emerging opportunities and threats.* Industries with promising opportunities and minimal threats on the near horizon are more attractive than industries with modest opportunities and imposing threats.
- *The presence of cross-industry strategic fit.* The more the industry's value chain and resource requirements match up well with the value chain activities of other industries in which the company has operations, the more attractive the industry is to a firm pursuing related diversification. However, cross-industry strategic fit may be of no consequence to a company committed to a strategy of unrelated diversification.
- *Resource requirements.* Industries having resource requirements within the company's reach are more attractive than industries where capital and other resource requirements could strain corporate financial resources and organizational capabilities.
- *Seasonal and cyclical factors.* Industries where buyer demand is relatively steady year-round and not unduly vulnerable to economic ups and downs tend to be more attractive than industries with wide seasonal or cyclical swings in buyer demand.
- *Social, political, regulatory, and environmental factors.* Industries with significant problems in such areas as consumer health, safety, or environmental pollution or that are subject to intense regulation are less attractive than industries where such problems are not burning issues.
- *Industry profitability.* Industries with healthy profit margins are generally more attractive than industries where profits have historically been low or unstable.
- *Industry uncertainty and business risk.* Industries with less uncertainty on the horizon and lower overall business risk are more attractive than industries whose prospects for one reason or another are quite uncertain.

Each attractiveness measure should be assigned a weight reflecting its relative importance in determining an industry's attractiveness; it is weak methodology to assume that the various attractiveness measures are equally important. The intensity of competition in an industry should nearly always carry a high weight (say, 0.20 to 0.30). Strategic-fit considerations should be assigned a high weight in the case of companies with related diversification strategies; but for companies with an unrelated diversification strategy, strategic fit with other industries may be given a low weight or even dropped from the list of attractiveness measures. Seasonal and cyclical factors generally are assigned a low weight (or maybe even eliminated from the analysis) unless a company has diversified into industries strongly characterized by seasonal demand and/or heavy vulnerability to cyclical upswings and downswings. The importance weights must add up to 1.0.

Next, each industry is rated on each of the chosen industry attractiveness measures, using a rating scale of 1 to 10 (where 10 signifies *high* attractiveness and 1 signifies *low* attractiveness). Weighted attractiveness scores are then calculated by multiplying the industry's rating on each measure by the

TABLE 8.1

Calculating Weighted Industry Attractiveness Scores

Rating scale: 1 = Very unattractive to company; 10 = Very attractive to company

Industry Attractiveness Measure	Importance Weight	Industry A Rating/Score	Industry B Rating/Score	Industry C Rating/Score	Industry D Rating/Score
Market size and projected growth rate	0.10	8/0.80	5/0.50	2/0.20	3/0.30
Intensity of competition	0.25	8/2.00	7/1.75	3/0.75	2/0.50
Emerging opportunities and threats	0.10	2/0.20	9/0.90	4/0.40	5/0.50
Cross-industry strategic fit	0.20	8/1.60	4/0.80	8/1.60	2/0.40
Resource requirements	0.10	9/0.90	7/0.70	5/0.50	5/0.50
Seasonal and cyclical influences	0.05	9/0.45	8/0.40	10/0.50	5/0.25
Societal, political, regulatory, and environmental factors	0.05	10/0.50	7/0.35	7/0.35	3/0.15
Industry profitability	0.10	5/0.50	10/1.00	3/0.30	3/0.30
Industry uncertainty and business risk	0.05	5/0.25	7/0.35	10/0.50	1/0.05
Sum of the assigned weights	1.00				
Overall weighted industry attractiveness scores		**7.20**	**6.75**	**5.10**	**2.95**

corresponding weight. For example, a rating of 8 times a weight of 0.25 gives a weighted attractiveness score of 2.00. The sum of the weighted scores for all the attractiveness measures provides an overall industry attractiveness score. This procedure is illustrated in Table 8.1.

Calculating Industry Attractiveness Scores

Two conditions are necessary for producing valid industry attractiveness scores using this method. One is deciding on appropriate weights for the industry attractiveness measures. This is not always easy because different analysts have different views about which weights are most appropriate. Also, different weightings may be appropriate for different companies—based on their strategies, performance targets, and financial circumstances. For instance, placing a low weight on financial resource requirements may be justifiable for a cash-rich company, whereas a high weight may be more appropriate for a financially strapped company.

The second requirement for creating accurate attractiveness scores is to have sufficient knowledge to rate the industry on each attractiveness measure. It's usually rather easy to locate statistical data needed to compare industries on market size, growth rate, seasonal and cyclical influences, and industry profitability. Cross-industry fit and resource requirements are also fairly easy to judge. But the attractiveness measure that is toughest to rate is that of intensity of competition. It is not always easy to conclude whether competition in one industry is stronger or weaker than in another industry. In the event that the available information is too skimpy to confidently assign a rating value to an industry on a particular attractiveness measure, then it is usually best to use a score of 5, which avoids biasing the overall attractiveness score either up or down.

Despite the hurdles, calculating industry attractiveness scores is a systematic and reasonably reliable method for ranking a diversified company's industries from most to least attractive.

Step 2: Evaluating Business-Unit Competitive Strength

The second step in evaluating a diversified company is to determine how strongly positioned its business units are in their respective industries. Doing an appraisal of each business unit's strength and competitive position in its industry not only reveals its chances for industry success but also provides a basis for ranking the units from competitively strongest to weakest. Quantitative measures of each business unit's competitive strength can be calculated using a procedure similar to that for measuring industry attractiveness. The following factors may be used in quantifying the competitive strengths of a diversified company's business subsidiaries:

- *Relative market share.* A business unit's *relative market share* is defined as the ratio of its market share to the market share held by the largest rival firm in the industry, with market share measured in unit volume, not dollars. For instance, if business A has a market-leading share of 40 percent and its largest rival has 30 percent, A's relative market share is 1.33. If business B has a 15 percent market share and B's largest rival has 30 percent, B's relative market share is 0.5.

- *Costs relative to competitors' costs.* There's reason to expect that business units with higher relative market shares have lower unit costs than competitors with lower relative market shares because of the possibility of scale economies and experience or learning curve effects. Another indicator of low cost can be a business unit's supply chain management capabilities.

- *Products or services that satisfy buyer expectations.* A company's competitiveness depends in part on being able to offer buyers appealing features, performance, reliability, and service attributes.

- *Ability to benefit from strategic fit with sibling businesses.* Strategic fit with other businesses within the company enhances a business unit's competitive strength and may provide a competitive edge.

- *Number and caliber of strategic alliances and collaborative partnerships.* Well-functioning alliances and partnerships may be a source of potential competitive advantage and thus add to a business's competitive strength.

- *Brand image and reputation.* A strong brand name is a valuable competitive asset in most industries.

- *Competitively valuable capabilities.* All industries contain a variety of important competitive capabilities related to product innovation, production capabilities, distribution capabilities, or marketing prowess.

- *Profitability relative to competitors.* Above-average returns on investment and large profit margins relative to rivals are usually accurate indicators of competitive advantage.

After settling on a set of competitive strength measures that are well matched to the circumstances of the various business units, weights indicating each

TABLE 8.2

Calculating Weighted Competitive Strength Scores for a Diversified Company's Business Units

Rating scale: 1 = Very weak; 10 = Very strong

Competitive Strength Measure	Importance Weight	Business A in Industry A Rating/Score	Business B in Industry B Rating/Score	Business C in Industry C Rating/Score	Business D in Industry D Rating/Score
Relative market share	0.15	10/1.50	1/0.15	6/0.90	2/0.30
Costs relative to competitors' costs	0.20	7/1.40	2/0.40	5/1.00	3/0.60
Ability to match or beat rivals on key product attributes	0.05	9/0.45	4/0.20	8/0.40	4/0.20
Ability to benefit from strategic fit with sister businesses	0.20	8/1.60	4/0.80	4/0.80	2/0.60
Bargaining leverage with suppliers/ buyers; caliber of alliances	0.05	9/0.45	3/0.15	6/0.30	2/0.10
Brand image and reputation	0.10	9/0.90	2/0.20	7/0.70	5/0.50
Competitively valuable capabilities	0.15	7/1.05	2/0.30	5/0.75	3/0.45
Profitability relative to competitors	0.10	5/0.50	1/0.10	4/0.40	4/0.40
Sum of the assigned weights	1.00				
Overall weighted competitive strength scores		7.85	2.30	5.25	3.15

measure's importance need to be assigned. As in the assignment of weights to industry attractiveness measures, the importance weights must add up to 1.0. Each business unit is then rated on each of the chosen strength measures, using a rating scale of 1 to 10 (where 10 signifies competitive *strength* and a rating of 1 signifies competitive *weakness*). If the available information is too skimpy to confidently assign a rating value to a business unit on a particular strength measure, then it is usually best to use a score of 5. Weighted strength ratings are calculated by multiplying the business unit's rating on each strength measure by the assigned weight. For example, a strength score of 6 times a weight of 0.15 gives a weighted strength rating of 0.90. The sum of weighted ratings across all the strength measures provides a quantitative measure of a business unit's overall market strength and competitive standing. Table 8.2 provides sample calculations of competitive strength ratings for four businesses.

Using a Nine-Cell Matrix to Evaluate the Strength of a Diversified Company's Business Lineup   The industry attractiveness and business strength scores can be used to portray the strategic positions of each business in a diversified company. Industry attractiveness is plotted on the vertical axis and competitive strength on the horizontal axis. A nine-cell grid emerges from dividing the vertical axis into three regions (high, medium, and low attractiveness) and the horizontal axis into three regions (strong, average, and weak competitive strength). As shown in Figure 8.3, high attractiveness is associated with scores of 6.7 or greater on a rating scale of 1 to 10, medium attractiveness to scores of 3.3 to 6.7, and low attractiveness to scores below 3.3. Likewise, high competitive strength is defined as a score greater than 6.7, average strength as scores of 3.3 to 6.7, and low strength as scores below 3.3. *Each business unit is plotted on the nine-cell matrix according to its overall attractiveness and strength scores, and then shown as a "bubble."* The size of each bubble is scaled to what percentage of revenues the business generates relative to total corporate revenues. The bubbles in Figure 8.3 were located on the grid using the four industry attractiveness scores from Table 8.1 and the strength scores for the four business units in Table 8.2.

The locations of the business units on the attractiveness–competitive strength matrix provide valuable guidance in deploying corporate resources.

FIGURE 8.3   **A Nine-Cell Industry Attractiveness–Competitive Strength Matrix**

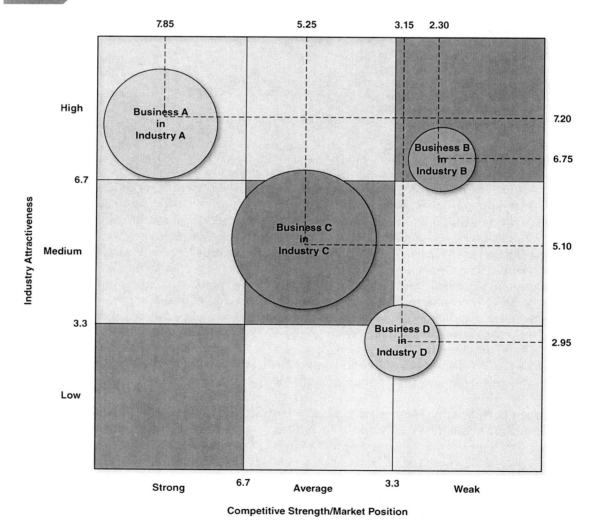

Note: Circle sizes are scaled to reflect the percentage of companywide revenues generated by the business unit.

In general, *a diversified company's best prospects for good overall performance involve concentrating corporate resources on business units having the greatest competitive strength and industry attractiveness.* Businesses plotted in the three cells in the upper left portion of the attractiveness–competitive strength matrix have both favorable industry attractiveness and competitive strength and should receive a high investment priority. Business units plotted in these three cells (such as business A in Figure 8.3) are referred to as "grow and build" businesses because of their capability to drive future increases in shareholder value.

Next in priority come businesses positioned in the three diagonal cells stretching from the lower left to the upper right (businesses B and C in Figure 8.3). Such businesses usually merit medium or intermediate priority in the parent's resource allocation ranking. However, some businesses in the medium-priority diagonal cells may have brighter or dimmer prospects than others. For example, a small business in the upper right cell of the matrix (like business B), despite being in a highly attractive industry, may occupy too weak a competitive position in its industry to justify the investment and resources needed to turn it into a strong market contender. If, however, a business in the upper right cell has attractive opportunities for rapid growth and a good potential for winning a much stronger market position over time, management may designate it as a grow and build business—the strategic objective here would be to move the business leftward in the attractiveness–competitive strength matrix over time.

Businesses in the three cells in the lower right corner of the matrix (business D in Figure 8.3) typically are weak performers and have the lowest claim on corporate resources. Such businesses are typically good candidates for being divested or else managed in a manner calculated to squeeze out the maximum cash flows from operations. The cash flows from low-performing/low-potential businesses can then be diverted to financing expansion of business units with greater market opportunities. In exceptional cases where a business located in the three lower right cells is nonetheless fairly profitable or has the potential for good earnings and return on investment, the business merits retention and the allocation of sufficient resources to achieve better performance.

The nine-cell attractiveness–competitive strength matrix provides clear, strong logic for why a diversified company needs to consider both industry attractiveness and business strength in allocating resources and investment capital to its different businesses. A good case can be made for concentrating resources in those businesses that enjoy higher degrees of attractiveness and competitive strength, being very selective in making investments in businesses with intermediate positions on the grid, and withdrawing resources from businesses that are lower in attractiveness and strength unless they offer exceptional profit or cash flow potential.

Step 3: Determining the Competitive Value of Strategic Fit in Multibusiness Companies

The potential for competitively important strategic fit is central to making conclusions about the effectiveness of a company's related diversification strategy. This step can be bypassed for diversified companies whose businesses are all unrelated (because, by design, no cross-business strategic fit is present). Checking the competitive advantage potential of cross-business strategic fit involves evaluating how much benefit a diversified company can gain from value chain matchups that present:

> The greater the value of cross-business strategic fit in enhancing a company's performance in the marketplace or the bottom line, the more powerful is its strategy of related diversification.

1. Opportunities to combine the performance of certain activities, thereby reducing costs and capturing economies of scope.
2. Opportunities to transfer skills, technology, or intellectual capital from one business to another.
3. Opportunities to share use of a well-respected brand name across multiple product and/or service categories.

But more than just strategic-fit identification is needed. The real test is what competitive value can be generated from this fit. To what extent can cost savings be realized? How much competitive value will come from cross-business transfer of skills, technology, or intellectual capital? Will transferring a potent brand name to the products of sibling businesses grow sales significantly? Absent significant strategic fit and dedicated company efforts to capture the benefits, one has to be skeptical about the potential for a diversified company's businesses to perform better together than apart.

Step 4: Evaluating Resource Fit

The businesses in a diversified company's lineup need to exhibit good resource fit. **Resource fit** exists when (1) businesses, individually, strengthen a company's overall mix of resources and capabilities and (2) the parent company has sufficient resources that add customer value to support its entire group of businesses without spreading itself too thin.

> **CORE CONCEPT**
>
> A diversified company exhibits **resource fit** when its businesses add to a company's overall mix of resources and capabilities and when the parent company has sufficient resources to support its entire group of businesses without spreading itself too thin.

> **CORE CONCEPT**
>
> A strong **internal capital market** allows a diversified company to add value by shifting capital from business units generating *free cash flow* to those needing additional capital to expand and realize their growth potential.

Financial Resource Fit   One important dimension of resource fit concerns whether a diversified company can generate the internal cash flows sufficient to fund the capital requirements of its businesses, pay its dividends, meet its debt obligations, and otherwise remain financially healthy. While additional capital can usually be raised in financial markets, it is also important for a diversified firm to have a healthy **internal capital market** that can support the financial requirements of its business lineup. The greater the extent to which a diversified company is able to fund investment in its businesses through internally generated free cash flows rather than from equity issues or borrowing, the more powerful its financial resource fit and the less dependent the firm is on external financial resources.

A *portfolio approach* to ensuring financial fit among the firm's businesses is based on the fact that different businesses have different cash flow and investment characteristics. For example, business units in rapidly growing industries are often **cash hogs**—so labeled because the cash flows they generate from internal operations aren't big enough to fund their expansion. To keep pace with rising buyer demand, rapid-growth businesses frequently need sizable annual capital infusions—for new facilities and equipment, for technology improvements, and for additional working capital to support inventory expansion. Because a cash hog's financial resources must be provided by the corporate parent, corporate managers have to decide whether it makes good financial and strategic sense to keep pouring new money into a cash hog business.

> **CORE CONCEPT**
>
> A **cash hog** generates operating cash flows that are too small to fully fund its operations and growth; a cash hog must receive cash infusions from outside sources to cover its working capital and investment requirements.

In contrast, business units with leading market positions in mature industries may be **cash cows**—businesses that generate substantial cash surpluses over what is needed to adequately fund their operations. Market leaders in slow-growth industries often generate sizable positive cash flows *over and above what is needed for growth and reinvestment* because the slow-growth nature of their industry often entails relatively modest annual investment requirements. Cash cows, though not always attractive from a growth standpoint, are valuable businesses from a financial resource perspective. The surplus cash flows they generate can be used to pay corporate dividends, finance acquisitions, and provide funds for investing in the company's promising cash hogs. It makes good financial and strategic sense for diversified companies to keep cash cows in healthy condition, fortifying and defending their market position to preserve their cash-generating capability over the long term and thereby have an ongoing source of financial resources to deploy elsewhere.

> **CORE CONCEPT**
>
> A **cash cow** generates operating cash flows over and above its internal requirements, thereby providing financial resources that may be used to invest in cash hogs, finance new acquisitions, fund share buyback programs, or pay dividends.

A diversified company has good financial resource fit when the excess cash generated by its cash cow businesses is sufficient to fund the investment requirements of promising cash hog businesses. Ideally, investing in promising cash hog businesses over time results in growing the hogs into self-supporting *star businesses* that have strong or market-leading competitive positions in attractive, high-growth markets and high levels of profitability. Star businesses are often the cash cows of the future—when the markets of star businesses begin to mature and their growth slows, their competitive strength should produce self-generated cash flows more than sufficient to cover their investment needs. The "success sequence" is thus cash hog to young star (but perhaps still a cash hog) to self-supporting star to cash cow.

If, however, a cash hog has questionable promise (because of either low industry attractiveness or a weak competitive position), then it becomes a logical candidate for divestiture. Aggressively investing in a cash hog with an uncertain future seldom makes sense because it requires the corporate parent to keep pumping more capital into the business with only a dim hope of turning the cash hog into a future star. Such businesses are a financial drain and fail the resource-fit test because they strain the corporate parent's ability to adequately fund its other businesses. Divesting a less-attractive cash hog business is usually the best alternative unless (1) it has highly valuable strategic fit with other business units or (2) the capital infusions needed from the corporate parent are modest relative to the funds available, and (3) there's a decent chance of growing the business into a solid bottom-line contributor.

Aside from cash flow considerations, two other factors to consider in assessing the financial resource fit for businesses in a diversified firm's portfolio are:

- *Do individual businesses adequately contribute to achieving companywide performance targets?* A business exhibits poor financial fit if it soaks up a disproportionate share of the company's financial resources, while making subpar or insignificant contributions to the bottom line. Too many underperforming businesses reduce the company's overall performance and ultimately limit growth in shareholder value.

- *Does the corporation have adequate financial strength to fund its different businesses and maintain a healthy credit rating?* A diversified company's strategy fails the resource fit test when the resource needs of its portfolio unduly stretch the company's financial health and threaten to impair its credit rating. Many of the world's largest banks, including Royal Bank of Scotland, Citigroup, and HSBC, recently found themselves so undercapitalized and financially overextended that they were forced to sell some of their business assets to meet regulatory requirements and restore public confidence in their solvency.

Examining a Diversified Company's Nonfinancial Resource Fit

A diversified company must also ensure that the nonfinancial resource needs of its portfolio of businesses are met by its corporate capabilities. Just as a diversified company must avoid allowing an excessive number of cash hungry businesses to jeopardize its financial stability, it should also avoid adding to the business lineup in ways that overly stretch such nonfinancial resources as managerial talent, technology and information systems, and marketing support.

- *Does the company have or can it develop the specific resources and competitive capabilities needed to be successful in each of its businesses?*[11] Sometimes the resources a company has accumulated in its core business prove to be a poor match with the competitive capabilities needed to succeed in businesses into which it has diversified. For instance, BTR, a multibusiness company in Great Britain, discovered that the company's resources and managerial skills were quite well suited for parenting industrial manufacturing businesses but not for parenting its distribution businesses (National Tyre Services and Texas-based Summers Group). As a result, BTR decided to divest its distribution businesses and focus exclusively on diversifying around small industrial manufacturing.

> Resource fit extends beyond financial resources to include a good fit between the company's resources and core competencies and the key success factors of each industry it has diversified into.

- *Are the company's resources being stretched too thinly by the resource requirements of one or more of its businesses?* A diversified company has to guard against overtaxing its resources, a condition that can arise when (1) it goes on an acquisition spree and management is called upon to assimilate and oversee many new businesses very quickly or (2) when it lacks sufficient resource depth to do a creditable job of transferring skills and competencies from one of its businesses to another.

Step 5: Ranking Business Units and Setting a Priority for Resource Allocation

Once a diversified company's businesses have been evaluated from the standpoints of industry attractiveness, competitive strength, strategic fit, and resource fit, the next step is to use this information to rank the performance prospects of the businesses from best to worst. Such rankings help top-level executives assign each business a priority for corporate resource support and new capital investment.

The locations of the different businesses in the nine-cell industry attractiveness/competitive strength matrix provide a solid basis for identifying high-opportunity businesses and low-opportunity businesses. Normally, competitively strong businesses in attractive industries have significantly better performance prospects than competitively weak businesses in unattractive industries. Also, normally, the revenue and earnings outlook for businesses in fast-growing businesses is better than for businesses in slow-growing businesses. As a rule, *business subsidiaries with the brightest profit and growth prospects, attractive positions in the nine-cell matrix, and solid strategic and resource fit should receive top priority for allocation of corporate resources.* However, in ranking the prospects of the different businesses from best to worst, it is usually wise to also consider each business's past performance as concerns sales growth, profit growth, contribution to company earnings, return on capital invested in the business, and cash flow from operations. While past performance is not always a reliable predictor of future performance, it does signal whether a business already has good to excellent performance or has problems to overcome.

Allocating Financial Resources   Figure 8.4 shows the chief strategic and financial options for allocating a diversified company's financial resources. Divesting businesses with the weakest future prospects and businesses that lack adequate strategic fit and/or resource fit is one of the best ways of generating additional funds for redeployment to businesses with better opportunities and better strategic and resource fit. Free cash flows from cash cow businesses also add to the pool of funds that can be usefully redeployed. *Ideally, a diversified company will have sufficient financial resources to strengthen or grow its existing businesses, make any new acquisitions that are desirable, fund other promising business opportunities, pay off existing debt, and periodically increase dividend payments to shareholders and/or repurchase shares of stock.* But, as a practical matter, a company's financial resources are limited. Thus, for top executives to make the best use of the available funds, they must steer resources to those businesses with the best opportunities and performance prospects and allocate little if any resources to businesses with marginal or dim prospects—this is why ranking the performance prospects of the various businesses from best to worst is so crucial. Strategic uses of

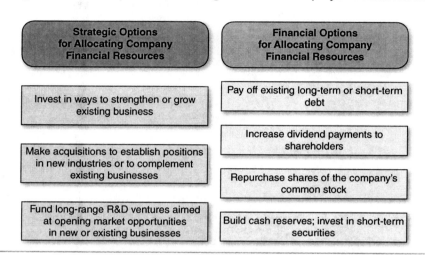

FIGURE 8.4 The Chief Strategic and Financial Options for Allocating a Diversified Company's Financial Resources

corporate financial resources (see Figure 8.4) should usually take precedence unless there is a compelling reason to strengthen the firm's balance sheet or better reward shareholders.

Step 6: Crafting New Strategic Moves to Improve the Overall Corporate Performance

LO5 Understand a diversified company's four main corporate strategy options for solidifying its diversification strategy and improving company performance.

The conclusions flowing from the five preceding analytical steps set the agenda for crafting strategic moves to improve a diversified company's overall performance. The strategic options boil down to four broad categories of actions:

1. Sticking closely with the existing business lineup and pursuing the opportunities these businesses present.
2. Broadening the company's business scope by making new acquisitions in new industries.
3. Divesting some businesses and retrenching to a narrower base of business operations.
4. Restructuring the company's business lineup and putting a whole new face on the company's business makeup.

Sticking Closely with the Existing Business Lineup The option of sticking with the current business lineup makes sense when the company's present businesses offer attractive growth opportunities and can be counted on to generate good earnings and cash flows. As long as the company's set of existing businesses puts it in a good position for the future and these businesses have good strategic and/or resource fit, then rocking the boat with major changes in the company's business mix is usually unnecessary. Corporate executives can concentrate their attention on getting the best performance from each of the businesses, steering corporate resources into those areas of greatest potential and profitability. However, in the event that corporate executives are not entirely satisfied with the opportunities they see in the company's present set of businesses, they can opt for any of the three strategic alternatives listed in the following sections.

Broadening the Diversification Base   Diversified companies sometimes find it desirable to add to the diversification base for any one of the same reasons a single-business company might pursue initial diversification. Sluggish growth in revenues or profits, vulnerability to seasonality or recessionary influences, potential for transferring resources and capabilities to other related businesses, or unfavorable driving forces facing core businesses are all reasons management of a diversified company might choose to broaden diversification. An additional, and often very important, motivating factor for adding new businesses is to complement and strengthen the market position and competitive capabilities of one or more of its present businesses. Procter & Gamble's acquisition of Gillette strengthened and extended P&G's reach into personal care and household products—Gillette's businesses included Oral-B toothbrushes, Gillette razors and razor blades, Duracell batteries, Braun shavers and small appliances (coffeemakers, mixers, hair dryers, and electric toothbrushes), and toiletries (Right Guard, Foamy, Soft & Dry, White Rain, and Dry Idea).

Divesting Some Businesses and Retrenching to a Narrower Diversification Base   A number of diversified firms have had difficulty managing a diverse group of businesses and have elected to get out of some of them. Selling a business outright to another company is far and away the most frequently used option for divesting a business. Ford divested its Jaguar and Land Rover brands to the Tata Group of India in 2009

> Focusing corporate resources on a few core and mostly related businesses avoids the mistake of diversifying so broadly that resources and management attention are stretched too thin.

and then sold its Volvo brand to a Chinese conglomerate in 2010. But sometimes a business selected for divestiture has ample resources and capabilities to compete successfully on its own. In such cases, a corporate parent may elect to spin off the unwanted business as a financially and managerially independent company, either by selling shares to the public via an initial public offering or by distributing shares in the new company to shareholders of the corporate parent. Online travel company Expedia, Inc., spun off Trip Advisor as a public company in 2011, distributing shares to its shareholders. Expedia itself was spun off from IAC/InterActiveCorp in 2005.

Retrenching to a narrower diversification base is usually undertaken when top management concludes that its diversification strategy has ranged too far afield and that the company can improve long-term performance by concentrating on building stronger positions in a smaller number of core businesses and industries. But there are other important reasons for divesting one or more of a company's present businesses. Sometimes divesting a business has to be considered because market conditions in a once-attractive industry have badly deteriorated. A business can become a prime candidate for divestiture because it lacks adequate strategic or resource fit, because it is a cash hog with questionable long-term potential, or because it is weakly positioned in its industry with little prospect of earning a decent return on investment. Sometimes a company acquires businesses that, down the road, just do not work out as expected even though management has tried all it can think of to make them profitable. Other business units, despite adequate financial performance, may not mesh as well with the rest of the firm as was originally thought. For instance, PepsiCo divested its group of fast-food restaurant businesses to focus its resources on its core soft drink and snack foods businesses, where its resources and capabilities could add more value.

Evidence indicates that pruning businesses and narrowing a firm's diversification base improves corporate performance.[12] Corporate parents often end up selling businesses too late and at too low a price, sacrificing shareholder value.[13] A useful guide to determine whether or when to divest a business subsidiary is to ask, "If we were not in this business today, would we want to get into it now?"[14] When the answer is no or probably not, divestiture should be considered. Another signal that a business should become a divestiture candidate is whether it is worth more to another company than to the present parent; in such cases, shareholders would be well served if the company were to sell the business and collect a premium price from the buyer for whom the business is a valuable fit.[15]

Selling a business outright to another company is far and away the most frequently used option for divesting a business. But sometimes a business selected for divestiture has ample resources to compete successfully on its own. In such cases, a corporate parent may elect to spin the unwanted business off as a financially and managerially independent company, either by selling shares to the investing public via an initial public offering or by distributing shares in the new company to existing shareholders of the corporate parent.

Broadly Restructuring the Business Lineup through a Mix of Divestitures and New Acquisitions

Corporate restructuring strategies involve divesting some businesses and acquiring others so as to put a new face on the company's business lineup. Performing radical surgery on a company's group of businesses is an appealing corporate strategy when its financial performance is squeezed or eroded by:

> **CORE CONCEPT**
>
> **Corporate restructuring** involves radically altering the business lineup by divesting businesses that lack strategic fit or are poor performers and acquiring new businesses that offer better promise for enhancing shareholder value.

- Too many businesses in slow-growth, declining, low-margin, or otherwise unattractive industries.

- Too many competitively weak businesses.

- An excessive debt burden with interest costs that eat deeply into profitability.

- Ill-chosen acquisitions that haven't lived up to expectations.

Candidates for divestiture in a corporate restructuring effort typically include not only weak or up-and-down performers or those in unattractive industries but also business units that lack strategic fit with the businesses to be retained, businesses that are cash hogs or that lack other types of resource fit, and businesses incompatible with the company's revised diversification strategy (even though they may be profitable or in an attractive industry).

CONCEPTS & CONNECTIONS 8.1

KRAFT FOODS' CORPORATE RESTRUCTURING PLAN TO PURSUE GROWTH AND BOOST SHAREHOLDER VALUE

In 2012, Kraft Foods, the 90-year-old darling of the consumer packaged goods industry, moved to improve its long-term performance by *restructuring* the corporation—the latest move in a series by CEO Irene Rosenfeld, who was brought in to turn around the company's performance. In addition to trimming operations, the restructuring plan called for dividing the enterprise into two separate units: a $32 billion fast-growing global snacks business that included Oreo and Cadbury (the British confectionary acquired in 2010), and a North American grocery unit that included Kraft Macaroni and Cheese, Oscar Mayer, and other nonsnack brands. With this radical new operational structure in place, Kraft hoped to improve its ability to focus on new opportunities and pursue profitable growth.

Managing these two large and very different businesses jointly had made it difficult for Kraft to act nimbly and adapt to changing market conditions. It also inhibited the company from executing new strategies free from significant portfolio-wide considerations. In announcing her intention to split the company in September 2011, CEO Irene Rosenfeld said, "Simply

put, we have now reached a point where North American grocery and global snacks will each benefit from standing on its own and focusing on its unique drivers for success." She noted that as separate businesses, "each will have the leadership, resources, and mandate to realize its full potential."

Before the split, Kraft undertook additional restructuring efforts in its U.S. sales operations, including reducing the number of management centers and selling some underperforming brands. Although in refashioning the company Kraft loses some of the operational benefits it enjoyed as a single entity, managers and investors hope the move will ultimately improve the company's ability to sustain profitable growth and increase shareholder value.

Developed with Maximilian A. Pinto.

Sources: Sam Webb, "New Reality Makes Kraft Split Vital," *Food Global News*, September 2011; E. J. Schultz, "Could Kraft Split Be a Blueprint for Blue Chips?" *Advertising Age* 82, no. 29 (August 8, 2011); www.nytimes.com/2007/02/21/business/21kraft.html (accessed March 2, 2012); http://stocks.investopedia.com/stock-analysis/2012/Cozying-Up-To-Kraft-KFT-CPB-K-HNZ0227.aspx#axzz1nzOMjDex (accessed March 2, 2012).

As businesses are divested, corporate restructuring generally involves aligning the remaining business units into groups with the best strategic fit and then redeploying the cash flows from the divested business to either pay down debt or make new acquisitions.

Over the past decade, corporate restructuring has become a popular strategy at many diversified companies, especially those that had diversified broadly into many different industries and lines of business. VF Corporation, maker of North Face and other popular "lifestyle" apparel brands, has used a restructuring strategy to provide its shareholders with returns that are more than five times greater than shareholder returns for competing apparel makers. Since its acquisition and turnaround of North Face in 2000, VF has spent nearly $5 billion to acquire 19 additional businesses, including about $2 billion in 2011 for Timberland. New apparel brands acquired by VF Corporation include 7 For All Mankind sportswear, Vans skateboard shoes, Nautica, John Varvatos, Reef surf wear, and Lucy athletic wear. By 2012, VF Corporation had become one of the most profitable apparel and footwear companies in the world, with net earnings of nearly $1.1 billion on revenues of $10.9 billion. It was listed as number 277 on *Fortune*'s 2012 list of the 500 largest U.S. companies. Concepts & Connections 8.1 discusses how Kraft Foods underwent a major restructuring that split the corporation into two companies in an attempt to boost shareholder value.

KEY POINTS

1. The purpose of diversification is to build shareholder value. Diversification builds shareholder value when a diversified group of businesses can perform better under the auspices of a single corporate parent than they would as independent, stand-alone businesses—the goal is to achieve not just a $1 + 1 = 2$ result but rather to realize important $1 + 1 = 3$ performance benefits. Whether getting into a new business has potential to enhance shareholder value hinges on whether a company's entry into that business can pass the attractiveness test, the cost-of-entry test, and the better-off test.

2. Entry into new businesses can take any of three forms: acquisition, internal development, or joint venture/strategic partnership. Each has its pros and cons, but acquisition usually provides quickest entry into a new entry; internal development takes the longest to produce home-run results; and joint venture/strategic partnership tends to be the least durable.

3. There are two fundamental approaches to diversification—into related businesses and into unrelated businesses. The rationale for *related* diversification is based on cross-business *strategic fit:* Diversify into businesses with strategic fit along their respective value chains, capitalize on strategic-fit relationships to gain competitive advantage, and then use competitive advantage to achieve the desired $1 + 1 = 3$ impact on shareholder value.

4. *Unrelated diversification* strategies surrender the competitive advantage potential of strategic fit. Given the absence of cross-business strategic fit, the task of building shareholder value through a strategy of unrelated diversification hinges on the ability of the parent company to (1) do a superior job of identifying and acquiring new businesses that can produce consistently good earnings and returns on investment; (2) do an excellent job of negotiating favorable acquisition prices; and (3) do such a good job of overseeing and parenting the collection of businesses that they perform at a higher level than they would on their own efforts. The greater the number of businesses a company has diversified into and the more diverse these businesses are, the harder it is for corporate executives to select capable managers to run each business, know when the major strategic proposals of business units are sound, or decide on a wise course of recovery when a business unit stumbles.

5. Evaluating a company's diversification strategy is a six-step process:

    *   Step 1: *Evaluate the long-term attractiveness of the industries into which the firm has diversified.* Determining industry attractiveness involves developing a list of industry attractiveness measures, each of which might have a different importance weight.

    *   Step 2: *Evaluate the relative competitive strength of each of the company's business units.* The purpose of rating each business's competitive strength is to gain clear understanding of which businesses are strong contenders in their industries, which are weak contenders, and the underlying reasons for their strength or weakness. The conclusions about industry attractiveness can be joined with the conclusions about competitive strength by drawing an industry attractiveness–competitive strength matrix that helps identify the prospects of each business and what priority each business should be given in allocating corporate resources and investment capital.

    *   Step 3: *Check for cross-business strategic fit.* A business is more attractive strategically when it has value chain relationships with sibling business units

that offer the potential to (1) realize economies of scope or cost-saving efficiencies; (2) transfer technology, skills, know-how, or other resources and capabilities from one business to another; and/or (3) leverage use of a well-known and trusted brand name. Cross-business strategic fit represents a significant avenue for producing competitive advantage beyond what any one business can achieve on its own.

- Step 4: *Check whether the firm's resources fit the requirements of its present business lineup.* Resource fit exists when (1) businesses, individually, strengthen a company's overall mix of resources and capabilities and (2) a company has sufficient resources to support its entire group of businesses without spreading itself too thin. One important test of financial resource fit involves determining whether a company has ample cash cows and not too many cash hogs.

- Step 5: *Rank the performance prospects of the businesses from best to worst and determine what the corporate parent's priority should be in allocating resources to its various businesses.* The most important considerations in judging business-unit performance are sales growth, profit growth, contribution to company earnings, cash flow characteristics, and the return on capital invested in the business. Normally, strong business units in attractive industries should head the list for corporate resource support.

- Step 6: *Crafting new strategic moves to improve overall corporate performance.* This step entails using the results of the preceding analysis as the basis for selecting one of four different strategic paths for improving a diversified company's performance: *(a)* Stick closely with the existing business lineup and pursue opportunities presented by these businesses, *(b)* broaden the scope of diversification by entering additional industries, *(c)* retrench to a narrower scope of diversification by divesting poorly performing businesses, and *(d)* broadly restructure the business lineup with multiple divestitures and/or acquisitions.

 ## ASSURANCE OF LEARNING EXERCISES

1. See if you can identify the value chain relationships that make the businesses of the following companies related in competitively relevant ways. In particular, you should consider whether there are cross-business opportunities for *(a)* transferring competitively valuable resources, expertise, technological know-how and other capabilities, *(b)* cost sharing where value chain activities can be combined, and/or *(c)* leveraging use of a well-respected brand name.

LO1, LO2, LO3, LO4

connect

OSI Restaurant Partners

- Outback Steakhouse.
- Carrabba's Italian Grill.
- Roy's Restaurant (Hawaiian fusion cuisine).
- Bonefish Grill (market-fresh fine seafood).
- Fleming's Prime Steakhouse & Wine Bar.
- Lee Roy Selmon's (Southern comfort food).
- Cheeseburger in Paradise.
- Blue Coral Seafood & Spirits (fine seafood).

L'Oréal

- Maybelline, Lancôme, Helena Rubinstein, Kiehl's, Garner, and Shu Uemura cosmetics.
- L'Oréal and Soft Sheen/Carson hair care products.
- Redken, Matrix, L'Oréal Professional, and Kerastase Paris professional hair care and skin care products.
- Ralph Lauren and Giorgio Armani fragrances.
- Biotherm skin care products.
- La Roche–Posay and Vichy Laboratories dermocosmetics.

Johnson & Johnson

- Baby products (powder, shampoo, oil, lotion).
- Band-Aids and other first-aid products.
- Women's health and personal care products (Stayfree, Carefree, Sure & Natural).
- Neutrogena and Aveeno skin care products.
- Nonprescription drugs (Tylenol, Motrin, Pepcid AC, Mylanta, Monistat).
- Prescription drugs.
- Prosthetic and other medical devices.
- Surgical and hospital products.
- Acuvue contact lenses.

LO1, LO2, LO3, LO4

2. Peruse the business group listings for United Technologies shown below and listed at its website (www.utc.com). How would you characterize the company's corporate strategy? Related diversification, unrelated diversification, or a combination related-unrelated diversification strategy? Explain your answer.

Carrier—the world's largest provider of air-conditioning, heating, and refrigeration solutions.

Hamilton Sundstrand—technologically advanced aerospace and industrial products.

Otis—the world's leading manufacturer, installer, and maintainer of elevators, escalators, and moving walkways.

Pratt & Whitney—designs, manufactures, services, and supports aircraft engines, industrial gas turbines, and space propulsion systems.

Sikorsky—a world leader in helicopter design, manufacture, and service.

UTC Fire & Security—fire and security systems developed for commercial, industrial, and residential customers.

UTC Power—a full-service provider of environmentally advanced power solutions.

LO1, LO2, LO3, LO4, LO5

connect

3. ITT is a technology-oriented engineering and manufacturing company with the following business divisions and products:

Industrial Process Division—industrial pumps, valves, and monitoring and control systems; aftermarket services for the chemical, oil and gas, mining, pulp and paper, power, and biopharmaceutical markets.

Motion Technologies Division—durable brake pads, shock absorbers, and damping technologies for the automotive and rail markets.

Interconnect Solutions—connectors and fittings for the production of automobiles, aircraft, railcars and locomotives, oil field equipment, medical equipment, and industrial equipment.

Control Technologies—energy absorption and vibration dampening equipment, transducers and regulators, and motion controls used in the production of robotics, medical equipment, automobiles, sub-sea equipment, industrial equipment, aircraft, and military vehicles.

Based on the above listing, would you say that ITT's business lineup reflects a strategy of related diversification, unrelated diversification, or a combination of related and unrelated diversification? What benefits are generated from any strategic fit existing between ITT's businesses? Also, what types of companies should ITT consider acquiring that might improve shareholder value? Justify your answer.

 ## EXERCISES FOR SIMULATION PARTICIPANTS

1. In the event that your company had the opportunity to diversify into other products or businesses of your choosing, would you opt to pursue related diversification, unrelated diversification, or a combination of both? Explain why.
   LO1, LO2, LO3

2. What specific resources and capabilities does your company possess that would make it attractive to diversify into related businesses? Indicate what kinds of strategic fit benefits could be captured by transferring these resources and competitive capabilities to newly acquired related businesses.
   LO1, LO2

3. If your company opted to pursue a strategy of related diversification, what industries or product categories could your company diversify into that would allow it to achieve economies of scope? Name at least two or three such industries/product categories and indicate the specific kinds of cost savings that might accrue from entry into each of these businesses/product categories.
   LO1, LO2

4. If your company opted to pursue a strategy of related diversification, what industries or product categories could your company diversify into that would allow your company to capitalize on using your company's present brand name and corporate image to good advantage in these newly entered businesses or product categories? Name at least two or three such industries or product categories and indicate *the specific benefits* that might be captured by transferring your company's brand name to each of these other businesses/product categories.
   LO1, LO2, LO3, LO4, LO5

   Would you prefer to pursue a strategy of related or unrelated diversification? Why?

 ## ENDNOTES

1. Constantinos C. Markides, "To Diversify or Not to Diversify," *Harvard Business Review* 75, no. 6 (November–December 1997).

2. Michael E. Porter, "From Competitive Advantage to Corporate Strategy," *Harvard Business Review* 45, no. 3 (May–June 1987).

3. Michael E. Porter, *Competitive Strategy: Techniques for Analyzing Industries and Competitors* (New York: Free Press, 1980).

4. Yves L. Doz and Gary Hamel, *Alliance Advantage: The Art of Creating Value through Partnering* (Boston: Harvard Business School Press, 1998).

5. Michael E. Porter, *Competitive Advantage* (New York: Free Press, 1985); and Constantinos C. Markides and Peter J. Williamson, "Corporate Diversification and Organization Structure: A Resource-Based View," *Academy of Management Journal* 39, no. 2 (April 1996).

6. Jeanne M. Liedtka, "Collaboration across Lines of Business for Competitive Advantage," *Academy of Management Executive* 10, no. 2 (May 1996).

7. Kathleen M. Eisenhardt and D. Charles Galunic, "Coevolving: At Last, a Way to Make Synergies Work," *Harvard Business Review* 78, no. 1 (January–February 2000); and Constantinos C. Markides and Peter J. Williamson, "Related Diversification, Core Competencies and Corporate Performance," *Strategic Management Journal* 15 (Summer 1994).

8. A. Campbell, M. Goold, and M. Alexander, "Corporate Strategy: The Quest for Parenting Advantage," *Harvard Business Review* 73, no. 2 (March–April 1995); and Cynthia A. Montgomery and Birger Wernerfelt, "Diversification, Ricardian Rents, and Tobin-Q," *RAND Journal of Economics* 19, no. 4 (1988).

9. Patricia L. Anslinger and Thomas E. Copeland, "Growth through Acquisitions: A Fresh Look," *Harvard Business Review* 74, no. 1 (January–February 1996).

10. Lawrence G. Franko, "The Death of Diversification? The Focusing of the World's Industrial Firms, 1980–2000," *Business Horizons* 47, no. 4 (July–August 2004).

11. Andrew Campbell, Michael Gould, and Marcus Alexander, "Corporate Strategy: The Quest for Parenting Advantage," *Harvard Business Review* 73, no. 2 (March–April 1995).

12. Constantinos C. Markides, "Diversification, Restructuring, and Economic Performance," *Strategic Management Journal* 16 (February 1995).

13. Lee Dranikoff, Tim Koller, and Antoon Schneider, "Divestiture: Strategy's Missing Link," *Harvard Business Review* 80, no. 5 (May 2002).

14. Peter F. Drucker, *Management: Tasks, Responsibilities, Practices* (New York: Harper & Row, 1974).

15. David J. Collis and Cynthia A. Montgomery, "Creating Corporate Advantage," *Harvard Business Review* 76, no. 3 (May–June 1998).

Ethics, Corporate Social Responsibility, Environmental Sustainability, and Strategy

LEARNING OBJECTIVES

LO1 Understand why the standards of ethical behavior in business are no different from ethical standards in general.

LO2 Recognize conditions that give rise to unethical business strategies and behavior.

LO3 Gain an understanding of the costs of business ethics failures.

LO4 Learn the concepts of corporate social responsibility and environmental sustainability and how companies balance these duties with economic responsibilities to shareholders.

Clearly, a company has a responsibility to make a profit and grow the business, but just as clearly, a company and its personnel also have a duty to obey the law and play by the rules of fair competition. But does a company have a duty to go beyond legal requirements and operate according to the ethical norms of the societies in which it operates? And does it have a duty or obligation to contribute to the betterment of society independent of the needs and preferences of the customers it serves? Should a company display a social conscience and devote a portion of its resources to bettering society? Should its strategic initiatives be screened for possible negative effects on future generations of the world's population?

This chapter focuses on whether a company, in the course of trying to craft and execute a strategy that delivers value to both customers and shareholders, also has a duty to (1) act in an ethical manner, (2) demonstrate socially responsible behavior by being a committed corporate citizen, and (3) adopt business practices that conserve natural resources, protect the interest of future generations, and preserve the well-being of the planet.

What Do We Mean by *Business Ethics?*

LO1 Understand why the standards of ethical behavior in business are no different from ethical standards in general.

Business ethics is the application of ethical principles and standards to the actions and decisions of business organizations and the conduct of their personnel.[1] Ethical principles in business are not materially different from ethical principles in general because business actions have to be judged in the context of society's standards of right and wrong. There is not a special set of rules that businesspeople decide to apply to their own conduct. If dishonesty is considered unethical and immoral, then dishonest behavior in business—whether it relates to customers, suppliers, employees, or shareholders—qualifies as equally unethical and immoral. If being ethical entails adhering to generally accepted norms about conduct that is right and wrong, then managers must consider such norms when crafting and executing strategy.

> ### CORE CONCEPT
> **Business ethics** involves the application of general ethical principles to the actions and decisions of businesses and the conduct of their personnel.

While most company managers are careful to ensure that a company's strategy is within the bounds of what is legal, evidence indicates they are not always so careful to ensure that their strategies are within the bounds of what is considered ethical. In recent years, there have been revelations of ethical misconduct on the part of managers at such companies as Enron, Tyco International, HealthSouth, Adelphia, Royal Dutch/Shell, Parmalat (an Italy-based food products company), Rite Aid, Mexican oil giant Pemex, AIG, Citigroup, several leading brokerage houses, mutual fund companies and investment banking firms, and a host of mortgage lenders. The consequences of crafting strategies that cannot pass the test of moral scrutiny are manifested in sharp drops in stock price that cost shareholders billions of dollars, devastating public relations hits, sizable fines, and criminal indictments and convictions of company executives.

Drivers of Unethical Strategies and Business Behavior

Apart from "the business of business is business, not ethics" kind of thinking apparent in recent high-profile business scandals, three other main drivers of unethical business behavior also stand out:[2]

> **LO2** Recognize conditions that give rise to unethical business strategies and behavior.

- *Overzealous pursuit of wealth and other selfish interests.* People who are obsessed with wealth accumulation, greed, power, status, and other selfish interests often push ethical principles aside in their quest for self-gain. Driven by their ambitions, they exhibit few qualms in skirting the rules or doing whatever is necessary to achieve their goals. The first and only priority of such corporate "bad apples" is to look out for their own best interests, and if climbing the ladder of success means having few scruples and ignoring the welfare of others, so be it. The U.S. government has been conducting a multiyear investigation of insider trading, the illegal practice of exchanging confidential information to gain an advantage in the stock market. Focusing on the hedge fund industry and nicknamed "Operation Perfect Hedge," the investigation has brought to light scores of violations and led to more than 60 guilty pleas or convictions by early 2012. Among the most prominent of those convicted was Raj Rajaratnam, the former head of Galleon Group, who was sentenced to 11 years in prison and fined $10 million. In January 2012, seven hedge fund managers, described as a "circle of friends who formed a criminal club," were charged with reaping nearly $62 million in illegal profits on trades of Dell Inc.[3]

- *Heavy pressures on company managers to meet or beat performance targets.* When key personnel find themselves scrambling to meet the quarterly and annual sales and profit expectations of investors and financial analysts or to hit other ambitious performance targets, they often feel enormous pressure to *do whatever it takes* to protect their reputation for delivering good results. As the pressure builds, they start stretching the rules further and further, until the limits of ethical conduct are overlooked.[4] Once people cross ethical boundaries to "meet or beat their numbers," the threshold for making more extreme ethical compromises becomes lower. In 2010, ATM maker Diebold, Inc., was fined $25 million for engaging in a fraudulent accounting scheme to inflate the company's earnings. Three of Diebold's former financial executives were also charged with manipulating the company's books to meet earnings forecasts.[5] More recently, an investigation into a decade-long cover-up of investment losses by the Japanese camera maker Olympus resulted in the 2012 arrest of seven executives on suspicion of violation of Japanese securities laws.

- *A company culture that puts profitability and good business performance ahead of ethical behavior.* When a company's culture spawns an ethically corrupt or amoral work climate, people have a company-approved license to ignore "what's right" and engage in most any behavior or employ most any strategy they think they can get away with. Such cultural norms as "everyone else does it" and "it is OK to bend the rules to get the job done" permeate the work environment. At such companies, ethically immoral or amoral people are certain to play down observance of ethical strategic actions and business conduct. Moreover, cultural pressures to utilize unethical means if circumstances become challenging can prompt otherwise honorable people to behave unethically. Enron's leaders created a culture that pressured company personnel to be innovative and aggressive in figuring out how to grow current earnings—regardless of the methods. Enron's annual "rank and yank" performance evaluation process, in which the lowest-ranking 15 to 20 percent of employees were let go, made it abundantly clear that bottom-line results were what mattered most. The name of the game at Enron became devising clever ways to boost revenues and earnings, even if this sometimes meant operating outside established policies. In fact, outside-the-lines behavior was celebrated if it generated profitable new business.

The Business Case for Ethical Strategies

LO3 Gain an understanding of the costs of business ethics failures.

While it is undoubtedly true that unethical business behavior may sometimes contribute to higher company profits (*so long as such behavior escapes public scrutiny*), deliberate pursuit of unethical strategies and tolerance of unethical conduct is a risky practice from both a shareholder perspective and a reputational standpoint. Figure 9.1 shows the wide-ranging costs a company can incur when unethical behavior is discovered and it is forced to make amends for its behavior. The more egregious a company's ethical violations, the higher are the costs and the bigger the damage to its reputation (and to the reputations of the company personnel involved). In high-profile instances, the costs of ethical misconduct can easily run into the hundreds of millions and even billions of dollars, especially if they provoke widespread public outrage and many people were harmed.

The fallout of ethical misconduct on the part of a company goes well beyond just the costs of making amends for the misdeeds. Buyers shun companies known for their shady behavior. Companies known to have engaged in unethical conduct have difficulty recruiting and retaining talented employees.[6] Most ethically upstanding people don't want to get entrapped in a compromising situation, nor do they want their personal reputations tarnished by the actions of an unsavory employer. A company's unethical behavior risks considerable damage to shareholders in the form of lost revenues, higher costs, lower profits, lower stock prices, and a diminished business reputation. To a significant degree, therefore, ethical strategies and ethical conduct are *good business*. Many companies have a code of ethics governing how they will conduct business—in the United States, the Sarbanes-Oxley Act, enacted in 2002, requires that

> Shareholders suffer major damage when a company's unethical behavior is discovered and punished. Making amends for unethical business conduct is costly, and it takes years to rehabilitate a tarnished company reputation.

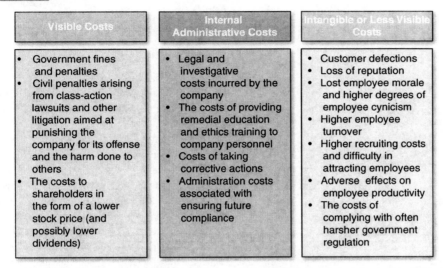

FIGURE 9.1   **The Costs Companies Incur When Ethical Wrongdoing Is Discovered and Punished**

Visible Costs	Internal Administrative Costs	Intangible or Less Visible Costs
• Government fines and penalties • Civil penalties arising from class-action lawsuits and other litigation aimed at punishing the company for its offense and the harm done to others • The costs to shareholders in the form of a lower stock price (and possibly lower dividends)	• Legal and investigative costs incurred by the company • The costs of providing remedial education and ethics training to company personnel • Costs of taking corrective actions • Administration costs associated with ensuring future compliance	• Customer defections • Loss of reputation • Lost employee morale and higher degrees of employee cynicism • Higher employee turnover • Higher recruiting costs and difficulty in attracting employees • Adverse effects on employee productivity • The costs of complying with often harsher government regulation

Source: Adapted from Terry Thomas, John R. Schermerhorn, and John W. Dienhart, "Strategic Leadership of Ethical Behavior," *Academy of Management Executive* 18, no. 2 (May 2004), p. 58.

companies whose stock is publicly traded have a code of ethics or else explain in writing to the Securities and Exchange Commission why they do not.

Ensuring a Strong Commitment to Business Ethics in Companies with International Operations

Notions of right and wrong, fair and unfair, moral and immoral, ethical and unethical are present in all societies, organizations, and individuals. But there are three schools of thought about the extent to which the ethical standards travel across cultures and whether multinational companies can apply the same set of ethical standards in all of the locations where they operate. Concepts & Connections 9.1 describes the difficulties Apple has faced in trying to enforce a common set of ethical standards across its vast global supplier network.

The School of Ethical Universalism

According to the school of **ethical universalism**, some concepts of what is right and what is wrong are *universal* and transcend most all cultures, societies, and religions.[7] For instance, being truthful strikes a chord of what's right in the peoples of all nations. Ethical norms considered universal by many ethicists include honesty, trustworthiness, respecting the rights of others, practicing the Golden Rule, and avoiding

CORE CONCEPT

According to the school of **ethical universalism,** the same standards of what's ethical and what's unethical resonate with peoples of most societies regardless of local traditions and cultural norms; hence, common ethical standards can be used to judge employee conduct in a variety of country markets and cultural circumstances.

CONCEPTS & CONNECTIONS 9.1

APPLE'S CHALLENGES IN ENFORCING ITS SUPPLIER CODE OF CONDUCT

Apple requires its suppliers to comply with the company's Supplier Code of Conduct as a condition of being awarded contracts. To ensure compliance, Apple has a monitoring program that includes audits of supplier factories, corrective action plans, and verification measures. In the company's 26-page 2012 progress report on supplier responsibility, Apple reported that in 2011 it conducted 229 audits of supplier facilities in such countries as China, the Czech Republic, Malaysia, the Philippines, Singapore, South Korea, Taiwan, Thailand, and the United States. More than 100 of these audits were first-time audits.

Apple distinguishes among the seriousness of infractions, designating "core violations" as those that go directly against the core principles of its Supplier Code of Conduct and must be remedied immediately. During the 2011 audits, core violations were discovered in 35 facilities, including cases of underage labor, excessive recruitment fees, improper hazardous waste disposal, and deliberately falsified audit records. Apple responded by ensuring that immediate corrective actions were taken, placing violators on probation, and planning to audit them again in a year's time.

While Apple's final-assembly manufacturers had high compliance scores for most categories, suppliers did not fare very well in terms of working hours. At 93 of the audited facilities, workers were required to work more than 60 hours per week—Apple sets a maximum of 60 hours per week (except in unusual or emergency circumstances). In 90 of the audited facilities, workers were found to have been required to work more than six consecutive days a week at least once per month—Apple requires at least one day of rest per seven days of work (except in unusual or emergency circumstances). At 108 facilities, Apple also found that overtime wages had been calculated improperly, resulting in underpayment of overtime compensation.

Apple requires suppliers to provide a safe working environment and to eliminate physical hazards to employees where possible. But the 2011 audits revealed that workers were not wearing appropriate protective personal equipment at 58 facilities. Violations were found at 126 facilities where unlicensed workers were operating equipment. Moreover, the audits revealed that 74 supplier facilities did not have any personnel assigned to ensuring compliance with Apple's Supplier Code of Conduct.

For Apple, the audits represent a starting point for bringing its suppliers into compliance, through greater scrutiny, education and training of suppliers' personnel, and incentives. Apple collects quarterly data to hold its suppliers accountable for their actions and makes procurement decisions based, in part, on these numbers. Suppliers that are unable to meet Apple's high standards of conduct ultimately end up losing Apple's business.

Sources: Apple, *Apple Supplier Responsibility 2012 Progress Report*, January 13, 2012, http://images.apple.com/supplierresponsibility/pdf/Apple_SR_2012_Progress_Report.pdf (accessed June 25, 2013); Nick Wingfield and Charles Duhigg, "Apple Lists Its Suppliers for 1st Time," *Nytimes.com*, January 13, 2012, www.nytimes.com/2012/01/14/technology/apple-releases-list-of-its-suppliers-for-the-first-time.html (accessed March 2, 2012).

unnecessary harm to workers or to the users of the company's product or service.[8] *To the extent there is common moral agreement about right and wrong actions and behaviors across multiple cultures and countries, there exists a set of universal ethical standards to which all societies, companies, and individuals can be held accountable.* The strength of ethical universalism is that it draws upon the collective views of multiple societies and cultures to put some clear boundaries on what constitutes ethical business behavior no matter what country market its personnel are operating in. This means that in those instances where basic moral standards really do not vary significantly according to local cultural beliefs, traditions, or religious convictions, a multinational company can develop a code of ethics that it applies more or less evenly across its worldwide operations.

The School of Ethical Relativism

Beyond widely accepted ethical norms, many ethical standards likely vary from one country to another because of divergent religious beliefs, social customs, and prevailing political and economic doctrines (whether a country leans more toward a capitalistic market economy or one heavily dominated by socialistic or communistic principles). The school of **ethical relativism** holds that when there are national or cross-cultural differences in what is deemed an ethical or unethical business situation, it is appropriate for local moral standards to take precedence over what the ethical standards may be in a company's home market. The thesis is that whatever a culture thinks is right or wrong really is right or wrong for that culture.[9]

> **CORE CONCEPT**
>
> According to the school of **ethical relativism,** different societal cultures and customs create divergent standards of right and wrong—thus, what is ethical or unethical must be judged in the light of local customs and social mores and can vary from one culture or nation to another.

A company that adopts the principle of ethical relativism and holds company personnel to local ethical standards necessarily assumes that what prevails as local morality is an adequate guide to ethical behavior. This can be ethically dangerous; it leads to the conclusion that if a country's culture generally accepts bribery or environmental degradation or exposing workers to dangerous conditions, then managers working in that country are free to engage in such activities. Adopting such a position places a company in a perilous position if it is required to defend these activi-

> Codes of conduct based upon ethical relativism can be *ethically dangerous* by creating a maze of conflicting ethical standards for multinational companies.

ties to its stakeholders in countries with higher ethical expectations. Moreover, from a global markets perspective, ethical relativism results in a maze of conflicting ethical standards for multinational companies. Imagine, for example, that a multinational company in the name of ethical relativism takes the position that it is acceptable for company personnel to pay bribes and kickbacks in countries where such payments are customary but forbids company personnel from making such payments in those countries where bribes and kickbacks are considered unethical or illegal. Having thus adopted conflicting ethical standards for operating in different countries, company managers have little moral basis for enforcing ethical standards companywide—rather, the clear message to employees would be that the company has no ethical standards or principles of its own, preferring to let its practices be governed by the countries in which it operates.

Integrative Social Contracts Theory

Integrative social contracts theory provides a middle position between the opposing views of universalism and relativism.[10] According to **integrative social contracts theory**, the ethical standards a company should try to uphold are governed both by (1) a limited number of universal ethical principles that are widely recognized as putting legitimate ethical boundaries on actions and behavior in *all* situations and (2) the circumstances of local cultures, traditions, and shared values that further prescribe what constitutes ethically permissible

CORE CONCEPT

According to **integrative social contracts theory,** universal ethical principles based on collective views of multiple cultures combine to form a "social contract" that all employees in all country markets have a duty to observe. Within the boundaries of this social contract, there is room for host-country cultures to exert *some* influence in setting their own moral and ethical standards. However, *"first-order"* universal ethical norms always take precedence over *"second-order"* local ethical norms in circumstances where local ethical norms are more permissive.

behavior and what does not. This "social contract" by which managers in all situations have a duty to serve provides that *"first-order" universal ethical norms always take precedence over "second-order" local ethical norms in circumstances where local ethical norms are more permissive.* Integrative social contracts theory offers managers in multinational companies clear guidance in resolving cross-country ethical differences: Those parts of the company's code of ethics that involve universal ethical norms must be enforced worldwide, but within these boundaries there is room for ethical diversity and opportunity for host-country cultures to exert *some* influence in setting their own moral and ethical standards.

A good example of the application of integrative social contracts theory involves the payment of bribes and kickbacks. Bribes and kickbacks seem to be common in some countries, but does this justify paying them? Just because bribery flourishes in a country does not mean that it is an authentic or legitimate ethical norm. Virtually all of the world's major religions (Buddhism, Christianity, Confucianism, Hinduism, Islam, Judaism, Sikhism, and Taoism) and all moral schools of thought condemn bribery and corruption.[11] Therefore, a multinational company might reasonably conclude that the right ethical standard is one of refusing to condone bribery and kickbacks on the part of company personnel no matter what the second-order local norm is and no matter what the sales consequences are. An example of the application of integrative social contracts theory that allows second-order local customs to set ethical boundaries involves employee recruiting and selection practices. A company that has adopted a first-order universal norm of equal opportunity in the workplace might allow applicants to include photographs with résumés in countries where such is the norm. Managers in the United States are prohibited by law from accepting employment applications including a photograph, but managers in Europe would find it very unusual for an application to not be accompanied by a photograph of the applicant. A policy that prohibited managers from accepting applications containing a photo of the applicant would result in almost all applications being rejected. But even with the guidance provided by integrative social contracts theory, there are many instances where cross-country differences in ethical norms create "gray areas" where it is tough to draw a line in the sand between right and wrong decisions, actions, and business practices.

LO4 Learn the concepts of corporate social responsibility and environmental sustainability and how companies balance these duties with economic responsibilities to shareholders.

Strategy, Corporate Social Responsibility, and Environmental Sustainability

The idea that businesses have an obligation to foster social betterment, a much-debated topic in the past 50 years, took root in the nineteenth century when progressive companies in the aftermath of the industrial revolution began to provide workers with housing and other amenities. The notion that corporate executives should balance the interests of all stakeholders—shareholders, employees, customers, suppliers, the communities in which they operated, and society at large—began to blossom in the 1960s.

What Do We Mean by *Corporate Social Responsibility?*

The essence of socially responsible business behavior is that a company should balance strategic actions to benefit shareholders against the *duty* to be a good corporate citizen. The underlying thesis is that company managers should display a *social conscience* in operating the business and specifically consider how management decisions and company actions affect the well-being of employees, local communities, the environment, and society at large.[12] Acting in a socially responsible manner thus encompasses more than just participating in community service projects and donating monies to charities and other worthy social causes. Demonstrating **corporate social responsibility (CSR)** also entails undertaking actions that earn trust and respect from all stakeholders—operating in an honorable and ethical manner, striving to make the company a great place to work, demonstrating genuine respect for the environment, and trying to make a difference in bettering society. Corporate social responsibility programs commonly involve:

> **CORE CONCEPT**
>
> **Corporate social responsibility (CSR)** refers to a company's *duty* to operate in an honorable manner, provide good working conditions for employees, encourage workforce diversity, be a good steward of the environment, and actively work to better the quality of life in the local communities where it operates and in society at large.

- *Efforts to employ an ethical strategy and observe ethical principles in operating the business.* A sincere commitment to observing ethical principles is a necessary component of a CSR strategy simply because unethical conduct is incompatible with the concept of good corporate citizenship and socially responsible business behavior.

- *Making charitable contributions, supporting community service endeavors, engaging in broader philanthropic initiatives, and reaching out to make a difference in the lives of the disadvantaged.* Some companies fulfill their philanthropic obligations by spreading their efforts over a multitude of charitable and community activities—for instance, Microsoft and Johnson & Johnson support a broad variety of community, art, and social welfare programs. Others prefer to focus their energies more narrowly. McDonald's, for example, concentrates on sponsoring the Ronald McDonald House program (which provides a home away from home for the families of seriously ill children receiving treatment at nearby hospitals). British Telecom gives 1 percent of its profits directly to communities, largely for education—teacher training, in-school workshops, and digital technology. Leading prescription drug maker GlaxoSmithKline and other pharmaceutical companies either donate or heavily discount medicines for distribution in the least-developed nations. Companies frequently reinforce their philanthropic efforts by encouraging employees to support charitable causes and participate in community affairs, often through programs that match employee contributions.

- *Actions to protect the environment and, in particular, to minimize or eliminate any adverse impact on the environment stemming from the company's own business activities.* Corporate social responsibility as it applies to environmental protection entails actively striving to be good stewards of the environment. This means using the best available science and technology to reduce environmentally harmful aspects of its operations *below the levels required by prevailing environmental regulations.* It also means putting time and money into improving the environment in ways that extend past a company's own industry boundaries—such as participating in recycling projects, adopting energy conservation practices, and supporting efforts to clean up local water supplies.

- *Actions to create a work environment that enhances the quality of life for employees.* Numerous companies exert extra effort to enhance the quality of life for their employees, both at work and at home. This can include on-site day care, flexible work schedules, workplace exercise facilities, special leaves to care for sick family members, work-at-home opportunities, career development programs and education opportunities, special safety programs, and the like.

- *Actions to build a workforce that is diverse with respect to gender, race, national origin, and other aspects that different people bring to the workplace.* Most large companies in the United States have established workforce diversity programs, and some go the extra mile to ensure that their workplaces are attractive to ethnic minorities and inclusive of all groups and perspectives.

The particular combination of socially responsible endeavors a company elects to pursue defines its **corporate social responsibility strategy.** Concepts & Connections 9.2 describes Burt's Bees' approach to corporate social responsibility. But the specific components emphasized in a CSR strategy vary from company to company and are typically linked to a company's core values. General Mills, for example, builds its CSR strategy around the theme of "nourishing lives" to emphasize its commitment to good nutrition as well as philanthropy, community building, and environmental protection.[13] Starbucks's CSR strategy includes four main elements (ethical sourcing, community service, environmental stewardship, and farmer support), all of which have touch points with the way that the company procures its coffee—a key aspect of its product differentiation strategy.[14]

> **CORE CONCEPT**
>
> A company's **corporate social responsibility strategy** is defined by the specific combination of socially beneficial activities it opts to support with its contributions of time, money, and other resources.

Corporate Social Responsibility and the Triple Bottom Line   CSR initiatives undertaken by companies are frequently directed at improving the company's "triple bottom line"—a reference to three types of performance metrics: *economic, social, environmental.* The goal is for a company to succeed simultaneously in all three dimensions.[15] The three dimensions of performance are often referred to in terms of the three pillars of "people, planet, and profit." The term *people* refers to the various social initiatives that make up CSR strategies, such as corporate giving and community involvement. *Planet* refers to a firm's ecological impact and environmental practices. The term *profit* has a

CONCEPTS & CONNECTIONS 9.2

BURT'S BEES: A STRATEGY BASED ON CORPORATE SOCIAL RESPONSIBILITY

Burt's Bees is a leading company in natural personal care, offering nearly 200 products including its popular beeswax lip balms and skin care creams. The brand has enjoyed tremendous success as consumers have begun to embrace all-natural, environmentally friendly products, boosting Burt's Bees' revenues to more than $160 million in 2012. Much of Burt's Bees' success can be attributed to its skillful use of corporate social responsibility (CSR) as a strategic tool to engage customers and differentiate itself from competitors.

While many companies have embraced corporate social responsibility, few companies have managed to integrate CSR as fully and seamlessly throughout their organizations as Burt's Bees. The company's business model is centered on a principle refered to as "The Greater Good," which specifies that all company practices must be socially responsible. The execution of this strategy is managed by a special committee dedicated to leading the organization to attain its CSR goals with respect to three primary areas: natural well-being, humanitarian responsibility, and environmental sustainability.

Natural well-being is focused on the ingredients used to create Burt's Bees products. Today, the average Burt's Bees product contains over 99 percent natural ingredients; by 2020, the brand expects to produce only 100 percent natural products.

Burt's Bees' humanitarian focus is centered on its relationships with employees and suppliers. A key part of this effort involves a mandatory employee training program that focuses on four key areas: outreach, wellness, world-class leadership, and the environment. Another is the company's responsible sourcing mission, which lays out a carefully prescribed set of guidelines for sourcing responsible suppliers and managing supplier relationships.

A focus on caring for the environment is clearly interwoven into all aspects of Burt's Bees. By focusing on environmentally efficient processes, the company uses its in-house manufacturing capability as a point of strategic differentiation.

Burt's Bees faced some consumer backlash when it was purchased in 2007 by The Clorox Company, whose traditional image is viewed in sharp contrast to Burt's Bees' values. But while Burt's Bees is still only a small part of Clorox's total revenue, it has become its fastest-growing division.

Developed with Ross M. Templeton.

Sources: Company websites; Louise Story, "Can Burt's Bees Turn Clorox Green?" *The New York Times,* January 6, 2008; Bill Chameides, "Burt's Bees Are Busy on the Sustainability Front," *Huffington Post,* June 25, 2010; Katie Bird, "Burt's Bees' International Performance Weaker Than Expected," *CosmeticsDesign.com,* January 6, 2011; "Burt's Bees, Marks & Spencer Share Staff Engagement Tactics," *EnvironmentalLeader.com,* May 31, 2011; http://blogs.newsobserver.com/business/investor-icahn-pushes-for-sale-of-burts-bees-parent-clorox#storylink=cpy (accessed March 1, 2012).

broader meaning with respect to the triple bottom line than it does otherwise. It encompasses not only the profit a firm earns for its shareholders but also the economic impact the company has on society more generally. Triple-bottom-line (TBL) reporting is emerging as an increasingly important way for companies to make the results of their CSR strategies apparent to stakeholders.

What Do We Mean by *Sustainability* and *Sustainable Business Practices?*

The term *sustainability* is used in a variety of ways. In many firms, it is synonymous with corporate social responsibility; it is seen by some as a term that is gradually replacing CSR in the business lexicon. Indeed, sustainability reporting and TBL reporting are often one and the same. More often, however, the term takes on a more focused meaning, concerned with the relationship of a company to its *environment* and its use of *natural resources,* including land, water, air, minerals, and fossil fuels. Since corporations are the biggest users of finite natural resources, managing and maintaining these resources is critical for the long-term economic interests of corporations.

For some companies, this issue has direct and obvious implications for the continued viability of their business model and strategy. Pacific Gas and Electric has begun measuring the full carbon footprint of its supply chain to become not only "greener" but also a more efficient energy producer.[16] For other companies, the connection is less direct, but all companies are part of a business ecosystem whose economic health depends on the availability of natural resources. In response, most major companies have begun to change *how* they do business, emphasizing the use of **sustainable business practices,** defined as those capable of meeting the needs of the present without compromising the ability to meet the needs of the future.[17] Many have also begun to incorporate a consideration of environmental sustainability into their strategy-making activities.

> **CORE CONCEPT**
>
> **Sustainable business practices** are those that meet the needs of the present without compromising the ability to meet the needs of the future.

Environmental sustainability strategies entail deliberate and concerted actions to operate businesses in a manner that protects and maybe even enhances natural resources and ecological support systems, guards against outcomes that will ultimately endanger the planet, and is therefore sustainable for centuries.[18] Sustainability initiatives undertaken by companies are directed at improving the company's triple bottom line— its performance on economic, environment, and social metrics.[19] Unilever, a diversified producer of processed foods, personal care, and home cleaning products, is among the most committed corporations pursuing environmentally sustainable business practices. The company tracks 11 sustainable agricultural indicators in its processed-foods business and has launched a variety of programs to improve the environmental performance of its suppliers. Examples of such programs include special low-rate financing for tomato suppliers choosing to switch to water-conserving irrigation systems and training programs in India that have allowed contract cucumber growers to reduce pesticide use by 90 percent, while improving yields by 78 percent.

> **CORE CONCEPT**
>
> **Environmental sustainability** involves deliberate actions to protect the environment, provide for the longevity of natural resources, maintain ecological support systems for future generations, and guard against the ultimate endangerment of the planet.

Unilever has also reengineered many internal processes to improve the company's overall performance on sustainability measures. For example, the company's factories have reduced water usage by 50 percent and manufacturing waste by 14 percent through the implementation of sustainability initiatives. Unilever has also redesigned packaging for many of its products to conserve natural resources and reduce the volume of consumer waste. The company's Suave shampoo bottles in the United States were reshaped to save almost 150 tons of plastic resin per year, which is the equivalent of 15 million fewer empty bottles. As the producer of Lipton Tea, Unilever is the world's largest purchaser of tea leaves; the company has committed to sourcing all of its tea from Rainforest Alliance Certified farms by 2015, due to Unilever's comprehensive triple-bottom-line approach toward sustainable farm management. Because 40 percent of Unilever's sales are made to consumers in developing countries, the company also is committed to addressing societal needs of consumers in those countries. Examples of the company's social performance include free laundries in poor neighborhoods in developing countries, start-up assistance for women-owned micro businesses in India, and free drinking water provided to villages in Ghana.

Sometimes cost savings and improved profitability are drivers of corporate sustainability strategies. DuPont's sustainability initiatives regarding energy usage have resulted in energy conservation savings of more than $2 billion between 1990 and 2005. Procter & Gamble's Swiffer cleaning system, one of the company's best-selling new products, was developed as a sustainable product; not only does the Swiffer system have an earth-friendly design, but it also outperforms less ecologically friendly alternatives. Although most consumers probably aren't aware that the Swiffer mop reduces demands on municipal water sources, saves electricity that would be needed to heat water, and doesn't add to the amount of detergent making its way into waterways and waste treatment facilities, they are attracted to purchasing Swiffer mops because they prefer Swiffer's disposable cleaning sheets to filling and refilling a mop bucket and wringing out a wet mop until the floor is clean.

Crafting Corporate Social Responsibility and Sustainability Strategies

While striving to be socially responsible and to engage in environmentally sustainable business practices, there's plenty of room for every company to make its own statement about what charitable contributions to make, what kinds of community service projects to emphasize, what environmental actions to support, how to make the company a good place to work, where and how workforce diversity fits into the picture, and what else it will do to support worthy causes and projects that benefit society. A company may choose to focus its social responsibility strategy on generic social issues, but social responsibility strategies linked to its customer value proposition or key value chain activities may also help build competitive advantage.[20] For example, while carbon emissions may be a generic social issue for a financial institution such as Wells Fargo, Toyota's social responsibility strategy aimed at reducing carbon emissions has produced both competitive advantage and environmental benefits. Its Prius hybrid electric/gasoline-powered automobile not only is among the least polluting automobiles, but also is the best-selling hybrid vehicle in the United States and has earned the company the loyalty of fuel-conscious buyers and given Toyota a green image.

> CSR strategies that have the effect of both providing valuable social benefits and fulfilling customer needs in a superior fashion can lead to competitive advantage. Corporate social agendas that address generic social issues may help boost a company's reputation, but are unlikely to improve its competitive strength in the marketplace.

The Business Case for Socially Responsible Behavior

It has long been recognized that it is in the enlightened self-interest of companies to be good citizens and devote some of their energies and resources to the betterment of employees, the communities in which they operate, and society in general. In short, there are several reasons the exercise of corporate social responsibility is good business:

- *Such actions can lead to increased buyer patronage.* A strong visible social responsibility strategy gives a company an edge in differentiating itself from rivals and in appealing to those consumers who prefer to do business with companies that are good corporate citizens. Ben & Jerry's, Whole Foods Market, Stonyfield Farm, and The Body Shop have definitely expanded their customer bases because of their visible and well-publicized activities as socially conscious companies.

- *A strong commitment to socially responsible behavior reduces the risk of reputation-damaging incidents.* Companies that place little importance on operating in a socially responsible manner are more prone to scandal and embarrassment. Consumer, environmental, and human rights activist groups are quick to criticize businesses whose behavior they consider to be out of line, and they are adept at getting their message into the media and onto the Internet. For many years, Nike received stinging criticism for not policing sweatshop conditions in the Asian factories that produced Nike footwear, causing Nike co-founder and former CEO Phil Knight to observe, "Nike has become synonymous with slave wages, forced overtime, and arbitrary abuse."[21] In 1997, Nike began an extensive effort to monitor conditions in the 800 factories of the contract manufacturers that produced Nike shoes. As Knight said, "Good shoes come from good factories and good factories have good labor relations." Nonetheless, Nike has continually been plagued by complaints from human rights activists that its monitoring procedures are flawed and that it is not doing enough to correct the plight of factory workers.

- *Socially responsible actions yield internal benefits (particularly for employee recruiting, workforce retention, and training costs) and can improve operational efficiency.* Companies with deservedly good reputations for contributing time and money to the betterment of society are better able to attract and retain employees compared to companies with tarnished reputations. Some employees just feel better about working for a company committed to improving society.[22] This can contribute to lower turnover and better worker productivity. Other direct and indirect economic benefits include lower costs for staff recruitment and training. For example, Starbucks is said to enjoy much lower rates of employee turnover because of its full benefits package for both full-time and part-time employees, management efforts to make Starbucks a great place to work, and the company's socially responsible practices. When a U.S. manufacturer of recycled paper, taking eco-efficiency to heart, discovered how to increase its fiber recovery rate, it saved the equivalent of 20,000 tons of waste paper—a factor that helped the company become the industry's lowest-cost producer. By helping two-thirds of its employees stop smoking and investing in a number of wellness programs for employees, Johnson & Johnson has saved $250 million on its health care costs over the past decade.[23]

- *Well-conceived social responsibility strategies work to the advantage of shareholders.* A two-year study of leading companies found that improving environmental compliance and developing environmentally friendly products can enhance earnings per share, profitability, and the likelihood of winning contracts. The stock prices of companies that rate high on social and environmental performance criteria have been found to perform 35 to 45 percent better than the average of the 2,500 companies comprising the Dow Jones Global Index.[24] A review of some 135 studies indicated there is a positive, but small, correlation between good corporate behavior and good financial performance; only 2 percent of the studies showed that dedicating corporate resources to social responsibility harmed the interests of shareholders.[25]

In sum, companies that take social responsibility seriously can improve their business reputations and operational efficiency while also reducing their risk exposure and encouraging loyalty and innovation. Overall, companies that take special pains to protect the environment (beyond what is required by law), are active in community affairs, and are generous supporters of charitable causes and projects that benefit society are more likely to be seen as good investments and as good companies to work for or do business with. Shareholders are likely to view the business case for social responsibility as a strong one, even though they certainly have a right to be concerned about whether the time and money their company spends to carry out its social responsibility strategy outweigh the benefits and reduce the bottom line by an unjustified amount.

 KEY POINTS

1. Business ethics concerns the application of ethical principles and standards to the actions and decisions of business organizations and the conduct of their personnel. Ethical principles in business are not materially different from ethical principles in general.

2. The three main drivers of unethical business behavior stand out:
    *   Overzealous or obsessive pursuit of personal gain, wealth, and other selfish interests.
    *   Heavy pressures on company managers to meet or beat earnings targets.
    *   A company culture that puts profitability and good business performance ahead of ethical behavior.

3. Business ethics failures can result in visible costs (fines, penalties, civil penalties arising from lawsuits, stock price declines), the internal administrative or "cleanup" costs, and intangible or less visible costs (customer defections, loss of reputation, higher turnover, harsher government regulations).

4. There are three schools of thought about ethical standards for companies with international operations:
    *   According to the *school of ethical universalism,* the same standards of what's ethical and unethical resonate with peoples of most societies regardless of local traditions and cultural norms; hence, common ethical standards can be used to judge the conduct of personnel at companies operating in a variety of international markets and cultural circumstances.

- According to the *school of ethical relativism*, different societal cultures and customs have divergent values and standards of right and wrong—thus, what is ethical or unethical must be judged in the light of local customs and social mores and can vary from one culture or nation to another.

- According to *integrative social contracts theory*, universal ethical principles or norms based on the collective views of multiple cultures and societies combine to form a "social contract" that all individuals in all situations have a duty to observe. Within the boundaries of this social contract, local cultures can specify other impermissible actions; however, universal ethical norms always take precedence over local ethical norms.

5. The term *corporate social responsibility* concerns a company's *duty* to operate in an honorable manner, provide good working conditions for employees, encourage workforce diversity, be a good steward of the environment, and support philanthropic endeavors in local communities where it operates and in society at large. The particular combination of socially responsible endeavors a company elects to pursue defines its corporate social responsibility (CSR) strategy.

6. The triple bottom line refers to company performance in three realms: economic, social, environmental. Increasingly, companies are reporting their performance with respect to all three performance dimensions.

7. Sustainability is a term that is used variously, but most often it concerns a firm's relationship to the environment and its use of natural resources. Environmentally sustainable business practices are those capable of meeting the needs of the present without compromising the world's ability to meet future needs. A company's environmental sustainability strategy consists of its deliberate actions to protect the environment, provide for the longevity of natural resources, maintain ecological support systems for future generations, and guard against ultimate endangerment of the planet.

8. There are also solid reasons CSR and environmental sustainability strategies may be good business—they can be conducive to greater buyer patronage, reduce the risk of reputation-damaging incidents, provide opportunities for revenue enhancement, and lower costs. Well-crafted CSR and environmental sustainability strategies are in the best long-term interest of shareholders, for the reasons above and because they can avoid or preempt costly legal or regulatory actions.

ASSURANCE OF LEARNING EXERCISES

LO1, LO4 1. Ikea is widely known for its commitment to business ethics and environmental sustainability. After reviewing the About Ikea section of its website (www.ikea.com/ms/en_US/about_ikea/index.html), prepare a list of 10 specific policies and programs that help the company achieve its vision of creating a better everyday life for people around the world.

LO2, LO3 2. Prepare a one- to two-page analysis of a recent ethics scandal using your university library's access to Lexis-Nexis or other Internet resources. Your report should (a) discuss the conditions that gave rise to unethical business strategies and behavior and (b) provide an overview of the costs resulting from the company's business ethics failure.

3. Based on the information provided in Concepts & Connections 9.2 explain how Burt's Bees' CSR strategy has contributed to its success in the marketplace. How are its various stakeholder groups affected by its commitment to social responsibility? How would you evaluate its triple-bottom-line performance?

    L04
    ■ connect

4. Go to www.nestle.com and read the company's latest sustainability report. What are Nestlé's key environmental sustainability policies? How do these initiatives relate to the company's principles, values, and culture? How do these initiatives help build competitive advantage in the food industry?

    L04
    ■ connect

 EXERCISES FOR SIMULATION PARTICIPANTS

1. Is your company's strategy ethical? Why or why not? Is there anything that your company has done or is now doing that could legitimately be considered as "shady" by your competitiors?

    L01

2. In what ways, if any, is your company exercising corporate social responsibility? What are the elements of your company's CSR strategy? What changes to this strategy would you suggest?

    L04

3. If some shareholders complained that you and your co-managers have been spending too little or too much on corporate social responsibility, what would you tell them?

    L03, L04

4. Is your company striving to conduct its business in an environmentally sustainable manner? What specific *additional* actions could your company take that would make an even greater contribution to environmental sustainability?

    L04

5. In what ways is your company's environmental sustainability strategy in the best long-term interest of shareholders? Does it contribute to your company's competitive advantage or profitability?

    L04

ENDNOTES

1. James E. Post, Anne T. Lawrence, and James Weber, *Business and Society: Corporate Strategy, Public Policy, Ethics*, 10th ed. (New York: McGraw-Hill Irwin, 2002).

2. John F. Veiga, Timothy D. Golden, and Kathleen Dechant, "Why Managers Bend Company Rules," *Academy of Management Executive* 18, no. 2 (May 2004).

3. Basil Katz and Grant McCool, "US Charges 7 in $62 Million Dell Insider-Trading Case," Reuters, January 18, 2012, www.reuters. com/ article/2012/01/18/ us-insidertrading-arrests-idUSTRE80H18920120118 (accessed February 15, 2012).

4. Ronald R. Sims and Johannes Brink-mann, "Enron Ethics (Or: Culture Matters More Than Codes)," *Journal of Business Ethics* 45, no. 3 (July 2003).

5. Marcy Gordon, "Diebold-SEC Fraud Settlement Reached: Former Voting Machine Maker to Pay $25 Million," *HuffPost Business*, June 2, 2010, http://www.huffmg tonpost.com/2010/06/02/diebold sec-fraud-settleme_n_598627.html (accessed February 16, 2012).

6. Archie B. Carroll, "The Four Faces of Corporate Citizenship," *Business and Society Review* 100/101 (September 1998).

7. Mark S. Schwartz, "Universal Moral Values for Corporate Codes of Ethics," *Journal of Business Ethics* 59, no. 1 (June 2005).

8. Mark S. Schwartz, "A Code of Ethics for Corporate Codes of Ethics," *Journal of Business Ethics* 41, nos. 1–2 (November–December 2002).

9. T. L. Beauchamp and N. E. Bowie, *Ethical Theory and Business* (Upper Saddle River, NJ: Prentice Hall, 2001).

10. Thomas Donaldson and Thomas W. Dunfee, "Towards a Unified Conception of Business Ethics: Integrative Social Contracts Theory," *Academy of Management Review* 19, no. 2 (April 1994); Thomas Donaldson and Thomas W. Dunfee, *Ties That Bind: A Social Contracts Approach*

to Business Ethics (Boston: Harvard Business School Press, 1999); and Andrew Spicer, Thomas W. Dunfee, and Wendy J. Bailey, "Does National Context Matter in Ethical Decision Making? An Empirical Test of Integrative Social Contracts Theory," Academy of Management Journal 47, no. 4 (August 2004).

11. P. M. Nichols, "Outlawing Transnational Bribery through the World Trade Organization," Law and Policy in International Business 28, no. 2 (1997).

12. Timothy M. Devinney, "Is the Socially Responsible Corporation a Myth? The Good, the Bad, and the Ugly of Corporate Social Responsibility," Academy of Management Perspectives 23, no. 2 (May 2009).

13. "General Mills' 2010 Corporate Social Responsibility Report Highlights New and Longstanding Achievements in the Areas of Health, Community, and Environment," CSRwire, April 15, 2010, www.csrwire.com/press_releases/29347-General-Mills-2010-Corporate-Social Responsibility-report-now-available.html.

14. Arthur A. Thompson and Amit J. Shah, "Starbucks' Strategy and Internal Initiatives to Return to Profitable Growth," 2010.

15. Gerald I.J.M. Zwetsloot and Marcel N. A. van Marrewijk, "From Quality to Sustainability," Journal of Business Ethics 55 (December 2004), pp. 79–82.

16. Tilde Herrera, "PG&E Claims Industry First with Supply Chain Footprint Project," GreenBiz.com,

June 30, 2010, www.greenbiz.com/news/2010/06/30/pge-claims-industry-first-supply-chain-carbon-footprint-project.

17. This definition is based on the Brundtland Commission's report, which described sustainable development in a like manner: United Nations General Assembly, "Report of the World Commission on Environment and Development: Our Common Future," 1987, www.un-documents.net/wced-ocf.htm, transmitted to the General Assembly as an annex to document A/42/427—"Development and International Cooperation: Environment" (accessed February 15, 2009).

18. Robert Goodland, "The Concept of Environmental Sustainability," Annual Review of Ecology and Systematics 26 (1995); and J. G. Speth, The Bridge at the End of the World: Capitalism, the Environment, and Crossing from Crisis to Sustainability (New Haven, CT: Yale University Press, 2008).

19. Gerald I. J. M. Zwetsloot and Marcel N. A. van Marrewijk, "From Quality to Sustainability," Journal of Business Ethics 55 (December 2004); and John B. Elkington, Cannibals with Forks: The Triple Bottom Line of 21st Century Business (Oxford: Capstone Publishing, 1997).

20. Michael E. Porter and Mark R. Kramer, "Strategy & Society: The Link between Competitive Advantage and Corporate Social Responsibility," Harvard Business Review 84, no. 12 (December 2006).

21. Tom McCawley, "Racing to Improve Its Reputation: Nike Has Fought to Shed Its Image as an Exploiter of Third-World Labor Yet It Is Still a Target of Activists," Financial Times, December 2000.

22. N. Craig Smith, "Corporate Responsibility: Whether and How," California Management Review 45, no. 4 (Summer 2003), p. 63; see also World Economic Forum, "Findings of a Survey on Global Corporate Leadership," www.weforum.org/corporatecitizenship (accessed October 11, 2003).

23. Michael E. Porter and Mark Kramer, "Creating Shared Value," Harvard Business Review 89, nos. 1–2 (January–February 2011).

24. James C. Collins and Jerry I. Porras, Built to Last: Successful Habits of Visionary Companies, 3rd ed. (London: HarperBusiness, 2002).

25. Joshua D. Margolis and Hillary A. Elfenbein, "Doing Well by Doing Good: Don't Count on It," Harvard Business Review 86, no. 1 (January 2008); Lee E. Preston and Douglas P. O'Bannon, "The Corporate Social-Financial Performance Relationship," Business and Society 36, no. 4 (December 1997); Ronald M. Roman, Sefa Hayibor, and Bradley R. Agle, "The Relationship between Social and Financial Performance: Repainting a Portrait," Business and Society 38, no. 1 (March 1999); and Joshua D. Margolis and James P. Walsh, People and Profits (Mahwah, NJ: Lawrence Erlbaum, 2001).

CPSIA information can be obtained
at www.ICGtesting.com
Printed in the USA
FFOW01n1055270717
38175FF